JACOB S. HACKER

THE GREAT RISK SHIFT

The New Economic Insecurity and the Decline of the American Dream

EXPANDED & FULLY REVISED
SECOND EDITION

OXFORD
UNIVERSITY PRESS

OXFORD
UNIVERSITY PRESS

Oxford University Press is a department of the University of Oxford. It furthers
the University's objective of excellence in research, scholarship, and education
by publishing worldwide. Oxford is a registered trade mark of Oxford University
Press in the UK and certain other countries.

Published in the United States of America by Oxford University Press
198 Madison Avenue, New York, NY 10016, United States of America.

Library of Congress Cataloging-in-Publication Data
Names: Hacker, Jacob S.
Title: The great risk shift : the new economic insecurity and the decline of
the American dream / Jacob S. Hacker.
Description: Second edition. | New York : Oxford University Press, [2019] |
Includes bibliographical references and index.
Identifiers: LCCN 2018048198 (print) | LCCN 2018053842 (ebook) |
ISBN 9780190844158 (Universal PDF) | ISBN 9780190844165 (E-pub) |
ISBN 9780190844141 (Paperback : alk. paper)
Subjects: LCSH: Economic security—United States. | Risk—United States. |
United States—Economic conditions. | American Dream.
Classification: LCC HD7125 (ebook) | LCC HD7125 .H24 2019 (print) |
DDC 330.973—dc23
LC record available at https://lccn.loc.gov/2018048198

1 3 5 7 9 8 6 4 2

Printed by Sheridan Books, Inc., United States of America

To my mother and father and to Anneke

"A brilliant diagnosis of how the American dream has dissolved, and what might be done to resurrect it. With cool intelligence but also great compassion, Jacob Hacker shows how both corporate and governmental safety nets have been systematically dismantled, leaving average Americans at the mercy of an increasingly risky global economy."

—Charles Ferguson, director of *Inside Job*

"His most ambitious work yet."

—*The New York Times Book Review*

"A fresh diagnosis of a familiar complex of problems from structural unemployment to the erosion of retirement plans you can retire on."

—*The Atlantic*

"A valuable new book . . . he presents data explaining the new sense of economic dread hanging over Americans. We all know that in this globalized, ultra-competitive age, job security has been beggared, but Hacker attaches startling numbers to the national anxiety."

—*New York Magazine*

"Jacob Hacker's research on the uneven state of the American safety net has made the young Yale University political scientist a top idea merchant to Democratic think tanks."

—*Businessweek*

"Hacker's is one of those prescient books that names and anatomizes a potent, ubiquitous trend that has been hidden in plain view. . . . His book deserves the widest possible audience, for having nailed the most powerful and underappreciated economic trend of our era, thereby inviting a discussion of the political opportunities."

—Robert Kuttner, *American Prospect*

"As Jacob Hacker argues persuasively in *The Great Risk Shift*, America's middle class finds itself living with far more risk and income volatility than it did a generation ago."

—Christopher Hayes, *The Nation*

"Jacob S. Hacker, a 35-year-old political science professor at Yale, has become something of an intellectual 'It boy' in the Democratic Party over the last decade. . . . The patchwork safety net created in the decades after World War II truly is shriveling, and there will be rewards for the party that comes up with a convincing solution. Hacker has done the Democrats a favor by developing a story and a catchphrase—the great risk shift—to describe the problem."

—David Leonhardt, *New York Times*

CONTENTS

INTRODUCTION
On the Edge

This is a book that began with a surprising discovery—two, in fact. It was the early 2000s, and I was just starting out as an assistant professor. Though my field was political science, I was reading a lot in economics. What I wanted to know was why, in polls at the time, working Americans expressed so much anxiety about their finances when many of the statistics I saw suggested the economy was roaring. And what surprised me was that economists didn't really study insecurity: they looked at poverty (inadequate income or wealth) and inequality (disparities of income or wealth) or they studied very specific kinds of economic dislocations, such as job loss and catastrophic medical costs. Yet somehow insecurity—the risk of losing income or wealth or having unexpected big expenses—didn't get much notice.

That was my first discovery. It led to my second. For it turned out that some economists *had* been examining trends related to insecurity, even if they didn't use the term. The focus of these pioneering researchers was *volatility*—the fluctuation of economic standing over time—and they had developed sophisticated techniques for studying it. Yet what they were looking at was the volatility of workers' earnings, and even more specifically of *male workers'* earnings. It seemed as if the volatility of male earnings had gone up, but nobody had really delved into the natural follow-up questions: Had family incomes become more volatile? Were households now on an economic roller coaster, with higher highs and lower lows? And could that be part of the reason they weren't as happy about the ostensibly strong economy as might be expected?

So I did the calculations myself, with the help of a young graduate student from Cornell named Nigar Nargis. (She now directs economic research for the American Cancer Society.) And I published my findings not only in an academic article, but also in an op-ed in *The New York Times*. The op-ed was titled "Call It the Family Risk Factor," and what was perhaps most notable about the piece was the large line chart that appeared alongside the text (reprinted on the next page, in updated form, as Figure I.1). The chart, taking up a good chunk of the *Times* op-ed page, showed the post-1970s volatility of household income—the incomes of all adults in a family, from all sources, public and private, not just the earnings of working men.[1] (My *Times* op-ed appeared in 2004, so the spike in volatility that began in the latter half of the 2000s amid the financial crisis still lay in the future.)

Volatility is an accepted measure of the riskiness of stocks. Rather than showing the level of a stock's return, it shows how uncertain, or risky, those returns are likely to be. And what the skyrocketing line on the chart made

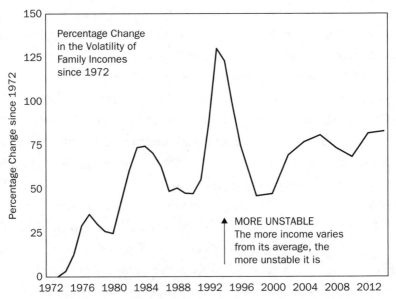

Figure I.1. The Rising Volatility of American Family Incomes: 1972–2014
Source: Panel Study of Income Dynamics, University of Michigan; analysis traces the transitory variance of before-tax family incomes, adjusted for family size, of individuals aged twenty-five through sixty-one. The PSID switched to biennial surveys in 1996, so thereafter no odd-number years have estimates. The trend line shown is a two-year moving average.

clear, even to those unversed in statistics, is that the volatility of family incomes had gone way up. Americans had gotten richer (though neither as quickly nor as evenly as sometimes believed), but they had also faced rapidly growing economic instability. Family incomes rose and fell ever more sharply. In fact, the volatility of household incomes nearly doubled from the early 1970s to the early 2010s.

I had hoped for some response to my op-ed. But writing about complex economic trends (with a graph, no less), I didn't have high hopes. I was wrong: the letters and emails poured in. Experts on pension plans wrote to tell me about the risks and challenges that retirement savings accounts like 401(k)s presented. Health policy specialists shared horror stories about the medically uninsured. Economists, including a Nobel laureate, inquired about my evidence.

But most gratifying—and troubling—were the responses from nonexperts who just wanted to share their experiences and views. There was Robert, who had tried to set up a health clinic for the working poor but then succumbed to an unexpected sickness and ended up living "four and a half years of sheer hell" trying to gain assistance from America's "safety net." There was Elizabeth, a well-educated consultant who said she "felt responsible for herself" but feared what would happen if either she or her husband were laid off, because, with two kids and unstable incomes, they hadn't been able to "save to the extent that we have a good safety net." There was the Yale undergraduate whose middle-class but chronically ill parents couldn't find a company that would even sell them a health insurance policy. There were tales of lost jobs and lost income, unexpected setbacks and unwelcome hardships. And then there was the graceful yet angry email of Andrea Case.

"I am in one of the families of which you speak," Andrea's note began. Then she proceeded to explain how she and her husband, a computer engineer, had been slammed by the exploding tech bubble. They had watched for months as her husband's firm sank, both fearing his job would go down with it at any time. The family's earnings plummeted, but the bills just kept coming: the mortgage payments for their new house, the tuition for the Montessori school they'd enrolled their son in because he had learning problems, statements for the gas, electric, telephone, car, and on and on.

In the space of a few months they had gone from taking their lives—and smooth upward path—for granted, to worrying about paying the utilities. Their income dropped by more than a third. Andrea went from sleeping soundly to lying awake asking herself tough questions. Should they pull their son from the school? Sell the house? Should Andrea go back to work—and if so, full time? What about health care? Her husband had eventually jumped to a lower-paying job, but under its stingy health plan, the family had to pay nearly $10,000 in health premiums and out-of-pocket medical costs.

Their freefall stopped when her husband found another position with better benefits, though even lower pay. Yet Andrea still did not feel secure, and she didn't know where to turn. "Who is the candidate for people like me?" her email closed:

> Where is the AARP for families? I feel like we need the equivalent of the Million Mom March to let candidates know that parents with young children are hurting. How can busy, overwhelmed parents be educated and motivated? How can we have our voice heard above those of huge PACs and corporations? I know this is nearly a rant, but I am angry and frustrated and don't know where to turn to be effective in getting the leadership this country needs.

I reached out to Andrea after her email, and the two of us talked by phone some months later. She was pushing her preschool-age daughter on the swing near their New Jersey home. I could hear her nine-year-old son playing in the background. Until the economic U-turn, she said, "everything exceeded our expectations." Out of college, she and her husband were riding the upward tide of the tech economy. Their combined income was high enough to allow them to move out of a Manhattan apartment near Battery Park, just a few blocks from the World Trade Center, into a three-bedroom, two-bath home on a cul-de-sac in suburban New Jersey—nothing as spectacular as the big homes with granite kitchens nearby, but grand compared with their old apartment. It also allowed Andrea to leave work to have kids. Then, the stock-market bubble burst; the 9/11 attacks occurred; her husband's firm started shedding workers; his pay dropped sharply. Everything seemed to come undone at once, and the low seemed all the lower because the high had been so high.

The low seemed lower, too, because their situation was at odds with everything they'd been told. Here they were, college-educated, frugal, responsible—and suddenly facing a very different life than they'd had or thought they'd have. In an instant everything had changed. It was as if their old life had been swept away by a hurricane.

Economic risk is a lot like a hurricane. Hurricanes strike powerfully and suddenly. They rip apart what they touch: property, landscape, and lives. They are common enough to affect many, yet rare enough still to shock. And although they can be prepared for, they cannot be prevented. Some people will inevitably suffer and require help; others will be spared. Recovery is inevitably traumatic and slow. And so it is with families whose lives have been touched by economic risk. What happens in an instant may change a life forever.

The comparison is not just metaphorical: for more than half a century, Americans responded to economic risk as if it were a natural disaster largely beyond the control or responsibility of those it struck.[2] In the wake of the Great Depression in the 1930s, which left a "third of the nation," in FDR's famous telling, "ill-housed, ill-clad, ill-nourished," political and business leaders put in place new institutions designed to spread broadly the burden of key economic risks, including the risk of poverty in retirement, the risk of unemployment and disability, and the risk of widowhood due to the premature death of a breadwinner.[3] These public and private institutions did not let the individual off the hook; they required contributions and work and proof of eligibility. But they were based on an ideal known as "social insurance"—the notion that certain risks can be effectively dealt with only through institutions that spread their costs across rich and poor, healthy and sick, able-bodied and disabled, young and old.

What struck me after speaking with Andrea Case—and hearing from and studying the economic lives of so many other Americans—is that this fabric of mutual protection has unraveled. No longer do institutions inspired by the ideal of social insurance connect and protect us in good times and bad. No longer do political and corporate leaders generally embrace the notion that catastrophic risks represent misfortunes largely beyond individual control. Instead of pooling risks through social insurance, those with the power to make policy have been offloading them—and they've been doing so with little interruption for more than a generation.

The result has been a massive transfer of economic risk from broad structures of insurance, including those sponsored by the corporate sector as well as by government, onto the fragile balance sheets of American families. This shift has fundamentally reshaped Americans' relationships to their government, their employers, and each other. And it has altered and sometimes dashed the most fundamental expectations associated with the American Dream: a stable middle-class income, an affordable place to live, a guaranteed pension, good health insurance coverage, greater economic security for one's kids.

In short, the stories I was tracing weren't just isolated instances of hardship; they signaled a fundamental transformation of our economy. Some ended well; some didn't. But that was precisely the point. In their diversity and their frequency, in their happy endings and especially their unhappy ones, they all shared one thing in common: risk.

I decided to call this transformation "The Great Risk Shift," and the phrase became the title of the first edition of this book, which came out more than a decade ago. My aim in 2006 wasn't to predict the next big downturn. (Even economists aren't very good at that.) It was to show that the typical up-and-down waves of the economy had been occurring alongside a rising tide of family insecurity, and that this tide had seeped into almost every corner of Americans' financial lives. Income volatility was just the loss leader, so to speak, in my catalog of evidence—one sign among many that Americans were more and more on their own in dealing with the "hazards and vicissitudes" of a changing economy.

The response to *The Great Risk Shift* was positive, but not universally so. One reviewer described the insecure Americans whose lives I showcased as "whiny"; another accused me of "poor-mouthing prosperity." Less personally distressing but more telling, the generally appreciative reception didn't really evidence the kind of urgency I believed was essential. It was as if I had described a Category 5 hurricane, and people had gotten out their umbrellas.

Then, on September 15, 2008, Lehman Brothers Holding Company filed for bankruptcy. The financial crisis that Lehman's collapse signaled ushered in the deepest recession since the 1930s, when FDR uttered his memorable words and put in place the foundation of America's distinctive response to economic insecurity. Some called the post-2008 downturn "The Great Recession." The economist Brad DeLong suggested it should be labeled "The Lesser Depression." Call it what you will, it was a shocking reminder of how fragile the finances of American families were. When an economy persistently falls short of its potential, economists speak of "output losses"—the prosperity we've missed out on because of reduced growth. Based on trends prior to the crisis, DeLong estimated that America's cumulative output losses exceeded 78 percent of America's annual GDP by the end of 2014.[4] Put another way, if the post-2007 crisis hadn't happened, the economy would have had to shut down completely for more than nine months to equal the total income losses experienced by Americans.

Or consider another number: $57,000. That sum amounts to the household wealth—assets minus debts, including housing—of the typical family in 2010. You won't be surprised that this number is below where it was before the Great Recession. You might be surprised that it is lower than at any point since *1969*.[5]

In the wake of the downturn, commentators suddenly started paying a lot more attention to insecurity. Yet far too many assumed the problem was merely a product of the crash. As I had argued in 2006, however, the Great Risk Shift far predated the Great Recession. I didn't know then when the bubble would pop. But I did know that household debt had exploded and that this spelled trouble. I didn't know then that corruption and recklessness had become the new normal on Wall Street. But I did know that anxiety and dislocation were becoming the new normal on Main Street—even when the overall economy was relatively stable. More important, I knew that risks weren't just rising among the poor and poorly educated; they were rising across the income spectrum, across the racial divide, across lines of geography and gender. Increasingly, they were affecting people such as Andrea Case: educated, upper-middle-class Americans—men and women who thought that by staying in school, by buying a home, by investing in their 401(k)s, they had bought a ticket to upward mobility and economic stability. Increasingly, economic insecurity spoke to the common "us" rather than to the insular, marginalized "them."

I also knew that the problem wasn't inevitable. Despite the metaphorical affinity between economic risks and natural disasters, the Great Risk Shift isn't a natural occurrence—a financial hurricane beyond human control. Sweeping changes in the global and domestic economy have helped propel it, but America's corporate and political leaders could have responded to these powerful forces by reinforcing the floodwalls that protect families from economic risk. Instead, in the name of personal responsibility, many of these leaders have been tearing the floodwalls down. Proponents of these changes speak of a nirvana of individual economic management—a society of empowered consumers, in which Americans are free to choose. What these advocates have been creating, however, is very different: a harsh new world of economic insecurity, in which far too many Americans are free to lose.

The Great Recession made this new reality undeniable, and as it deepened, I delved back into the insecurity explosion. Along with a team of political scientists and economists, and with the support of the Rockefeller Foundation, I developed a new measure of economic security that showed not only that large income drops had gone up, but also that families faced greater risk of catastrophic medical spending that suddenly reduced how much of their variable income they had for other needs. We also showed that vanishingly few families had enough wealth to insure themselves against these twin risks. What's more, we found similar trends across all three of the major data sets that analysts use to examine family income dynamics.[6]

We also fielded a multi-wave survey of our own, asking a representative sample of Americans about their experiences and attitudes at two separate intervals in 2009. The results were striking: during the eighteen months preceding September 2009, nearly nine in ten Americans reported experiencing at least one substantial economic loss related to employment or earnings, wealth, health care, or family structure (for example, divorce or the death of a spouse). Not surprisingly, losses of household wealth were the most common reported source of insecurity. Yet more than two-thirds (70 percent) of all Americans experienced a loss that wasn't wealth-related. And these losses were often quite substantial. During these eighteen months, almost a quarter of all households reported a decline in earnings totaling 25 percent or more of their previous annual income. Meanwhile, less than a third said their household could go six months or longer without hardship if their earnings were to stop. Nearly half said they could go no longer than two months, and one in five said they could last no more than two weeks.[7]

But here's what may be most shocking: when we compared our survey responses with previous surveys that had asked people about their economic worries—surveys done just before the Great Recession—we found that Americans had been pretty worried back then, too. With regard to unemployment and housing, concerns had understandably spiked due to the Great Recession. But these worries were already high before the crash, and worries about health insurance and debt were just as high. The downturn had intensified concerns, but it hadn't created them. It had laid bare the hidden insecurity of the vast majority of American families.

Nonetheless, much has changed since the first edition of this book—for better as well as for worse. In 2009 and 2010, we witnessed the passage of three landmark laws designed to reduce insecurity: the Affordable Care Act, aka "Obamacare"; the financial reform bill of 2010; and the 2009 economic recovery package, which sought to upgrade unemployment insurance and strengthen the safety net for lower-income families, among other reforms. The effects of these steps—and the fierce political and policy response to them—need to reckoned with every bit as much as the effects and legacies of the Great Recession.

That is what I seek to do in this fully revised edition. It not only updates the story I told in 2006, it also deepens and extends it. We know far more than we did about insecurity then. Alas, we also have far more to do to address it. For while we now understand just how bad economic hurricanes can be—even with all the warning signals and floodwalls built since the

1930s—too many of our political leaders and policy experts still argue that little can or should be done. The Great Risk Shift may no longer be hidden, but it's still happening—and it still can be stopped.

To understand the change, we must first understand what is changing. America's distinctive framework of economic protection grew out of specific political struggles and a unique set of values and beliefs. Less expansive than some hoped, more expansive than others desired, it was a curious and sometimes contradictory amalgam of goals and institutions. By the early 1970s, it worked tolerably well in insulating most middle-class Americans from the major financial risks of a dynamic capitalist economy. But today, despite some crucial recent expansions, it is falling apart under the weight of political attack and economic change—its conflicting elements falling in on each other, its gaps and traps growing by the day.

It is common to say that the United States does little to provide economic security compared with other rich capitalist democracies. Whether because of a deeply embedded mistrust of government, a constitutional structure that makes big policy reforms hard to achieve, the weakness of the American labor movement, or the depth of ethnic and racial divisions, the United States has provided infertile soil for the comprehensive welfare states that now dominate the economic landscape of most affluent countries. This is true, but it is only half the story. The United States does spend less on government benefits as a share of its economy, but it also relies more—far more—on private workplace benefits, such as health care and retirement pensions. Indeed, when these private benefits are factored into the mix, the U.S. framework of economic security is *not* smaller than the average system in other rich democracies; it is actually slightly larger.[8] With the help of hundreds of billions in tax breaks, American employers serve as the United States' unique mini-welfare states—the first line of defense for millions of workers buffeted by the winds of economic change.

The problem is that these mini-welfare states are coming undone, and in the process, risk is shifting back onto workers and their families. Employers want out of the social contract forged in the more stable economy of the past. And because they do not need to answer to the broader public that depends on the jerry-rigged systems of security they provide, employers are getting what they want. Meanwhile, America's framework of government support is also strained. Patently inadequate to deal with families' growing risks, it is nonetheless attacked for costing and doing too much—by critics who claim that the ideal of insurance is both outmoded and harmful to economic growth and advancement.

As private and public protections erode, workers and their families must bear a greater burden. This is the essence of the Great Risk Shift. Through the cutback and restructuring of workplace benefits, employers are seeking to offload more and more of the risk once pooled under their auspices. Facing fiscal constraints and political opposition, public social programs have eroded even as the demands on them have risen. And if critics have their way, these programs will erode even further. The next frontier in the Great Risk Shift is the transformation of existing programs—Medicare and Social Security chief among them—from guaranteed benefits defined by law to individualized private accounts that leave workers and families shouldering more and more of the risks that these programs once covered.

The Great Risk Shift might be less worrisome if work and family were stable sources of security themselves. Unfortunately, they are not. The job market has grown markedly more uncertain and unstable, especially for those who were once best protected from its vagaries. The family, once a refuge from economic risk, is creating new risks of its own. With families needing two earners to maintain a middle-class standard of living, families' economic calculus has changed in ways that accentuate many of the risks they face. At the same time, families are making greater, and more risky, investments in their futures—in buying a home, in gaining new skills, in raising well-educated children—and they are bearing the losses when those investments fail.

The goal of this book is to explain why the Great Risk Shift has played out, and how it can be countered. I start by demonstrating how dramatic the rise in insecurity is and dissecting one of its overarching causes, what I call "The Personal Responsibility Crusade"—a political drive to shift a growing amount of economic risk from government and the corporate sector onto ordinary Americans in the name of enhanced individual responsibility and control. Thanks in part to this crusade, even middle-class families are facing greater insecurity in the workplace, in the balancing of work and family, in planning for retirement, and in obtaining and paying for health care.

The shift of risk within these areas—how it has happened, who and what is behind it, and where it leaves us today—is the heart of my story. Work, family, and public and private benefits have all grown more risky at roughly the same time, which is one reason that the weakening of these traditional sources of security has proved so sweeping and so difficult to address. To take in the full scope of the Great Risk Shift, however, requires considering these transformations one by one: the new world of work, the increasingly risk-bound family, and America's enfeebled public-private framework of health insurance and retirement pensions, in which Americans have invested so much money, faith, and hope. The failures here are not small or fleeting. They are enormous and endemic—and the solutions proposed by the Personal Responsibility Crusade will only make them immeasurably worse.

These deep and worsening problems call for bold solutions. What we need are new ways of allowing families to save and insure against some of the most potent risks to their income, coupled with new ideas for revitalizing American social insurance and providing economic opportunity to all. A "security and opportunity" agenda would emphasize work and responsibility. But it would also provide real protection when families fall from the ladder of economic advancement, encouraging families to look to the future rather than fear the present. The old canard that ensuring security always hurts the economy turns out to be cruelly false. Economic security is vital to economic opportunity, and economic insecurity is one of the greatest barriers between American families and the American Dream.

1

The New Economic Insecurity

I was born in a small college town in Oregon in the early 1970s—just before the oil shocks, stagflation, and upheaval of the decade. I remember gas lines snaking around the block near my family's rented home, and my mother's dismay as prices in the supermarket, like unemployment, just kept rising. Underlying the surface calm was a growing unease—a sense that the nation was unsettled. My first real political memory was the Iranian hostage crisis; the first election I remember was Reagan's rout of Carter in 1980. What I didn't realize as I rode my red Raleigh bike through the quiet streets of my neighborhood was that a larger shift was also occurring in the wider world. An era was ending. A thirty-year period of shared prosperity in the United States was giving way to a new age of insecurity.

Today, the Internet, newspapers, and the airwaves are filled with debates over the changing American economy. We read story after story about the instabilities and hardships that affect middle-class families that resemble

Andrea Case's: workers recently laid off from well-paying jobs, parents struggling under the costs of a child's unexpected health problems, retirees forced to go back to work—in short, our next-door neighbors, our friends, the people we cross paths with everyday. The transformation began around the time of my youth, slowly eroding the confidence of middle-class Americans that they'd have stable jobs, generous benefits, and smooth upward mobility, and that their children would enjoy greater economic security than they'd had. But who killed economic security and why remains a mystery that we have only begun to plumb.

We all know something about rising *inequality* in the United States, the growing space between the rungs of America's economic ladder. We hear about the soaring incomes of princely executives who garner hundreds of millions in compensation even as workers at the middle and bottom fall farther and farther behind. Yet we have heard less about the causes and consequences of rising *insecurity,* the growing risk of slipping down the economic ladder itself. Perhaps that's because the stories here seem more random—blue-collar workers laid off after long years of service, college-educated middle managers whose upward trajectories have been abruptly halted, working families thrown off balance by catastrophic expenses, middle-class parents who find that health and retirement plans are shifting more costs and uncertainties onto them. It's easy to find the common thread when the subject is hardening divisions between two Americas— one marked by deprivation, the other by excess. It's harder to find it in stories of loss and anxiety whose common element is not constancy or stability, but sudden and often unexpected change.

Inequality and insecurity are of course deeply interwoven, but they are not the same. Inequality has indeed risen sharply. Between 1979 and 2013 the average pretax income of the richest 1 percent of Americans nearly tripled after adjusting for inflation, while that of middle-class Americans increased by around a third (accounting for all forms of income, including America's exorbitantly expensive health benefits).[1] Nonetheless, it is possible to look at rising inequality and still paint a somewhat positive picture. After all, Americans at all points on the income ladder have gotten richer—albeit at starkly unequal rates—and during this same period, our economy has expanded handsomely. A rising tide may not be lifting all boats as well as it did in the 1950s and 1960s, but it is lifting them nonetheless.

But another tide has been rising in the United States since my youth—the rising tide of risk. Americans may be modestly richer than they were in the 1970s, but they are also facing much greater economic insecurity. And this insecurity is increasingly plunging ordinary middle-class families into a sea of economic turmoil.

Consider some of the alarming facts. Personal bankruptcy has gone from a rare occurrence to a relatively common one, with the number of households filing for bankruptcy rising from fewer than 290,000 in 1980 to more than 2 million in 2005, when a strict new bankruptcy law demanded by the financial industry radically scaled back eligibility on the eve of the economic meltdown.[2] The bankrupt are pretty much like other Americans before they file: slightly better educated, more likely to be married and have children, roughly as likely to have had a good job, and modestly less likely to own a home.[3] They are not the persistently poor, the downtrodden looking for relief. They are refugees of the middle class, frequently wondering how they fell so far so fast.

Americans have also been losing their housing at record rates. Between the early 1970s and mid-2000s—even before the housing bubble burst—the mortgage foreclosure rate increased approximately fivefold.[4] From 2001 to 2005, an average of one in every sixty households with a mortgage fell into foreclosure each year—a legal process that begins when homeowners default on their mortgages and can end with homes being auctioned to the highest bidder in local courthouses.[5] In 2010, at the peak of the crisis, a startling one in twenty households entered the foreclosure process—compared with less than one in *three hundred* in the early 1970s.[6]

David Lamberger, a Michigan resident who has worked in the auto industry most of his life, can testify to just how shattering the process can be. David and his wife, Mary, purchased their two-story home in the metro Detroit area as an investment in the future for themselves and their four children. When David lost his job at an auto parts maker, he declared bankruptcy to delay foreclosure on the house. But the money he made working at a used-car lot hasn't been sufficient to keep them afloat, and now he's on the verge of losing his family's modest home.[7] For David and scores of other ordinary homeowners, the American Dream has mutated into what former U.S. comptroller of the currency Julie L. Williams calls "the American nightmare."[8]

The sociologist Matthew Desmond has recently cast a spotlight on another pervasive source of insecurity in the housing market: eviction. The growing gap between wages and rent in America's cities, as well as declining federal subsidies, have led lower-income renters to spend an enormous and growing share of their income on housing expenditures—in the majority of cases, more than half their income. According to Desmond, a startling 6 to 7 percent of the nation's 35 million or so renter-occupied households have eviction filings made against them annually, with around 2 to 3 percent ultimately facing eviction—again, *each year*.[9]

Meanwhile, the number of Americans who lack health insurance— after rising steadily with the expansion of employment-based insurance after World War II and the passage of Medicare and Medicaid in 1965— began to fall around 1980, as employers cut back on workplace coverage for employees and their dependents. By the late 2000s, roughly one out of three nonelderly Americans spent some time without health insurance over a two-year period—most of them workers, most of them uninsured for more than half a year.[10] Mark Herrara was one of them. A union carpenter who went out on his own to become an independent contractor, Herrara didn't think insurance was a pressing priority when he was using all his resources to get his business off the ground. Or at least he didn't until he woke up one morning with a "massive headache." Reluctant to go to the hospital for fear of the costs, he finally relented only to discover that he had suffered two strokes and his brain was bleeding. Ineligible for Medicaid, his bills rose and rose. "I've got a $225,000 debt and yeah, if I come into any money, well, the first people I got to pay back is for this medical coverage," said Herrara.[11]

Stories like these helped propel the passage of landmark legislation in 2010. The Affordable Care Act (aka "Obamacare") expanded Medicaid for low-income Americans and created new regulated marketplaces where those without insurance could buy subsidized coverage. The law's effects have proved dramatic: a dramatic drop in the share of Americans without health insurance, largely due to the Medicaid expansion—and without a feared spike in overall medical costs (in fact, the economic downturn and the law helped slow medical inflation to historic lows). But the Affordable Care Act still left nearly 30 million Americans uninsured for all of 2016— down from a peak of 44 million just before the law's implementation—it has faced fierce pushback from both national and state leaders, and costs are once again rising sharply.[12] For far too many Americans, security against ruinous medical expenditures and access to needed care remain as elusive as they were before the 2010 breakthrough.

At the same time that the financial threats associated with our jobs, our homes, and our health care have all increased, corporations have raced away from the promise of guaranteed benefits in retirement. Thirty-five years ago, 83 percent of medium and large firms offered traditional "defined-benefit" pensions that provided a predetermined monthly benefit for the remainder of a worker's life. Today, the share is a quarter.[13] Instead, companies that offer pensions provide "defined-contribution" plans, such as the 401(k), in which returns are neither predictable nor assured. Defined-contribution pensions can earn big returns, but they also embody big risks: the risk of stock market downturns, the risk of inadequate savings, the risk of outliving one's account balances. Between 1983 and 2010—an era in which 401(k) coverage exploded—the share of families whose retirement savings promised a level of income in retirement that experts deem adequate declined from more than two-thirds to less than half, as old-style guaranteed pensions rapidly became a thing of the past.[14]

If saving for retirement has become a difficult hill to climb, saving for a rainy day looks like Mount Everest. According to a survey that my research team fielded in 2009, more than 70 percent of Americans say they don't have enough saved to go more than six months without hardship if their earnings dry up (see Figure 1.1). Looking at families' balance sheets, researchers at the nonpartisan Pew Charitable Trusts determined that more than three-quarters of American households met at least one of three tests of "financial

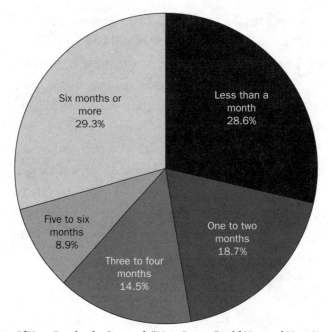

Figure 1.1. If Your Paychecks Stopped, "How Long Could You and Your Family Get By"?
Source: See Jacob S. Hacker, Philipp Rehm, and Mark Schlesinger, "The Insecure American: Economic Experiences, Financial Worries, and Policy Attitudes," *Perspectives on Politics* 11:1 (March 2013): 27.

fragility"—they had less than a month's income in savings, they spent more than or equal to what they made the prior year, or they spent more than 40 percent of their income paying their debts. The Pew researchers conclude: "Despite the national recovery, most families feel vulnerable and stressed, and could not withstand a serious financial emergency."[15]

These numbers are all the more striking, because—as we saw in the Introduction—American family incomes are now on an alarming roller coaster, rising and falling more sharply from year to year than they did forty years ago. In other words, not only have the gaps grown between the rungs on the ladder of the American economy, so too has the distance that people slip down the ladder when they lose their financial footing. And for most the personal safety net that might arrest their fall is far weaker than in the past as well.

Nor does this rising insecurity come with any obvious silver linings. The chance that families will see their income plummet has risen. The chance that they will experience long-term movement up the income ladder has not. For average families, the economic roller coaster takes them up and down. It doesn't leave them any higher than when they started. To the contrary, the chance an adult will end up with a higher family income than his or her parents has fallen dramatically in recent decades.[16] As David Lamberger, the Michigan man who is in the process of losing his house, puts it, "There have been years I made $80,000, and there have been years I made $28,000. . . . Sometimes we're able to pay bills and get by, but then stuff from the slow times never goes away. You can't catch up, and it comes back to haunt you."[17]

What's more, while these up-and-down swings are more severe for workers such as David Lamberger who lack a college education, the pace by which instability has increased since the 1970s has been almost exactly the same for workers who've received a college degree as it has been for those who haven't. Educated professionals may comfort themselves with the thought that they are more financially stable than the checkout clerk who never finished high school. But compared with educated professionals in the past, they are experiencing much greater income swings—swings in fact comparable to those experienced by less-educated workers in the 1970s.

And while national income and wealth have indeed grown handsomely during the era in which insecurity has risen, the economic standing of the American middle class has increased only modestly. The incomes of middle-class families aren't much higher today than they were in the 1970s—and they are much more at risk.

Economic insecurity strikes at the very heart of the American Dream. It is a fixed American belief that people who work hard, make good choices, and do right by their families can buy themselves stable membership in the middle class. The rising tide of economic risk swamps these expectations, leaving individuals who have worked hard to reach their present heights facing uncertainty about whether they can keep from falling. Economic inequality may stir up envy of those at the top or resentment of those at the bottom, but the prospect of economic insecurity—of being laid off, or losing health coverage, or having a serious illness befall a family member—stirs up anxiety. And anxiety, as we shall see, is just what millions of middle-class Americans feel.

THE RISK FACTOR

Pundits fixate on the current state of the economy: Is GDP growth accelerating or slowing? Is the job market expanding or contracting? Is the stock market rising or falling? These are important questions, but they are about the short-term waves of our economy—the movement on the surface, rather than the fundamental changes below. The Great Risk Shift isn't a wave. It's a rising tide that has increased the level of economic insecurity for nearly all Americans, in good times as well as bad.

We all know what risk is when we experience it. When we first get behind the wheel of a car, or traverse the edge of a perilous cliff, we feel the butterflies in our stomach, the lightheadness of fear. But conceptually, risk is not so easy to grasp. It turns all our conventional frames of reference upside down. We are used to thinking about averages, rather than about ranges; about what happens, rather than what could happen; about events at one point, rather than evolution over time—in sum, about levels, rather than dynamics.

Yet risk—the possibility of multiple outcomes, whether good or bad—is all about dynamics. Sophisticated investors in the stock market (the fearless surfers on the waves of risk) recognize this when they talk about the *volatility* of a stock as well as its return. If a stock has higher volatility, its price undergoes more substantial up-and-down shifts over time. These fluctuations in its price, or return, mean that the stock embodies greater risk for the investor, which is why savvy traders only snap up high-volatility stocks when they have high returns as well. Much of our increasingly sophisticated appreciation of risk comes from the efforts of economic players who deal with risk day in and day out to come up with new measures and new models for judging its magnitude and effects.

Risk is at the heart of some of capitalism's greatest successes. The entrepreneurs who financed the nation's first railroad tracks, prospected for oil, or bet on the success of microchips reaped outsized profits. Risk has also been the source of untold misery. For every story of a successful financial risk taken, there is one in which individuals lose their shirts. Risk is the reason companies go bankrupt, workers end up on the streets, and, at the extreme, financial markets crash. Seeing risk and understanding it, finding ways to quantify and share and manage it, gaining from its upsides while minimizing its downsides—these constitute some of the greatest achievements of the last two centuries. But while societies have the ability to master risk—to pool it across many people or address its root causes— societies also create risks: the risks of a dynamic investment market, the risks of interruption of earnings that arise in a division-of-labor economy in which people trade their work for pay, and, of course, the risks to health and the environment that modern production and consumption can pose.[18]

Economic insecurity lies on the dark side of risk. Although the term is rarely defined, *economic insecurity* can be understood as the psychologi- cally mediated experience of the prospect of hardship-causing economic losses. The psychology of insecurity is crucial, for it motivates many of our personal and social responses to risk—responses that can be either pos- itive (buying insurance, building up private savings, forming a family) or negative (suffering anxiety, withdrawing from social life, postponing investments in the future because of fear of loss). Yet a feeling of insecu- rity is not enough to say someone is insecure. Insecurity requires real risk that threatens real hardship. We know that Americans think they are inse- cure. What I will show is that they have good reason to think so—that, like the investor who buys a highly volatile stock, Americans are facing much greater risk of substantial economic loss. The Great Risk Shift is the story of how a myriad of risks that were once managed and pooled by government and private corporations have been shifted onto workers and their families, and how this has created both real hardship for millions and growing anx- iety for millions more.

Risk turns out to be a lot harder to capture precisely with people than with stocks. To know what the volatility of a stock is, we need only follow the ticker for a while (with the familiar caveat that past performance is no guarantee of future results). To know what the volatility of families' economic standing is, however, we need to trace a representative set of families over time, preferably long periods of time. We need to follow these families through all the normal and abnormal events of life: births, deaths, relocations, formation and destruction of families, and so on. We need, in short, to look at the economy the way people actually live it—as a moving picture, rather than an isolated snapshot.

That's not, however, what economic statistics typically do. Consider the growing body of research on inequality in the United States. We know the gap between the rich and the rest has grown dramatically over the last forty years, reaching levels not seen since before the 1930s. The spoils of our system are now so unevenly divided that we must reach back to the robber barons of the 1890s and Gatsbys of the 1920s for a similar comparison to today's gap between middle-income Americans and the super-rich. Between 1980 and 2014, according to comprehensive new data from inequality experts Thomas Piketty and Emmanuel Saez, the top 1 percent of U.S. households (average income in 2014: $1.31 million) saw their pretax income increase by 204 percent, on average. In comparison, households in the bottom half of the income distribution only saw a 1 percent average increase in their pretax income over this period.[19]

Yet as arresting as these statistics are, they're based on annual surveys that reach different people every year. These surveys can tell us how many people are rich and how many are poor, and how big the gap between the two is. But they cannot tell us whether the same people are rich or poor from year to year, or whether movement up (or down) the income ladder is greater or smaller than it used to be. We all know we'll never be as rich as Warren Buffett or Bill Gates. But can we depend, as our parents once did, on maintaining—or, even better, steadily augmenting—our income and standard of living? And how many people are experiencing the wild fluctuations in income (fluctuations that resemble some of our most volatile stocks) that David Lamberger's family has seen?

To answer these sorts of questions, we need to do more than take annual snapshots of income. We need to survey the same people over many years, following them even as they experience death, birth, marriage, pay raises, pay cuts, new jobs, lost jobs, relocations, and all the other events, good and bad, that mark the passage from childhood into old age. We need to see Mark Herrara ensconced in his union job as a carpenter as well as Mark Herrara, independent contractor, as he returns from the hospital, hundreds of thousands of dollars in debt. These kinds of surveys are called "panel surveys," and compared with the usual approach—contacting a different random group of people for each survey—they are exceedingly difficult to carry out. Surveyors must stay in contact with respondents (and their descendants) over long periods of time while periodically adding new respondents to keep the survey representative of a changing population.

Given the difficulties, it's perhaps understandable that no official economic statistic tries to assess directly the dynamics of family income. Curious citizens who spend a few hours on the websites of the Commerce Department or Census Bureau will come away with a wealth of snapshots of the financial health of American families—from annual wages and income to the gap between rich and poor. But they will search fruitlessly for even the most basic information about how the economic status of American families changes over time, much less about what causes these shifts. If they extend their search beyond official statistics, they will do better, but not much better. Many studies of income dynamics have been done. Yet when I began my research in the early 2000s, nobody had looked at the simple question of whether the up-and-down swing of family incomes—the volatility of the American family stock, if you will—had risen or fallen over the last generation.

The answer can be found in the Panel Study of Income Dynamics (PSID)—a nationally representative survey that has been tracking thousands of families from year to year since the late 1960s. Nearly fifty years into its operation, the survey has included more than 75,000 people, some of whom have been answering questions for their entire adult lives, others of whom have been in the survey since their birth.[20] As a result, the PSID is uniquely well-suited to examining how and why incomes rise and fall over time.[21]

And what becomes immediately clear is that family incomes rise and fall a lot—far more than one would suspect just looking at static income-distribution figures. To take just one simple measure, if we track family incomes over ten years, Americans aged twenty-five to sixty-one have less than half the income in the year they're poorest, on average, as they do in the year they're richest.[22] Over ten years, in other words, an average Betty who had $60,000 in her best year would have less than $30,000 in her worst.

These up-and-down swings are what get missed when we use annual snapshots to look at the income distribution. There are not just the well off and the poor. There are Americans who are doing well one year and poorly the next—and vice versa. In fact, a surprisingly big chunk of the inequality that we see across families at any point in time is due to transitory shifts of family income, rather than to permanent differences across families.

This is a point that the Personal Responsibility crowd loves. Sure, inequality is growing, they say, but mobility is alive and well, making any comparison of income groups misleading. The fact that Betty could make $20,000 one year and more than $60,000 in another just shows that the American Dream remains strong for those willing to pull themselves up by their own bootstraps.

But this conclusion is as wrongheaded as the image of a frozen class structure that is sometimes taken from income-distribution statistics. Upward mobility is real. Men like Mark Herrara do start their own businesses; David Lamberger does get his dream house. But upward mobility is usually not dramatic, and there is no evidence that it has increased in the contemporary era of rising inequality.[23] In the mid-2000s, the *Economist* magazine (no foe of American-style capitalism) reported that "a growing body of evidence suggests that the meritocratic ideal is in trouble in America. Income inequality is growing to levels not seen since the Gilded Age, around the 1880s. But social mobility is not increasing at anything like the same pace: would-be Horatio Algers are finding it no easier to climb from rags to riches, while the children of the privileged have a greater chance of staying at the top of the social heap."[24]

Since then, that "growing body of evidence" has only become bigger. The chance of moving into a higher income group—say, from the bottom fifth to the top fifth—is shockingly low and hasn't risen even as inequality has skyrocketed. The evidence shows, moreover, that income mobility across generations is actually lower in the United States than in other affluent nations. According to recent studies, there is more social mobility in European nations such as Sweden than in the United States, there is more social mobility in Canada (where the chances of moving from the bottom to the top is twice what it is in the United States), and in fact only Italy and Britain have as little mobility across generations.[25]

Meanwhile, the chance of children growing up to have a higher household income than their parents has plummeted: from around 90 percent for those born in the early 1940s to around 50 percent—a coin flip—for those born in the early 1980s[26]. With most gains going to the top, fewer and fewer young Americans can expect to do better than their parents. And "better" here doesn't just mean pulling down more income. As we will see, younger Americans are falling behind their parents when it comes to nearly all the trappings of middle-class life: secure housing, adequate savings, health and retirement protections, the means to invest in one's children. In effect, one of the biggest risks of all—reaching middle age without reaching the secure middle class—has exploded.

Plus, there's another glaring oversight of paeans to social mobility: what goes up also goes down. As we saw with David Lamberger, volatility of income can mean making $80,000 one year and freefalling to $28,000 the next, and the year of the freefall could be the year one loses not only one's job but also the family home.

The difference between these two scenarios is profound, because both research and common sense suggest that downward mobility is far more painful than upward mobility is pleasurable. In fact, in the 1970s, the psychologists Amos Tversky and Daniel Kahneman gave a name to this bias: "loss aversion."[27] Most people, it turns out, aren't just highly risk-averse—they prefer a bird in the hand to even a very good chance of two in the bush. They are also far more cautious when it comes to bad outcomes than when it comes to good outcomes of exactly the same magnitude. *The search for economic security is, in large part, a reflection of a basic human desire for protection against losing what one already has.*

Anybody who has watched the differing responses of a toddler to the pleasure of receiving a new toy and the pain of having one taken away knows about loss aversion. Yet it is something of a puzzle why adults behave like toddlers when it comes to things they own. After all, in classic economic theory, goods are simply tickets to enhanced welfare, and we should have no special attachment to things we already possess if other items could deliver welfare just as effectively. Aside from the "diminishing marginal utility" of income (the fact that every dollar buys slightly less happiness or well-being, making us value a $100 gain modestly less than we lament a $100 loss), people should, according to standard theory, value losses and gains in roughly equal terms.

Experiments show, however, that few actual people think this way. Even when given a trivial item, we suddenly become willing to pay a much higher price to retain it than we were willing to shell out to buy it. (One clever study involved giving college students mugs and pencils—seemingly trivial items—and finding that they insisted on selling their gift for much more than they'd earlier said they would pay for it.) Researchers call this the "endowment effect," and it helps explain myriad features of the economic world that are otherwise inexplicable: why, for example, wages don't generally fall during recessions; why stocks have historically had to pay much higher returns than bonds to entice people to take on the increased risk of loss—and why insurance against economic injury remains the most popular and extensive of all the activities that modern governments engage in. (In 2016, for example, spending by public and private social programs such as Medicare, Social Security, workplace retirement pensions, and unemployment insurance represented nearly 30 percent of our economy.)[28]

The endowment effect is surprisingly strong. Americans are famously opportunity-loving. But when asked in 2015 whether they preferred financial stability or upward mobility, 92 percent of Americans said they wanted financial stability; just 8 percent chose upward mobility.[29] In 1996 the Panel Study of Income Dynamics asked participants a similar question. Which would you choose: your present job with your current income for life, or a new job that offered a fifty-fifty chance of doubling your income and a fifty-fifty chance of cutting your income by a third?

On paper, the deal was pretty good. If John was making $30,000 and won the gamble, he'd have $60,000—a comparative fortune. If he lost the gamble, he'd make $20,000—not great, but not terrible compared with what he had. If John didn't worry at all about risk, the choice would be easy: since he has a fifty-fifty chance of ending up with $60,000 and a fifty-fifty chance of ending up with $20,000, the rational position would be to treat the gamble as offering $40,000 (the average of the two salaries)—an amount a third higher than his present income.

Few people who were asked whether they'd take the gamble were rational in this fashion: only 35 percent said they would roll the dice. Lowering the potential income loss budged some of the cautious, but surprisingly few. More than a third of respondents said they wouldn't accept even the most generous deal that the survey presented (which promised, on average, an almost 50 percent income increase). People like to gamble, but not, it seems, when their long-term economic security is on the line.

Loss aversion is a well-known phenomenon in behavioral economics—the study of how people actually reason about economic choices. But the implications of loss aversion for our understanding of the ups and downs of economic life are often missed. What loss aversion means is that drops in income, even when later compensated for by equal or even larger gains, are intensely psychologically difficult.[30] Upward mobility is nice; downward mobility is devastating, especially since it's on the downward trips that jobs, houses, savings, and the other things gained on the way up often get lost.

THE ECONOMIC ROLLER COASTER

Judged on these terms, what my evidence shows is troubling, to say the least. When I started out, I expected to see a modest rise in instability. But I was thunderstruck by what I found: instability of before-tax family incomes had skyrocketed. Income instability was much higher in the 1980s than the 1970s, and much higher in the 1990s than the 1980s. And while it dropped during the boom of the late 1990s, it never fell below 1.4 times its starting level, and it shot up in recent years (my data end in 2014) to more than twice what it was in the early 1970s.[31] Since the early 1970s, rising income inequality and rising income instability have gone hand in hand. The gap between Richie

Rich and Joe Citizen is a lot larger than it used to be, but so too is the gap between Joe Citizen in a good year and Joe Citizen in a bad year.

Isn't this just a problem of the less educated, the workers who've fallen farthest behind in our skills-based economy? The answer is no. Volatility is indeed higher for less-educated Americans than for more educated Americans.[32] (It is also higher for blacks and Hispanics than for whites, and for women than for men.) Yet, surprisingly, volatility has risen by roughly the same amount across all these groups over the last forty years. During the 1980s, people with less formal education experienced a large rise in volatility, while those with more formal education saw a modest rise. As Figure 1.2 shows, however, family income instability has steadily reached higher and higher up the educational ladder—first touching those who went to college but failed to receive a degree and then, by the early 2000s, spreading to college graduates and those even more highly educated. The story of the last few decades is the generalization of the income instability that once afflicted mostly the less educated and disadvantaged. Increasingly, more educated workers are riding the economic roller coaster once reserved for the working poor.

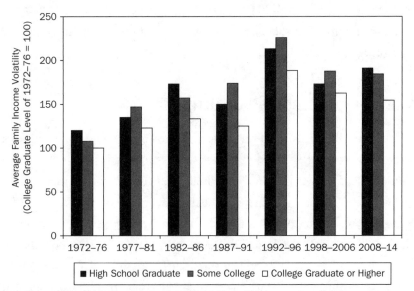

Figure 1.2. Instability Rose at Both High and Low Education Levels
Source: Panel Study of Income Dynamics.

This suggests that growing economic instability cannot easily be chalked up to poor personal choices. It might be argued that workers without a college degree could have gotten additional education (although this would leave open the question of who exactly would fill the millions of jobs that require little advanced training or skills). But how can we say that about workers who did stay in school and yet still experience high levels of volatility? The forces that have created the new economic roller coaster—growing workplace insecurity, the new risks of the contemporary family, and the erosion of stable social benefits—have swept through the lives of almost every American. Prudent choices can reduce exposure to this growing level of economic risk, but they can't eliminate it. Indeed, many of the choices that expose Americans to risk—from going to school to seeking a better job to building a family—are precisely the ones that most greatly benefit families and society as a whole. Families can give up many of these risks only by giving up on the American Dream.

A clue on this point is found in the PSID's questions about risk mentioned earlier, questions that measure the extent to which people are risk-seeking or risk-avoiding. If much of the volatility in income that we see in the PSID was caused by voluntary choices, then we would expect that people who are more worried about risk would be less likely to experience large income swings. After all, if you want to avoid risk and you have the power to do so, you are unlikely to put yourself in a position where your income is highly unstable. If you are risk-averse, you won't choose to go back to graduate school when you can continue working at the local bank, and you won't leave your cushy corporate job for that one-in-a-million opportunity to get your own business off the ground.

Yet the PSID data reveal few consistent relationships between how risk tolerant someone is and how unstable that person's income is. The risk tolerance of someone in the PSID turns out to be a terrible predictor of their income experience. People who are highly risk-seeking experience wild income swings, but so too do people who are highly risk-averse—which is not at all what one would expect if income volatility were mostly voluntary. It's as if a cautious grandmother and reckless teenager were each equally likely to take up bungee jumping, a sure sign that something other than unfettered free choice is at work.

Maybe so, but couldn't family breakup be driving the results? If a family divorces, for example, does one family become two, each with a lower income? The answer is yes, divorce does cause some instability in my measure, but that's because divorce is a real risk to family incomes. The analysis looks at how unstable people's incomes are, and family changes (birth, death, marriage, divorce, separation, and the like) are an important cause of income instability. Lest it be thought that rising divorce rates are the main reason for the rise in income instability, however, it's worth pointing out that the U.S. divorce rate actually peaked in the early 1980s and fell through the mid-2010s—even as economic instability climbed.[33]

How can we make sure that we aren't confusing instability with income growth? If Americans are getting richer and richer, wouldn't that show up as greater income variance? The answer is no. (The premise of the question is also wrong—most Americans are not flying into the income stratosphere.) Just as with the volatility of a stock, the volatility of family incomes is meant to capture how much income bounces around its average level. If the income of Americans is simply rising, that's not instability; it's prosperity.[34]

DROP ZONE

Still, it's hard to think about income instability in the same way we think about stock volatility. When most of us contemplate the financial risks in our lives, we don't worry about the up-and-down movement of our finances around some long-term path, even though that's technically what financial risk is. We think about downside risks, about drops in our income—and understandably so: we are loss averse, in major part, because losing what we have can require wrenching adjustments. We have to cut back, to go without, to adjust our expectations, to rethink our lives. When losses are catastrophic, people have to confront what the anthropologist Katherine Newman calls "falling from grace"—to contend "not only with financial hardship, but also with the psychological, social, and practical consequences" of losing our proper place.[35]

We can get a better sense of these "falls from grace" by looking specifically at *drops* in family income. About 45 percent of all nonelderly adults in the PSID experience a drop in real family income over a two-year period, and while the share rises and falls with the business cycle and has increased overall since the 1970s, it has remained fairly steady. Yet people who experience a family income drop fall farther than they used to. In the early 1970s, roughly 3 percent of individuals experienced drops in family income of 50 percent or greater over a two-year period; by the early 2010s, around 8 percent did, with the share peaking at almost 9 percent in 2010.[36] For a family with around $56,000 in annual income (the median for U.S. households in 2014), a 50 percent loss would mean an income drop of over $28,000.

Figure 1.3 tells the full story, charting the rising share of working-age Americans experiencing 50 percent or greater drops in their family income over two-year periods. The probability of a 50 percent or greater drop was as low as 2 percent in the late-1960s. It's risen dramatically since, and while (like income volatility) it has oscillated with the business cycle, it has risen through both good times and bad, reaching record levels during the Great Recession. Moreover, it has risen among those with advanced degrees as well as high school dropouts, among those in the middle of the income spectrum as well as people at the bottom. There is nothing extraordinary about "falling from grace." You can be perfectly average, and you're still roughly twice as likely to see your income plummet as an average person was forty years ago.

The most dramatic consequence of "falling from grace" is poverty—subsistence at a level below the federal poverty line (for 2018, an annual income of just over $12,000 for an individual and roughly twice that for a family of four).[37] Our conventional view of poverty envisions a distinct group—"the poor," "the truly disadvantaged," "the underclass"—whose experience of deprivation lasts for years, and perhaps even extends across generations. Yet long-term poverty, though real and worrisome, is rarer than we think. Most of the poor at any moment are not poor for long. Less

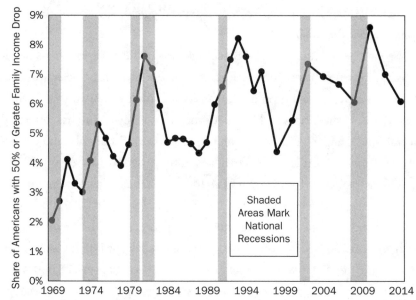

Figure 1.3. Working-Age Americans' Chance of a 50 Percent or Greater Income Drop
Source: Panel Study of Income Dynamics. The line traces the share of individuals aged twenty-five to sixty-one experiencing at least a 50 percent drop in family-size-adjusted real family income from one year to two years afterward.

than a tenth of Americans experience five consecutive years of poverty during their adult life.[38]

The flipside of this picture, however, is that poverty afflicts many more Americans at some point in their lives than is commonly believed. Take the U.S. child poverty rate of more than 20 percent—a rate roughly three times higher than the norm in northern Europe.[39] Most people look at this number and think that "only" one in five kids experience poverty in the United States. That's true in any given year, but the kids who are poor change from year to year. If we want to know how many kids experience poverty at some point in their childhood, we need to count up the total number who spend at least a year beneath the poverty line by the age of eighteen. The answer, it turns out, is shocking: roughly four out of ten of American kids spend at least a year in poverty by the time they're eighteen. Among black children, the share is three-quarters.[40]

The picture is similar for adults. Using the PSID, the sociologists Mark Rank has calculated that a stunning 62 percent of Americans will spend at least a year in poverty (defined in his analysis as falling below the twentieth percentile of the national income distribution) between the ages of twenty-five and sixty.[41] Worse, the chance of spending at least a year in poverty has increased substantially since the late 1960s, even for workers in their peak earning years.[42]

The statistics on income instability and loss provide a precise picture of the growing economic insecurity faced by ordinary workers and their families. And unlike other possible measures, they are about as direct and comprehensive as they come. They tell us by how much the roller coaster goes up and down, looking at every source of a family's income, from friends to employers to government. Rates of bankruptcy or home foreclosure might go up because financial meltdowns have lost their stigma or because people are making foolish choices about spending and debt or because laws have tightened or loosened. But nobody files for a major income drop or spends his or her way into an unstable paycheck. Income instability is a basic building block of economic insecurity. It is not just evidence of the Great Risk Shift; it is a force behind many other types of economic instability, from family breakup to loss of workplace benefits.

It is not, however, the whole of economic insecurity. Indeed, as troubling as the trends we have examined are, they vastly *understate* the true depth of the problem. The up-and-down movement of income among working-age Americans is a powerful indicator of the economic risks faced by families today. Yet economic insecurity is also driven by the rising threat to families' financial well-being posed by budget-busting expenses such as catastrophic medical costs, as well as by the declining security provided by household wealth—and increasing threat posed by household debt. Nor is economic insecurity just about income, expenses, and wealth. It also reflects the transformation of American's distinctive framework of economic protection: the declining scope and generosity of state unemployment benefits, the retreat of employers from generous health benefits, the massively increased risk that retirement has come to represent as more and more of the responsibility of planning for the post-work years has shifted onto Americans and their families. When we take in this larger picture, we see an economy not merely changed but fundamentally transformed.

WHAT'S GOING ON?

Over the years, I've revisited the old neighborhood where I once rode my bike. It looks essentially the same—a city in amber. The supermarket is still there. Close by, other neighborhoods have sprouted large new homes amid long stretches of green. The surface is tranquil, even improved. The old gas station where I remember oil-crisis lines is gone; a microbrewery has moved in nearby. But beneath the calm facade is a growing canker. Families whose lawns remain manicured fear not being able to meet their next mortgage payment. Having seen their salaries drop once, if not more than once, they question their ability to hang on.

What has changed? Why has economic security in the United States fallen so far, so fast? The potential causes are many, and the evidence often murky. Yet much of this book is devoted to unraveling the mystery of the Great Risk Shift. The answer is not as neat or simple as some fictional mysteries, but then again we are talking about momentous shifts in our economy, our society, and our nation's social policies. A change as big as the Great Risk Shift does not usually stem from a single grand cause.

The mystery, it turns out, is not just *why* Americans have come to face greater economic risk. There are straightforward reasons that workers and their families experience heightened financial instability in today's economy and society. The big puzzle is why political and corporate leaders have been so slow to respond. In fact, the puzzle is even deeper than that. Political and corporate leaders haven't simply failed to respond; they've actually piled on new risks even as Americans have become increasingly less secure.

To answer this puzzle requires not further statistical inquiries but a historical journey into the rise and decline of an ideal—the ideal of insurance. This is our next subject: America's sweeping transformation away from an all-in-the-same-boat philosophy of shared risk toward a go-it-alone vision of personal responsibility.

2

Risking It All

For more than four decades, our nation has been undergoing a fundamental revolution in its approach to widely distributed economic risks. Yet so sweeping, steady, and subterranean has this transformation been that few of us stop to consider how dramatically our experiences and assumptions have changed.

A generation ago, if we had been offered a retirement plan by our employer, it would have been a traditional guaranteed pension that looked much like Social Security. Today, those of us who are lucky enough to receive a pension are almost universally enrolled in individual account plans such as 401(k)s. Even the public sector, the last bastion of traditional defined-benefit pensions, has recently been retreating from them—though much more gradually than in the private sector.

A generation ago, if we had been offered a workplace health plan, it would have provided Blue Cross–style coverage, with most of the cost paid directly by our employer. Today, only around half (53 percent) of private-sector workers employed more than twenty hours a week receive health coverage (down from 70 percent in 1980), and old-style coverage with no-money-down care and free choice of physicians is virtually non-existent. Instead, if we find ourselves among the fortunate half of workers receiving coverage, our plan is likely to have one noticeable trait: it places a good chunk of medical costs onto our own financial shoulders. As recently as 2006, only 1 in 10 single-coverage workplace plans had a deductible of $1,000 or more. Today, more than 1 in 2 do. [1] Even the Affordable Care Act, the landmark health law championed by President Barack Obama, permits insurance plans to place very large cost-sharing requirements on patients, albeit with special protections for those with modest incomes.

And a generation ago, nobody in Washington talked about turning Medicare (the federal health program for the aged and disabled) into a system of competing private health plans, or capping spending on Medicaid (the joint state-federal health program for the poor that also pays for most nursing home care), or transforming employer-provided health insurance into a system of individual Health Savings Accounts (HSAs)—at least if they wanted their careers to continue.

Since the mid-1990s, however, cutbacks in social programs have dominated discussion in our nation's capital. Meanwhile, Washington has buzzed with proposals to encourage workers and their families to deal with economic risks on their own—from HSAs to college savings programs to the ever-expanding menu of tax-subsidized plans for retire-ment investments. Ideas that once elicited controversy and confusion now seem ho-hum. When HSAs were authorized under federal law in the early 2000s, few employers or workers seemed interested, and most Americans had no idea what they were. By 2016, with federal tax breaks for such ac-counts increasing, more than half of workers whose employers offered health benefits had access to an HAS or similar savings option, paired with high-deductible health insurance.[2]

What all these discussions have in common is the mantra of indi-vidual control and personal responsibility. The 2005 bankruptcy bill, which greatly tightened the nation's rules for filing personal bankruptcy, was signed by President George W. Bush with the explanation: "America is a nation of personal responsibility where people are expected to meet their obligations."[3] When Treasury Department officials issued the first guidelines for HSAs, they explained: "You own and you control the money in your HSA. Decisions on how to spend the money are made by you without relying on a third party or a health insurer. You will also decide what types of investments to make with the money in the account in order to make it grow."[4] Most famous of all, the Republican-crafted legislation to "end welfare as we know it" that was signed into law in 1996 by President Bill Clinton (who coined the "EWAWKI" credo during his 1992 campaign) was entitled "The Personal Responsibility and Work Opportunity Act."

The responsibility bandwagon stalled in 2005 when President George W. Bush spectacularly failed to pass legislation that would move future beneficiaries of Social Security into private retirement accounts. Yet it returned with a vengeance after the 2008 financial crisis. A huge bailout for Wall Street did not end the advocacy of personal responsibility for Main Street. To the contrary, the rhetoric ramped up, fueled in part by the conservative reaction to President Obama known as the Tea Party. The Tea Party began with a televised rant on the floor of the Chicago Mercantile Exchange by CNBC commentator Rick Santelli in 2009. Calling for a "Chicago Tea Party," Santelli railed against help for distressed homeowners. Rather than "subsidize the losers' mortgages," he declared to cheers from surrounding traders, government should "reward people that could carry the water instead of drink the water."[5] Within weeks, grass-roots organizers and deep-pocketed funders were arranging Tea Party protests at congressional town-hall discussions of the Affordable Care Act. A leading spokesman for the movement summed up its philosophy as "No public money for private failure."[6]

The most famous expression of this philosophy was of course offered by GOP presidential candidate Mitt Romney. At a private fundraiser during the 2012 presidential campaign, Romney singled out those who paid no federal income taxes (almost all of whom pay federal payroll taxes, as well as state and local taxes):

All right, there are 47 percent who . . . are dependent upon government, who believe they are victims, who believe the government has
a responsibility to care for them, who believe that they are entitled
to health care, to food, to housing, to you-name-it. That—that's an
entitlement. And the government should give it to them. And they
will vote for this President no matter what. . . . These are people who
pay no income tax. . . . My job is not to worry about those people.
I'll never convince them they should take personal responsibility and
care for their lives.[7]

Romney's secretly taped remarks became a major liability for him in the
2012 campaign. But he was hardly the only politician singing from the personal responsibility hymnal. According to Tea Party favorite Joni Ernst of
Iowa, who won a Senate seat in 2014, "What we have fostered, is really a
generation of people that rely on the government to provide absolutely everything for them. . . . We're at a point where the government will just give
away anything."[8]

The language of personal responsibility found its most eloquent
spokesman, however, in Representative Paul Ryan of Wisconsin, the self-
styled budget wonk who became chair of the House Budget Committee
in 2011, Romney's running mate in 2012, and then Speaker of the House
in 2015 (only to resign less than three years later as the party's fortunes
fell). Ryan made his name with a series of budget blueprints that slashed
taxes and public spending—especially spending on the poor—radically
scaled back health programs such as Medicare and Medicaid, cut Social
Security and diverted its financing into private accounts, and covered up
the resulting red ink with magic asterisks (proposing, for example, a 91 percent reduction in all spending outside of military expenditures and mandatory programs).[9] Though Ryan usually wrapped his ideas in the soothing
language of "empowerment," he occasionally let the mask slip. Selling his
budget plan, Ryan declared, "We don't want to turn the safety net into a
hammock that lulls able-bodied people to lives of dependency and compla-
cency, that drains them of their will and their incentive to make the most
of their lives."[10]

Ryan's words neatly encapsulate what I call the "Personal Responsibility Crusade," a set of activists, assumptions, and initiatives that have come to dominate debates over social policy in recent decades. The core assertion embodied in the Crusade is that Americans are best off dealing with economic risks on their own, without the overweening interference or expense of wider systems of risk sharing. Insurance, by protecting us from the full consequences of our choices, takes away our incentives to be productive and prudent. As Ryan put it in an elaborate PowerPoint presentation defending House Republicans' 2017 vote to scale back Medicaid and the Affordable Care Act, "Instead of using OPM—other people's money—to pay for health care [so] that you don't care what things cost, we want to harness the power of the marketplace, the power of the consumer." "What [a] Health Savings Account . . . does," Ryan argued, "is it helps hardworking taxpayers get access to affordable solutions, have them pay for their out-of-pocket costs, but it is also their skin in the game."[11]

The Personal Responsibility Crusade is all about putting more "skin in the game"—making people more responsible for the management and finance of the major economic risks they face. More skin means we reap the rewards when the game goes well. More skin also means we bear the losses when the game goes badly.

The Personal Responsibility Crusade is not a momentary response to the recent gains of antigovernment politicians. It is a movement that has been building steam for years, refining its arguments and strategies to challenge the very notion of shared risk. Its ideas are institutionalized in think tanks, embedded in our tax code, and increasingly, part of our most established social programs. Its intellectual and organizational leaders are the primary force pressing for plans to further transform American social protections. Its adherents are not coy about their larger goals, though they generally don't trumpet them in public. In early 2005, when President Bush was beginning his ill-fated campaign to privatize Social Security, a top White House aide wrote to his boss Karl Rove (with excessive hubris, it turns out): "For the first time in six decades, the Social Security battle is one we can win—and in doing so, we can help transform the political and philosophical landscape of the country. We have it within our grasp to move away from dependency on government and toward giving greater power and responsibility to individuals."[12] Ryan put it somewhat less eloquently at a 2017 "ideas summit" hosted by the conservative magazine *National Review*. Making the case for huge cutbacks in Medicaid, Ryan told the panel's moderator, "We've been dreaming of this since I've been around, since you and I were drinking out of kegs."[13]

How did economic risk become a matter of individual rather than shared responsibility? Why, at the same time that Americans are becoming more insecure, is more and more risk and responsibility being shifted onto them? What is at stake in the personal responsibility vision, for us and for American society? Who stands to win, and to lose, if that vision is fulfilled? And what will the brave new world of individually managed risks look like? To understand the full scope of the transformation—and thus the distance we've come—we must travel back to the beginning: 1935, the year of Social Security's birth, and the moment when a powerful new ideal of insurance was planted in America's famously individualistic soil.

THE BIRTH OF AMERICAN SOCIAL INSURANCE

It was spring 1935, and Edwin Witte was worried. The mild-mannered University of Wisconsin professor had come to the nation's capital in 1934 at the request of Labor Secretary Frances Perkins. Cautious and self-effacing, Witte was no firebrand. But his charge was ambitious, even radical—to assist with the development of what was being called the Economic Security Act. The scope of the effort was dauntingly broad, "embracing," Witte later wrote, "all measures to promote recovery and to develop a more stable economic system, as well as assistance to the victims of insecurity and maladjustment"—including health insurance, unemployment insurance, and old-age protections.[14]

By early 1935, however, Witte was far from certain the effort would succeed. "Practically all of the letters which the member of Congress received on the economic security bill," he lamented, "were critical or hostile"—leaving the "net impression . . . that there was serious opposition to the bill and no real support."[15] Worse, a private insurance consultant successfully lobbied the Senate to amend the bill so that those corporations that operated private retirement plans for their workers could opt out of the proposed federal retirement system and not pay the required taxes. Witte knew that this provision was a poison pill that could kill the entire retirement program, preventing it from spreading risks broadly across all workers.

Witte's pessimism, of course, proved unwarranted. The bill, renamed the "Social Security Act," passed in the summer of 1935. At the eleventh hour, Congress dropped the proposal to let companies with private pensions opt out of public old-age insurance. The threat of an old-age program with warring public and private components had been averted.

Nonetheless, the new retirement program (which soon appropriated the label "Social Security" all for itself) was scarcely the crown jewel of U.S. social policy it would later become. True, it was the only fully national program in the 1935 legislation. Yet only half of workers were initially covered, benefits were meager (and failed to rise until after World War II), and nearly all blacks were excluded (due to the exemption of domestic and agricultural workers from coverage—a provision sought by southern conservatives). Moreover, a program for health insurance did not make it into the bill. Though Roosevelt considered the idea, the opposition of the American Medical Association (AMA) helped convince him to put it aside, creating the opening for the predominantly private insurance system of health insurance that the United States has today.[16]

And while the Social Security Act was more ambitious than what most business leaders and Republicans wanted, it was a disappointment to many on the Left, who had called for more fundamental restructuring of the economy and more extensive redistribution of wealth. The act aimed to stabilize capitalism, not stab it. It was about giving workers "a floor of protection," rather than a luxurious carpet of wealth. In describing the act a year after its passage, Witte noted with unconcealed pride that "only in a very minor degree did [the Social Security Act] modify the distribution of wealth and it does not alter at all the fundamentals of our capitalistic and individualist economy."[17]

The breakthrough of 1935 was momentous all the same, for Social Security embodied a bold new imperative of government action: *insurance.*

The word rings familiar today, but it once had a radical air. Insurance was an affirmation of free will over fate. If not an effort to stay the hand of God, it was an attempt to soften his blow. And it rested on modern statistics and actuarial science—which were being employed with increasing sophistication by America's growing network of insurance companies in the 1930s. Witte, in fact, packed the technical working group that was developing the Economic Security Act with private insurance experts willing to deploy the intelligence of insurance on behalf of the nation's economic future.

The intelligence of insurance became genius when insurance principles were coupled with the power of the state to require participation and ensure adequate and affordable coverage. "Social insurance," as it was called, transformed individual misfortunes into common problems. It made the inevitable dislocations of capitalist society risks that could be managed and redistributed, rather than blows of fate that could only be feared and suffered. The "insurance" in social insurance came from the power of aggregation: risks that could devastate an individual or community could be managed if they were spread across many individuals and many communities. The "social" in social insurance came from the principle of shared fate, the reassurance that "we're all in this together." All insurance pools risks. Only social insurance pools risks on terms that enable the poor as well as the rich, the aged as well as the young, the ill as well as the healthy to afford protection. The crafters of the Economic Security Act believed that insurance had to be available and within the means of those who needed insurance most.

At the heart of this belief was a simple conviction: broadly distributed threats to economic well-being—sickness, injury, disability, unemployment, penurious old age—were not the responsibility of individuals alone. They were a widespread and often unavoidable feature of an interdependent industrial society. And because they were, the cost of these risks should be distributed widely across the citizenry, not concentrated on those unlucky enough to experience them—a goal made possible by the unique power of government to compel participation and require contributions. Government could pool the risks of millions of citizens. It could guarantee that even workers of limited means were able to afford basic protection. And it could require that everyone contributed to this common pool throughout their lives, rather than waiting until they fell on hard times or disaster struck, when—for all but the richest—it would be too late.

Today, critics of Social Security often describe it as "outmoded"—a program built for a very different set of circumstances. But the ideal of insurance wasn't meant to deal with the calamity of the Depression; it was meant to provide a secure foundation for economic activity and advancement for decades to come. The architects of the Social Security Act contrasted insurance for working Americans with relief for those who were already destitute. Relief was reactive, demeaning, inevitably stingy. Insurance was proactive, uplifting, generous. Relief was backward looking; insurance was forward looking. By creating a basic floor of protection, it allowed Americans to seize on economic opportunities they might otherwise view with anxiety and fear.

The wealthy had long taken basic economic security of this sort for granted, in part because of long-standing protections for businesses and entrepreneurs whose investments went sour.[18] Social insurance extended economic security to those least capable of obtaining it on their own—namely, those with modest means or a high probability of needing assistance. FDR put it best in a 1938 address commemorating the third anniversary of the Social Security Act: "We must face the fact that in this country we have a rich man's security and a poor man's security and that the Government owes equal obligations to both. National security is not a half and half matter: it is all or none."[19]

INSURING AMERICA

In the three decades after Roosevelt's 1938 speech, what he had called the "frontier of insecurity" shrunk dramatically.[20] A massively expanded Social Security program, disability insurance, Medicare and Medicaid to provide health insurance to the elderly and the poor—all expressed a commitment to protect Americans against the "hazards and vicissitudes" of modern industrial life.[21]

Nor was government the only force pushing back the borders of American insecurity. Pressed on by an aggressive labor movement and flush with profits in an ascendant economy, corporate America also got into the act. Employers built extensive guaranteed pension plans on top of Social Security; they offered private health insurance as an alternative to public protections. The result was a vast system of private security—subsidized by the tax code and regulated by the government—that shielded millions from uncertainty and fear. When this private system was factored into the mix, many better-off and unionized Americans received insurance benefits that were as large, or larger, than those enjoyed by the citizens of such left-leaning European nations as Sweden.[22]

Indeed, the Social Security Act turned out to be a huge boon for private benefits. Life insurance flourished. Retirement pension plans grew more extensive and generous, particularly for highly paid workers. Even corporations that had fought the old-age insurance legislation, or argued that employers with private pensions should be exempted from it, came to recognize the substantial benefits of building their retirement plans on top of Social Security. The private pension consultant who had lobbied most actively for letting employers that operated private retirement plans opt out of Social Security later exclaimed: "It was the greatest mistake of my life. Business is booming as never before."[23]

Americans were also gaining private health insurance coverage at a record pace. Spurred in part by wartime wage controls that exempted workplace fringe benefits, private insurance coverage expanded to reach more than half of Americans in 1950.[24] Most of that coverage, moreover, came through Blue Cross, a nationwide network of hospital-run health plans. Blue Cross plans certainly weren't public programs, but they weren't really commercial insurance, either. Instead of sorting people by their expected cost and charging rates based on these risk categories, the Blues offered insurance to all enrollees at roughly the same premium. With the help of special enabling legislation that was enacted in most states, Blue Cross plans also aspired to enroll lower-income citizens as well as the highly paid. A 1939 press release declared: "The [Blue Cross] plans are a form of social insurance under nongovernmental auspices, not merely a form of private insurance under non-profit auspices."[25]

"Social insurance under nongovernmental auspices" seems an odd rallying cry for a private health plan. But it nicely indicates the extent to which the original vision of Social Security was picked up, and reworked, in the decades after the act's passage. Employers and insurers and, soon, labor unions all saw their own advantages in backing private benefits that pooled risks broadly, though never as broadly as government would have. These actors also demanded, successfully, that the federal tax code generously subsidize these benefits, and they defended them on terms remarkably similar to those that had been used to justify the Social Security Act itself. In the process, they created a unique public-private system of insurance that, for a few brief decades, united government and corporations in pursuit of a common goal—economic security.

PICTURE PERFECT

In the robust economy that followed World War II, many large employers embraced their invigorated role in ensuring economic security with true enthusiasm. Here, in the eyes of corporate leaders, was a distinctive American response to the problems that other nations had addressed through government programs. In 1965 the National Association of Manufacturers announced: "Private employee benefit plans with their inherent flexibility to adapt to the almost infinite requirements of employees and employers should be encouraged to grow and prosper within a favorable government policy and climate."[26] And for three decades after World War II, grow they did.

Consider the giant photo manufacturer Eastman Kodak, always on the forefront of these developments. Based in Rochester, New York, where it once employed a stunning fifth of the city's workforce, "Big Yellow"—as its employees called it—was a pioneer in benevolent welfare capitalism. The benefits offered by Kodak surpass even today's nostalgic accounts of corporate generosity in the 1950s: company housing, in-house health programs, production planning to minimize layoffs, profit-sharing, even jobless benefits paid out of Kodak's own private fund for the unemployed.[27] Kodak *was* its employees' security.

Kodak did not keep its business model to itself, either. Kodak's treasurer, Marion Folsom, served on the advisory committee that helped design Social Security and was secretary of the Department of Health, Education, and Welfare during the Eisenhower administration. Folsom, a southerner by birth who had served in the army during World War I and seemed to be involved in every major political debate over Social Security from 1935 until his death in 1968, was a tireless proselytizer for generous private benefits within corporate circles. In the 1940s Folsom helped Kodak initiate one of the nation's first pension plans that built on top of the nascent Social Security program by offering supplemental retirement benefits. In 1953 Kodak adopted the first medical plan for workers in manufacturing, and it created a health plan for retirees a year later.

Company leaders credited this private welfare system for Kodak's low turnover, high worker morale, and impenetrability to unions. Yet they also saw this system as a model for the *nation's* approach to economic insecurity. Looking back from the vantage point of the late 1960s, Folsom saw it only as a matter of time before the direction of Kodak was the direction of the country: "[W]e have made considerable progress in the last 50 years in protecting people against the major economic hazards of life.... We've still got a few gaps, but on the whole, we're making pretty good progress.... In other words, the two systems [private and public] are working together. Now we've got to extend the voluntary plans to cover these people that are not now covered, most in small unstable companies."[28]

Looking at the American economy of the late 1960s, one could be forgiven for thinking—as Folsom clearly did—that America's unique public-private system of insurance was on the verge of achieving something close to universal economic security. And yet that system was about to be hit with a series of shocks as cumulatively profound as those that had prompted the development of social insurance in the United States. What would emerge would be a very different vision of the role of insurance in American society.

THE ATTACK ON INSURANCE

Social insurance always had its share of critics. Yet rarely did those critics repudiate the ideal of insurance itself. Instead, they argued that the private sector could fill the need without the costly interventions of an overbearing federal government. By the 1960s many erstwhile foes of public social insurance did not even go this far. They merely insisted that government should not do too much to crowd out private protections. As Social Security expanded in the 1960s, the U.S. Chamber of Commerce meekly stated, "Social Security should be continued . . . at a reasonable level. Our only fear is that if Social Security grows too large, it will overtake everything else."[29] When Medicare and Medicaid were created in 1965, it looked as if protection against economic insecurity—once denounced as a fearsome Bolshevist plot—had come to be seen as American as apple pie.

Looks, however, can be deceiving. For even as moderate Republicans such as Folsom were offering effusive praise for America's public-private partnership, a new guard of critics was waiting in the wings. And this new guard had a new line of attack as well: insurance was grossly inefficient.

At the heart of this attack was a previously obscure insurance concept known as *moral hazard*. The essence of moral hazard is simple: protecting people against risks reduces the care people exercise in avoiding those risks. If we have health insurance, according to the logic of moral hazard, we won't take good care of ourselves. If we have coverage for medical costs, we'll spend more on health care. If we are guaranteed Social Security, we'll save less for retirement.

For centuries, insurers have recognized that protecting people against losses that are at least partially under their control gives people less reason to prevent such losses—and, indeed, can even prompt wholly induced or fraudulent claims (as in the classic example of the man who burns down his own home to collect on homeowners' insurance).[30] Moral hazard is an inevitable result of the economic incentives that insurance creates, and all insurers have to design their policies and monitor their payouts to prevent it from becoming too serious a problem. But in the new critique of insurance, moral hazard wasn't just a technical issue that insurers had to address.

It was a glaring flaw with insurance itself—and with government insurance in particular.

The wellspring of this new critique was not the political arena, at least not at first. It was economics. In the 1960s Kenneth Arrow (who would win the Nobel Prize in Economics in 1972) authored a pioneering analysis of the role of insurance in medical care, in which he argued that insurance was a rational and positive response to the inherent uncertainties of the medical field.[31] Arrow, a rigorous, wide-ranging scholar who was also known for his personal generosity and for refusing to engage in ideological squabbling, saw the message of his work as supporting government efforts to encourage broad insurance coverage. "The welfare case for insurance of all sorts is overwhelming," he wrote. "It follows that the government should undertake insurance where the market, for whatever reason, has failed to emerge."[32]

By the 1970s, however, many economists who, like Arrow, subscribed to the tenets of "neoclassical" economics were arguing quite the opposite: that government involvement in insurance could be a huge drag on a dynamic, efficient economy. The first volley came from a freshly minted University of Virginia PhD, Mark Pauly, who launched a no-holds-barred broadside against Arrow's enthusiastic endorsement of government insurance—in what would become "the single most influential article in the health economics literature."[33] Insurance didn't naturally make the medical market work better, Pauly argued. Indeed, it likely made it work worse. The reason was moral hazard, a problem that Pauly insisted had little to do with "moral perfidy" and everything to do with "rational economic behavior." If someone had insurance against medical costs, that person consumed excessive care, driving up premiums. He or she might recognize this fact, even deplore it. But the incentives were clear: get as much health care as possible, costs be damned. The result, said Pauly, wielding the sharpest rhetorical sword in his profession's arsenal, was "inefficiency."[34] And the only way that moral hazard could be countered, Pauly's critique implied, was by eliminating government involvement in insurance—or at the very least making sure insurance was designed properly.

"Designed properly," in the new efficiency critique of insurance, had two meanings, both of which struck at the heart of the argument for broad-based social insurance. "Designed properly" meant, first, that insurers had to charge subscribers in close accordance with their expected probability of requiring help, something private insurers only halfheartedly did, and government insurance virtually never did. Because they were known risks, people who had preexisting conditions, for example, a heart murmur or diabetes—would be asked to pay more or even be denied health insurance. People at greater risk of disability would need to pay more for disability insurance. Otherwise, by this line of logic, insurance would unfairly subsidize high-risk groups, increasing costs for the healthy and prudent, and for society as a whole.

"Designed properly" meant, second, that insurance had to aggressively monitor policyholders' behavior to make sure they didn't engage in insurance-induced opportunism—faking their conditions, or spending excessively on insured services, or doing anything that increased their exposure to risk. If some people with life insurance were routinely going skydiving, companies needed to write such people out of their contracts. If some people with health insurance were going to the doctor whenever they had the sniffles, such people had to be discouraged from overutilizing services—or excluded from coverage. At best, such moral hazard was costly to the insurer. At worst, by encouraging people to take excessive risks, it could worsen the very problems that insurance was meant to solve, further impairing efficiency. Like the child who sees his bicycle helmet as an invitation to ride in rush-hour traffic, insurance could turn people into risk-seeking opportunists, blind to the true costs of their reckless actions.

Of course, this critique—that insurance didn't charge premiums in close accordance with expected risk or aggressively monitor policyholders' behavior—was directly at odds with the conception of insurance that had emerged out of the New Deal. Social insurance (even when under "private auspices," as the proponents of Blue Cross health plans described their mission) was *supposed* to provide subsidized coverage to high-risk groups and those who couldn't easily purchase commercial policies. Social insurance was *supposed* to protect beneficiaries from the intrusive and stigmatizing interventions into private conduct that had been so characteristic of assistance policies in the past. But, according to the new science of moral hazard, these convictions were destined for history's dustbin. The appropriate standard, this perspective insisted, was not whether insurance created broad risk pools or provided economic security. It was *efficiency*, and to the critics, social insurance was anything but efficient.

The most influential of these critics was the most improbable of tenured radicals, Harvard economist Martin Feldstein. Balding, diminutive, and bespectacled, with an unassuming demeanor and amused smile, Feldstein looked every bit as threatening to the established economic consensus as a chihuahua to a Doberman. The Doberman, however, didn't stand a chance. Feldstein was prolific. He was a skilled teacher, commanding huge audiences in his introductory economics course, which he turned into a running pitch for neoclassical economics and its then-unconventional prescriptions. I remember taking his course as a student in the early 1990s, surrounded by hundreds of young, smart, impressionable freshmen in the grand wood pews of Sanders Theatre. The stained-glass windows gave the auditorium the feel of a church, and it was of sorts—the church of neoclassical economics. Our bible was Adam Smith's *Wealth of Nations*, our catechism the laws of supply and demand, our spiritual leader an unexceptional-looking professor in a drab gray suit whose high forehead glowed angelically under the theater lights.

Feldstein also had the ears of influential politicians. Rising stars in the invigorated conservative movement may not have read or understood his hundreds of articles, but they did understand that Feldstein was providing a sophisticated and credible version of what they were arguing: government was too big, too overbearing, too inefficient. A Feldstein article had two parts, now familiar after years of repetition by disciples and emulators. First, find a well-meaning law, regulation, or program that was designed to protect workers and their families from harm by indemnifying them against certain risks. Second, show that by reducing the costs of these risks, the law, regulation, or program created perverse incentives, making the problem it was meant to solve worse, or at least not much better. For example, Feldstein attacked both unemployment insurance and Social Security on the grounds that they encouraged the very thing they were supposed to prevent—namely, time out of the workforce and inadequate retirement income.[35] The Feldstein one-two punch was always backed up with impressive economic techniques and delivered with an air of regret rather than anger. "You may not like the truth," was Punch 1. "But you cannot deny it," was Punch 2.

Over the course of the 1970s, Feldstein churned out a series of highly technical but hugely influential studies showing that Americans, because of tax breaks and public programs, were excessively insured against health costs and other financial risks. Not only were all existing policies inefficient, Feldstein argued, but the taxes used to support them were a huge drain on the economy, drastically reducing the incentives of higher-income Americans to work and invest. (In his classes, Feldstein liked to describe the three U.S. tax rates as "high," "higher," and "highest.") When Ronald Reagan was elected in 1980, he tapped the forty-one-year-old economist to head the White House's Council of Economic Advisers.

The straightforward prescription of all these attacks was that government should dramatically cut back its role in insuring Americans against economic losses. Moral hazard, this growing body of criticism hammered home, was a greater problem than insecurity—and indeed, the critics suggested, one of insecurity's main causes.

THE PERSONAL RESPONSIBILITY CRUSADE

Politically influential critics of government did not take long to pick up the moral hazard mantra. The notion, after all, resonated deeply with long-standing elements of American political thought: the emphasis on individual self-reliance, the celebration of private markets, and the abiding concern about overweening government power. Implicit in the concept, too, was another potent theme that was gaining ground in the 1970s—a demand for individual self-restraint as the central means of dealing with crime, poverty, and other social ills, which were increasingly blamed on "permissive" government policies. Perhaps most important, moral hazard provided a pragmatic rationale for policy ideas that conservatives had once advocated on idealistic grounds. As moral hazard moved from economic circles into political debate, it thus quickly became an all-purpose critique not just of poorly designed insurance but of the perverse economic effects of government in general.

Efficiency was the lodestar of this new critique, and its most effective weapon. In the past, critics of an activist state had taken on government in broad philosophical tones. Now, they argued that government, whatever its intentions, was a *practical* failure because it impaired economic efficiency.[36] Government was not only incapable of providing economic security, in other words: it actually hurt it by harming the economy. Reagan, perhaps the most successful political figure to ride the antitax, antigovernment wave of the late 1970s, summed up the sentiment in his 1981 inaugural address: "In this present crisis, government is not the solution to our problem; government is the problem."[37]

This was—and is—the central message of the Personal Responsibility Crusade: government should get out of the way and let people succeed or fail on their own. Government insurance upsets the natural working of a free society. It takes from the most energetic individuals and enterprises in society to subsidize those who are a costly drag on a vibrant economy. "Government insurance," in the words of one critic, "taxes the most productive activities to redistribute to the most risky"—one reason "the government that governs least, governs best."[38] In the early 1980s, conservative scholar Charles Murray coined a simple syllogism to explain why good-intentioned programs inevitably went bad: "Any social transfer increases the net value of being in the condition that prompted the transfer."[39] In other words, helping people just creates more people who need help—moral hazard with a vengeance.

Perhaps the clearest statement of the new credo came not from an economist but from a prominent antifeminist, George Gilder, whose 1981 bestseller, *Wealth and Poverty*, swept through the emboldened Republican policy community like a conservative tsunami. (The *New York Times* observed that Gilder's book—which President Reagan handed out to friends and advisers and Reagan's budget director hailed as "Promethean"—was "embraced by Washington with a warmth not seen since the Kennedys adopted John

Kenneth Galbraith.")[40] Now best known for his defense of big tax cuts for the rich, Gilder actually began his indictment of present policy with a chapter entitled "The Moral Hazards of Liberalism." The chapter turned out to be a pithy summation of the conservative case against insurance, which, Gilder warned, had "upset the balance between risk and security." "There is abundant reason to believe," Gilder confidently declared, "that the American welfare state long ago passed its points of diminishing and counterproductive returns, that the insurance features of American society now so overbalance the risk features that everyone—rather than the direct victims of hardship or change—feels anxious and insecure." Here was the moral hazard mantra in all its interlocking dimensions: far from aiding the economy, insurance was creating "a collective danger of national sclerosis, an economy that is closed to the necessarily risk-fraught and unknown future." If Americans felt "anxious and insecure," this was only because they had too much insurance, not because they had too little.[41]

Thus, by the 1980s, the circle was complete. Insurance had been justified as a way of aiding the unfortunate—now it was criticized as a way of coddling the irresponsible. Insurance had been understood as a partial solution to social problems such as unemployment and poverty in old age—now it was condemned as worsening the very problems it was meant to solve. Insurance had been seen as a cushion against the sharp edges of a dynamic capitalist economy—now it was disparaged as an impediment to economic efficiency. When economists used the term "moral hazard," they focused on incentives rather than morality. But in the rhetoric of the Personal Responsibility Crusade, morality was never far beneath the surface. "What moral hazard means," according to James K. Glassman, a resident fellow of the conservative American Enterprise Institute (and a leading advocate of Social Security privatization), "is that, if you cushion the consequences of bad behavior, then you encourage that bad behavior."[42]

Statements such as these might suggest that the language of moral hazard resonated only on the fringes of conservative thought. Yet nothing could be further from the truth. The concept was powerful precisely because its core message—personal responsibility, self-reliance, individual discipline, private probity—resonated so strongly with so many Americans at a time when concern about the cost and economic impact of existing programs was rising. "Personal responsibility," notes the political theorist Yascha Mounk in his 2017 book, *The Age of Responsibility*, started "its life as a political watchword [and] slowly turned into a cultural phenomenon."[43] And yet, while millions of Americans happily repeated the mantra of responsibility, the message of moral hazard was, underneath it all, fundamentally in conflict with many Americans' strongest beliefs about fate, security, and justice. For as enduring as the faith in rugged individualism was—and continues to be—Americans had also come to accept and expect a substantial role for government and corporations in shielding workers from the major economic risks they faced. As soon would become clear, the message of moral hazard was directly in conflict with that role.

FROM INSURANCE TO INSECURITY

The role of corporations was the first to change. Beginning in the late 1970s, American business began to abandon and restructure private benefits to move risks and costs from their balance sheets onto families' bottom lines. The days of the benevolent corporation that *was* its employees' security, as "Big Yellow" once was, were over. Private health insurance declined steadily, as corporations imposed deductibles and dropped coverage, and the health insurance market fragmented into smaller and smaller risk pools.

Meanwhile, personal responsibility—and risk—was also on the rise in the area of retirement pensions. Workers who had traditional guaranteed pension plans held onto them, but new workers weren't given the option, and old-style plans weren't expanded. Instead, new workers whose employers provided a plan were offered 401(k)s and other defined-contribution plans that allowed them to save for their retirement but didn't provide any promise that the benefits would be sufficient for them to finance their old age. Workers had to put away their own money for their own retirement, and they had to manage the money capably themselves. If they didn't—if they failed to take advantage of 401(k) plans or made poor investment decisions or didn't plan their finances carefully enough—that was their problem, not a corporate concern.

To be sure, advocates of personal responsibility weren't directly responsible for these changes, which were driven by business concerns about competitiveness and a sense that workplace benefits no longer delivered the big rewards that companies such as Kodak had once celebrated. But proponents of personal responsibility did abet the shift in a variety of ways. One was by developing attractive new tax breaks to encourage individualized benefit plans that could compete with old-style health and pension benefits. In 1981, for example, the Reagan administration authorized the first 401(k) retirement plans under the terms of a little-noticed 1978 law. Reagan also pushed for massively expanded Individual Retirement Accounts (IRAs) as an alternative to both Social Security and traditional pensions. The floodgates quickly opened to a growing assortment of costly new tax breaks for IRAs, 401(k)s, education savings plans, health care accounts, and other account-style plans that, conservative supporters hoped, would not only reduce Americans' dependence on government programs but also bolster enthusiasm for new and expanded private options.

Conservative backers of individualized private options had plenty of reasons to support new tax-subsidized accounts. Such accounts were, after all, generous all-purpose savings and inheritance-planning devices for the wealthy and highly paid. If you made good money, IRAs and 401(k)s not only let you pass on much more to your children but also allowed you to enjoy more goodies yourself in your golden years. If that wasn't enough to get anti-tax conservatives on board, encouraging people to save for their own health care and retirement in tax-free accounts also undermined government programs by reducing tax revenues. And yet it was not lost on many of the most fervent backers of individualized private plans that tax-free accounts had another important salutary effect as well: having individuals manage their own risk created a powerful alternative to the existing public-private system of security. In strategy sessions, advocates went so far as to call private retirement and savings accounts a "parallel system"—parallel in the sense that it could operate alongside existing programs, gradually fostering a new constituency for private-sector alternatives and transforming popular conceptions of government's role in safeguarding security.[44] These strategists understood that America's system of economic security hadn't been built in a day, and it wouldn't be torn down in a day either. It had to be steadily undermined until—battered by hostile private-sector interests and an increasingly unsympathetic public, all but the poorest segments of which looked to the private sector, not government, for security—it would finally succumb.

This strategic rationale had been laid out as early as 1985 by a prominent conservative policy expert, Stuart Butler of the Heritage Foundation, who was at the center of the intellectual development of conservative proposals for social policy reform throughout the 1980s and 1990s. (Butler would later moderate some of his views and become a Senior Fellow at the center-left Brookings Institution; the move was a telling indicator not only of how mainstream his views had become within policy circles, but also of how far to the right the Heritage Foundation and other advocates of the Personal Responsibility Crusade transited in the 2000s and 2010s.)

British by birth, Butler was what might have been called, in his native country, a Red Tory—a conservative free-market enthusiast who nonetheless believed that government could and should play a positive role in people's lives, albeit an indirect one. What made Butler a behind-the-scenes player in nearly every major policy drive launched under the personal responsibility banner—the Waldo, if you will, of the conservative attack on the welfare state—was the unusual savvy with which he married political and policy analysis. A keen student of Margaret Thatcher, Butler believed that the only way to cut back government's role in providing economic security was to offer voters an attractive alternative vision of government's role that was rooted in the self-interest of powerful private actors. The route to victory, Butler argued, wasn't hectoring citizens or futilely chopping away at the margins of existing programs. It was to encourage the private sector—or, more precisely, affluent consumers and private benefit providers—to take matters into its own hands, creating a robust alternative to public programs that would not just benefit influential private actors but also create the institutional means to put the government out of the insurance business down the line.[45]

I had the chance to speak with Butler as I was writing this book, and he was quite candid about the long-term conservative strategy:

In general, an element of all of these [conservative policy approaches] is to create a parallel system based on more legitimate principles. In the process, you change people's view of risk—you get people to think differently. . . . You could just say, "Accept risk, walk it off." But what we say is "Let's essentially privatize the risk man-agement for health or retirement." You give people other vehicles to manage the risk of living too long or being sick. You wean people gradually off of social-insurance risk management into private risk management without making them fearful about it. You have got to do it in steps and have some government protection, at least at the beginning.[46]

The target of the Personal Responsibility Crusade therefore increasingly shifted from the means (government) to the end (insurance). Rather than calling for the *elimination* of government's role, conservatives demanded that this role shift from providing shared insurance against economic mis-fortune toward providing individual accounts that people could use to provide for themselves and their families. Yes, these accounts would be sponsored by government. Yes, they would be subsidized by taxpayers. Yes, they would be regulated; indeed, they would sometimes be mandatory. But they would shift risk onto individuals, and this made them consistent with personal responsibility. It also didn't hurt that they could be sold as tax cuts, and that most of their benefits went to upper-income taxpayers, who tended to be reliable Republican voters.

Perhaps most important, advocates of private accounts believed that they would ultimately transform how Americans viewed government and each other. By encouraging Americans to rely on themselves, tax-favored accounts would also make people more deeply invested in the market, more distrustful of direct government programs, more reluctant to join broader risk pools—and more likely to vote for conservative politicians. Shifting from public insurance to publicly encouraged ownership, in the triumphant declaration of James Glassman, will "shift the entire founda-tion of our domestic politics. Today's Entitlement Age, based on New Deal assumptions . . . will fade."[47] In the new conservative playbook, accounts wouldn't just strike at the heart of the insurance state; they would also peel off voters for a new conservative governing coalition.

This larger political goal has been described most grandiosely by Grover Norquist, the bearded antigovernment crusader who heads Americans for Tax Reform and helps coordinate the conservative movement for federal tax and spending cuts and privatization of public programs. New and expanded investment accounts lavishly subsidized through the tax code, Norquist has argued, will "change the national psyche: increasing the political constituency for lower taxes, stronger property rights, and greater personal responsibility and self-reliance."[48]

The embrace of government-subsidized accounts in pursuit of the Personal Responsibility Crusade adds a paradoxical twist to Reagan's famous credo. To the personal responsibility crusaders, government is the problem, but government is also the solution. For only government can tear Americans away from their dependence on public and private institutions of risk sharing and teach them to appreciate the age-old virtues of individual responsibility and personal thrift.

WHO'S AFRAID OF PERSONAL RESPONSIBILITY?

To pursue their attack on insurance, adherents of the Personal Responsibility Crusade have largely adopted strategies of stealth, seeking to transform existing arrangements beneath the radar screen of public awareness. Rather than tear existing arrangements out by the roots, advocates of personal responsibility have mostly worked to chip away at America's public-private framework of economic security, all the while blocking efforts to deal with the growing economic risks that American families face. To see their success thus requires looking for more than dramatic policy upheavals. It requires understanding why, in an era in which more and more risk and responsibility is shifting onto the shoulders of ordinary Americans, there is so little political discussion of the crucial role of insurance in ensuring the vibrancy and humanity of a dynamic capitalist economy.

The main motive for conservatives' strategies of stealth has been simple political pragmatism. Conservatives learned the hard way that for all the natural appeal of the rhetoric of personal responsibility, frontal assaults on existing programs are a nonstarter with most of the American public. Americans believe strongly that people should pull themselves up by their own bootstraps; but they also believe that people should be protected when they are buffeted by the winds of economic fortune.[49] Conservatives gained traction when they talked about the debilitating effects of government programs and taxes in general terms. Their wheels skidded, though, when they singled out specific programs of insurance for cutbacks, restructuring, or all-out dismantling—and so they focused on changing the *form* and *generosity* of insurance, rather than eliminating protections altogether.

Janis Joplin once sang, "Freedom's just another word for nothing left to lose." The Personal Responsibility Crusade offers a new twist: "*Insurance* is just another word for nothing left to lose." In the logic of social insurance, rules and incentives that encourage risk sharing are enabling—indeed, essential if citizens are to participate fully in the economy. In the logic of personal responsibility, *repealing* such rules and incentives is enabling. During the 2017 debate over Republicans' ill-fated health plan, a crystalline moment came when Congress's budget scorekeeper predicted that 22 million Americans would lose insurance due to the plan's cutbacks in Medicaid and private premium subsidies and its elimination of the requirement that people show proof of coverage. Paul Ryan responded, "It's not that people are getting pushed off a plan. It's that people will *choose* not to buy something that they don't like or want."[50]

To Ryan and the many who share his outlook, greater exposure to risk is liberating, not lamentable—freeing, not frightening. Freed from the shackles of old-style risk protections, we can plan for our own future, make our own decisions about how much risk to bear in the market, and enjoy the financial rewards of our newfound freedom as we alone wish. Freed from the specter of moral hazard, our government will be able to scale back its commitment to insurance protections that invite immoral opportunism and subsidize high-risk groups. The state will not wither away, but its role will be limited to providing people with the means—from private accounts to individual vouchers—to cope with economic risk largely on their own.

Picture our liberated worker. A hardworking professional, he takes time each morning to check the level of his IRA, rebalance the portfolio in his 401(k), see if his medical spending is depleting his HSA, and make sure the Education Savings Account he set up for his kids is accumulating enough for sixteen or more years of private schooling for his twin daughters. If he were to lose his job, he would draw on his Temporary Unemployment Savings Account—which, of course, he's diligently contributed to, knowing full well the risks that all professionals face in today's hyperdynamic, free-agent economy. If he were somehow disabled, he could draw on his Disability Savings Account, as well as the tax-advantaged private disability coverage that he purchased on his own and religiously renews each year.

His wife is staying home to care for their two new children, courtesy of a Caregivers' Account in which the couple socked away money from their first day out of college. Soon, they will draw on the Caregivers' Account to pay for a full-time nanny so his wife can go back to her own professional job. Ever resourceful, he has not only bought a standard life insurance policy but also set up a Long-Term HSA, which will cover his and his wife's expenses if they ever need nursing home care—and, like all the other ac-counts, can be passed on to the kids if they don't use the money by their deaths. He often finds himself shaking his head when he hears about young workers who have passed up all these extravagantly subsidized options. To each his own, he shrugs. He is certainly not going to bail them out when they find themselves out of a job or in need of round-the-clock care. And when his kids are older, he will tell them what he has learned from a life of hard work and prudent saving: the entitlement age is over.

Now let's turn to a real worker, Felix Meschke. On January 1, 2006, just before President Bush called for $156 billion over ten years in expanded support for HSAs in his State of the Union Address, Meschke took per-sonal responsibility for his family's health care and signed up his family for an HSA.[51] Less than two weeks later, he found himself in an emergency room, deciding whether or not to hospitalize his eleven-month-old son, whose ear infection had developed into a high fever and racking cough. Thankfully, his son recovered, but the family was left with a whopping bill, a bill that under an old-style insurance plan would have been fully covered.

Now the Meschkes alone would be responsible for the entire amount—whether or not they could afford to pay.

Here's the rub: Meschke was not your typical consumer. He was a business school professor at the University of Minnesota who taught courses in financial management and investment. If even the most educated and informed consumer with plenty of "skin in the game" struggles with health care decisions, how realistic is it to expect more of the rest of us? On the University of Minnesota's website, the HSA's description read: "you make decisions about how you spend your health care dollars."[52] But in the emergency room, faced with a decision on whether or not to hospitalize his son as his ear infection worsened, Felix Meschke did not feel much in control. "I realized that I neither had the bargaining power nor mental capacity," confided Meschke. "If you're negotiating a car, you can always say, 'I'll walk off the lot.' If your one-year-old kid has an IV in his arm, you don't have the same situation."[53]

Which of these two pictures of the new world of personal responsibility awaits us? Are we on the verge of a nirvana of empowered consumers, or a harsher reality of increasingly widespread economic risk and insecurity? The Personal Responsibility Crusade says the first. The changes taking place in the United States suggest the second.

3

Risky Jobs

Jeff Martinelli might be considered lucky. He grew up in poverty, sometimes going hungry as a child. Even today, he remembers with shame his family relying on welfare checks to get by and hauling groceries home through the snow on a tiny cart because his parents didn't have a car. Perhaps these hardships help explain why Jeff skipped college to go straight to work to earn a living. But then again, the work was good: a factory job with high pay and generous benefits, a direct route to middle-class life. Then, in 2001, when he was fifty, the bottom fell out of Jeff's American Dream. He was laid off, and despite his factory experience, he couldn't find work. Eventually, he scavenged a new job—in pest control—but he ended up making less than half what he used to. A sunny man, Jeff looks on the bright side: "At least I have a job. Some of the guys I worked with have still not found anything. A couple of guys lost their houses."[1]

Lisa Casino-Schuetz might well lose her home. In 2008 she had a well-paying job as a business consultant. With her graduate degree in organizational psychology, she never expected her own organizational footing to be at risk. But after she lost her job, the forty-eight-year-old shuttled between increasingly penurious and precarious positions—a $15 gig at a sports medical facility, a customer service job at an Amazon wholesaler—until she was making one-fifth of her original salary as a temp. Today, Casino-Schuetz does a different sort of consulting: offering advice to other laid-off workers adjusting to their unwelcome new circumstances. As a volunteer for Neighbors-helping-Neighbors, a self-help group for the long-term unemployed founded in 2011, she helps others confront the depression and anxiety that comes with long-term unemployment, the depression and anxiety that almost pulled her under. "You can't believe what's happening to you," she recalls. "You ask: 'Why me?', 'What did I do wrong?'" As time went by, her angst turned into fear—fear she wouldn't be able to make ends meet, fear she wouldn't be able to pull out of her economic and emotional tailspin. Her children were scared, too. "The pressure was enormous," she says.[2]

In comparison with Jeff and Lisa, Mark McClellan initially rose higher. He had it all: a big house in the nicest part of town, a swimming pool, a new Jeep. His wife didn't even have to work. "I was right in the middle of middle-class America, and I knew it and I loved it," he said. But when his management job at Kaiser Aluminum in Washington State was eliminated after the company filed for bankruptcy, he fell right out of the middle. Now, his savings depleted, he looks for work and dreams about opening a carwash. But most of his time—and money—goes to caring for his wife, who has a rare brain disease. Because he's no longer employed, it costs him a small fortune to buy basic health insurance and the medicine she needs to live. He cares for her on his own. "Am I scared just a little bit?" Mark asks. "Yeah, I am."[3]

Mark is not alone. Though his plight is stark, he feels what millions of workers feel: *fear*. But this fear isn't the kind we typically think of when we talk about "job insecurity"—the fear of losing a job during an economic downturn and then having to tread water for a short time until the economy picks up. Nor does this fear affect only low-wage workers in dead-end jobs, as we too often assume. The new workplace insecurity is different from these familiar portrayals: broader, more insidious, and often more damaging to workers' morale than the boom-and-bust layoffs of the past. It is driven by the growing recognition that no worker, no matter how educated, no matter how well trained, is free of the risk of sudden and large economic losses—when the economy is racing along as well as when it is struggling. Indeed, in America's new knowledge and service economy, with its huge and shifting differentials in pay and benefits and its growing role for part-time, erratic, and contingent work, the skills in which we invest our time, our money, and our passion are both more necessary to economic success and more fragile as guarantees of economic security than ever before.

Workers have always faced risks. Jobs come and go. Pay trends up or down. Hours expand and contract. What's changed is that these risks have become broader—they affect more workers and come from more sources—and the stakes have gone up. Workers now invest more in education to earn a middle-class living, and yet these costly investments are no guarantee of a high, stable, or upward-sloping path. The nation's official unemployment rate obscures just how often people find themselves displaced from even well-paying jobs. It also obscures how risky many sectors of the economy are even for those who keep their jobs. The service sector produces plenty of well-paid jobs, but it also features a mass of low-wage and part-time positions with little or no job security, opportunities for advancement, or benefits. The apotheosis of this transformation is the so-called gig economy of no-commitment contingent work—an increasing share of it managed through online platforms such as the ride service Uber and piece-work sites such as TaskRabbit and Amazon's Mechanical Turk. All these shifts have dramatically reshaped the expectations and experiences of a workforce that once operated under the assumption that employees could smoothly progress up the income ladder and move between jobs without enduring declines in their pay or benefits.

Job security isn't the same as job stability. You can be secure and have a constantly changing work life if you're getting the training and support you need to jump from job to job and your income and benefits aren't constantly at risk. Indeed, some European nations have tried to achieve what they call "flexicurity"—flexible labor markets with the security workers need to feel confident they can invest in their work and skills. What job security means, most fundamentally, is what FDR famously called "freedom from fear": the fear that a job will disappear entirely, the fear that specific investments in work will be lost, the fear that losing a job will mean losing other things of value—health care, retirement security, the income needed to maintain a middle-class standard of living. American workers today are not free from fear. And their reasons for fear are real and growing.

THE NEW WORK CONTRACT

We've heard much about how the American economy has changed and why. Global trade has increased, exposing once-sheltered jobs to international economic pressure. Cross-border financial flows have exploded, encouraging companies to shift their operations—and jobs—from nation to nation to maximize return. Short-term investment behavior driven by an emphasis on stock value has replaced the more slow-moving cash flows of the past, giving companies less room for error, less cushion against losses, and less reason to invest in their workers, as opposed to "incentivizing" their CEOs and big shareholders. Dramatic technological changes, from automation to digitalization to artificial intelligence, have transformed the nature of work, decimating traditional blue-collar jobs while boosting knowledge and service positions marked by large differentials in pay and benefits and, often, limited job security.

And yet, the sum of these changes still remains elusive. Books and articles take one side and then the other in the dispute over whether the new American worker is liberated or alienated, a free agent or a fall guy. The end result is often confusion rather than clarification—even though the basic contours of what has happened turn out to be abundantly clear.

The one aspect of the new American workplace that everyone seems to agree on is inequality: highly educated workers are pulling farther and farther ahead; less educated workers are falling farther and farther behind. There is much truth to this assertion, but it is incomplete. Only a small slice of the American workforce is truly excelling in the new world of work. (One study finds that only the top few percent of earners received wage gains as large as the overall growth of U.S. productivity in recent decades. The median hourly wage, by contrast, barely rose; wages for the bottom fifth of workers actually fell.)[4] What's more, inequality is rising *among* skilled workers as well as *between* the skilled and unskilled, and the previously most insulated workers are actually the ones who have seen the greatest erosion of their workplace preeminence over the past thirty years.[5]

Inequality is real and rising, but looking at the changing economic landscape only through its prism occludes as well as reveals. If we look at the landscape through the prism of risk instead, we see that the most fundamental transformation felt by most workers is much simpler and more profound: the loss of the belief that jobs provide a stable path to or guaranteed place in the American middle class—the loss, in a nutshell, of workplace security. And at the heart of this loss is the new American work contract.

By American work contract, I mean the formal rules and informal norms that once governed the mutually beneficial but inherently uneasy relationship between workers and their employers. The old contract—never enjoyed by all workers and almost always implicit, yet still a powerful private standard whose influence belied its less-than-complete reach—said that workers and employers shared the risk of uncertainty in the market as well as the gains of productivity from skills and innovation.

The shared gains we know much about, because the three decades after World War II are now widely recognized to have been a period of equalizing incomes and rapidly rising median wages. The shared risks we know less about, because they were less visible, hidden in the private practices of workers, unions, and employers. On the worker side, shared risks meant a certain degree of loyalty to the firm, a certain degree of commitment to the pay and welfare of fellow employees, a certain degree of restraint in demanding benefit and pay increases when times were good so that the fallout would be less painful when times were bad. On the employer side, shared risks meant an emphasis on the development of workers' skills, the provision of generous workplace benefits such as health care and pensions, and the buffering of workers from the risks of fluctuating demand. The bargain held because it worked for both parties—workers received job security, guaranteed benefits, and good pay; employers got loyal, productive workers who invested in skills specific to their jobs and didn't jump ship when times were tough.

Who killed the old contract? Was its death inevitable because of competitive pressures? Or was it an inside job, driven by changing corporate strategies or the desire of high-pay workers to go it alone? The answer unquestionably is both—but the specific form that the new contract took was most certainly not inevitable.

The competitive pressures on corporations have indeed intensified. Compared with the early postwar period, many firms face greater volatility in sales, employment, and profits, implying, as one analysis concludes, that "Americans now find their paychecks tied to increasingly rocky corporate ships."[6] Paradoxically, other sectors have seen concentration and consolidation, as the distinctive characteristics of the knowledge economy reward the biggest players who can leverage their huge networks of locked-in users and the near-zero cost of expanding those networks: companies such as Amazon, Apple, Facebook, and Google. But even these dominant firms worry that they can go from have-it-alls to has-beens overnight. Gene Sperling, former economic adviser to Bill Clinton and Barack Obama, has called this new era "the dynamism economy," one characterized by an acceleration of the "creative destruction" of innovation and restructuring that the great economist Joseph Schumpeter identified as the defining element of the market economy.[7] Another way to describe it, however, is as the "insecure economy," in which most of the costs of adjusting to new economic realities have been shifted from employers and the government onto workers and their families.

Yet, if the rise of the insecure economy was fueled by outside forces on companies, the corporate response was formulated in a particular context—the antigovernment era of the late 1970s and early 1980s, when organized labor and the ideal of insurance were both on the wane. Corporations and workers were thus left to forge a new bargain on their own, and not surprisingly, corporations usually had the upper hand.

The essence of the new contract was the idea that workers should be constantly pitted against what economists call the "spot market" for labor—the amount that they could command at a particular moment given particular skills and the particular contours of the economy at that time. Companies acknowledged that workers might jump ship if another better-paying job came calling. But that was the price to pay for the larger change they sought: shifting the major risks of skill obsolescence, unexpected benefit costs, and business fluctuations from corporations onto workers.

The old contract was about *shared fate*—workers and their companies rose and fell together. The new contract was about *individual gain*—workers and companies stayed together when it was beneficial to both, and only so long as it was beneficial to both. Consider the following not-atypical corporate statements of the new contract (these are from an employee memo penned by the CEO of General Electric during the mid-1980s): "The only job security is a successful business" and "If loyalty means that this company will ignore poor performance, then loyalty is off the table." At the telephone giant AT&T, executives described the change in terms eerily similar to those used by critics of the welfare state. From a system based on the ideals of a "fair day's pay, a secure future, and an opportunity to rise through the ranks," AT&T had moved to a system that "encouraged entrepreneurship, individual responsibility, and accountability."[8]

This change didn't mean a shift in pay or benefits per se. Workers who were highly valued outside the firm might do even better under the new system than the old. What it meant was a shift in risk. "If the traditional, lifetime employment relationship was like a marriage," University of Pennsylvania management expert Peter Cappelli says, "then the new employment relationship is like a lifetime of divorces and remarriages."[9] As with real marriages, some emerge from the "divorce" better off than they were before—they might even initiate it. Others fare less well. What they have to offer isn't valued at the moment; they've given their all and can't take what they've given with them; they find themselves forced to compete with younger "suitors" with attributes more highly sought after than theirs. In addition, the "marriage" itself is not based on equality in the first place.

Companies have the upper hand in deciding what the terms are, meaning that breakups usually favor them more than their erstwhile partners.

A seemingly mundane example can illustrate the profound difference between the old and new contracts. Taxicab drivers once were basically in-house employees of cab companies: the cabs were owned by the companies, which handled insurance and fuel, and cabbies split what they took in with the companies. Today, most cabbies lease their cabs from the companies, often paying more than a hundred dollars a day for the use of the licensed cab. They're responsible for fuel, and they have to buy insurance. In return, of course, they keep all their fares and tips—which can be very good or very bad. If they have a good day, they come away with a reasonable living. If they have a bad day, they end up losing money. The old world of the hit TV show *Taxi* is gone. Cabbies don't hang out at the company when business is slow. They work more hours, driving twelve or fourteen or sixteen hours a day, just to break even.

Now, of course, these workers are facing a new source of competitive pressure: ride hailing services such as Uber and Lyft. But the e-upstarts aren't emulating the old work contract; they're doubling down on the new one. Drivers for Uber makes in the range of $10 an hour after taking into account all their expenses and the 25 percent cut that Uber takes of the fares that it sets unilaterally. That's a poverty level wage for a family of two—and it comes without any benefits or job security. Like most contingent workers, Uber drivers are treated as "independent contractors," a special occupational category once reserved for high-wage free agents but now shared by many of the most vulnerable workers. Independent contractors are basically exempt from all traditional employment protections, from unemployment insurance to hours and wage rules. Perhaps not surprisingly, 96 percent of Uber drivers quit within their first year.[10]

Sereve Pekle hasn't—at least not yet. "I thought I was going to be having my own car, having my own schedule, making $1000 a week," says the former taxi driver. "The reality was completely different." Fuel, insurance, and Uber's cut—it all added up, and that wasn't counting depreciation on the new car he had to buy to comply with Uber's vehicle standards. Worse, Pekle wasn't just competing with those who've stayed in the taxi business;

Uber was pulling in more and more drivers during the peak hours when fares are highest, so it wouldn't have to resort to surge pricing. "You are not making anything," Pekle complains. "It's like minimum wage." He has even joined a union of sorts, an advocacy group for app-based drivers linked to the Teamsters. But the group has no formal recognition, and it's clear Uber isn't keen on feedback. Uber's founder, Travis Kalanick, remarked of one driver who said he went bankrupt because of Uber's strict policies, "Some people don't like to take responsibility for their own shit." It could be a motto for the gig economy: "Take responsibility for your own shit!" Unfortunately, much of that shit is being heaped onto employees by the companies they work for because those companies deny they are employees at all.[11]

The daily hustle of driving at first seems quite removed from the white-collar world of AT&T or GE. But the logic is the same: the risk is on workers, not shared between companies and workers. Workers might do better in this system, or they might not. But that's not the point. The point is that they face far more uncertainty and risk.

Is the new contract good or bad for workers? The answer is obviously good for some (those who are highly prized on the spot market at any moment) and bad for others (those who are not). The new contract is one of the reasons for rising inequality, especially the huge gains at the very top. Virtually all workers, however, are facing much greater insecurity as a result of the new contract, and the burden is being borne almost entirely by workers and their families on their own, rather than with the help of corporate or government measures that might pool and manage these growing risks.

GOOD JOBS GONE FOR GOOD

As the experiences of Jeff Martinelli, Lisa Casino-Schuetz, and Mark McClellan remind us, the uncertainties of the new world of work are never clearer than when work disappears. The unemployed, like the poor, have always been with us. Yet the nature of unemployment has dramatically shifted from its pattern in the immediate decades after World War II— and in keeping with the larger changes in the labor market just charted.

Traditionally, unemployment was "cyclical": workers lost their jobs when production contracted and were then re-employed in lines of work similar to their previous ones when production re-expanded. Today, however, unemployment is increasingly likely to be "structural"—persistent, perhaps even permanent, and ending only when workers accept a new job that often implies major cuts in pay, hours, or both.

The popular term for this shift is "downsizing," and it captures an essential element of the change: the idea that layoffs are not the result of (hopefully temporary) drops in the demand for a firm's products but instead of the decision of employers to shed certain workers permanently to raise share prices, deal with competitive pressures, or reorganize production processes. The change can be seen most clearly in the company policies of those employers that once promised extensive job security. The vast majority of large employers had abandoned policies of job security, such as no-layoff rules, by the late 1990s. An American Management Association survey at the time found that more and more of its thousand member companies were reporting at least one downsizing wave even as the economy was improving. The reason given for these layoffs also changed, from overall economic conditions to a desire to restructure. Indeed, most of the companies cutting back jobs were reporting profits even while eliminating positions—a strong indication that job cuts were structural rather than cyclical.[12]

The key difference between structural and cyclical unemployment concerns the nature of the risks faced by workers. While cyclical unemployment invariably causes temporary interruptions of earnings—which, historically, public programs such as unemployment insurance have aimed to address—structural unemployment leads to permanent reductions in income and may require retraining that is both economically costly and psychologically taxing. These distinctive features of structural unemployment, in turn, have important effects on workers' upfront investment in skills and commitment to their firms.

To see the extent of structural unemployment, we need to look beyond the unemployment rate to studies of job loss—involuntary separation from employment due to layoffs or downsizing, rather than voluntary quits or firing "for cause." The level of involuntary job loss in the American economy is higher than most might expect. Even during the boom of the late 1990s, roughly one in ten workers lost their jobs for reasons unrelated to their particular performance (a traditional "firing") in a three-year period, according to calculations by the Princeton economist Henry Farber using the Displaced Worker Survey, which began collecting data in the early 1980s and has been conducted by the federal government every two years since. The rate of job loss increased sharply during the recession of the early 2000s, despite only a tiny bump in the unemployment rate. It then spiked upward in the late 2000s to almost 16 percent. In other words, during the Great Recession, nearly one in six workers lost their jobs through no fault of their own every three years.[13]

Yet the really startling findings concern what happens *when* workers lose their jobs. Start with the simplest question: When workers lose their jobs, what's the chance they'll be employed when they're surveyed again two years later? The answer in the late 1990s was over 75 percent: Three-quarters of those who lost jobs were re-employed in subsequent surveys. During the recession of the early 2000s, only around 60 percent of job losers were re-employed, and the share barely budged upward throughout the decade. Then, during the Great Recession, the share plummeted to below 50 percent: more than half of workers who lost their jobs were not working when they were surveyed again. What's more, a growing share of those finding new jobs were employed part-time, rather than full-time: in 2000, the share of job losers re-employed as part-time workers—whose benefits and job security are typically much below full-timers'—was around one in seven. In 2010, it was around one in four.

Perhaps most striking, even those who found new full-time jobs—the lucky ones, so to speak—faced steep cuts in earnings. Consider the three-year period beginning in 2001, a mild downturn by historical standards. Even full-time workers who found new full-time jobs—the best-case scenario—ended up earning around 17 percent less than they would have had they not lost their jobs.[14] This steep earnings loss was actually greater than that experienced by full-time workers who found new full-time jobs during the Great Recession (presumably because only a select group of displaced workers were able to regain full-time jobs in the late-2000s).

Statistics on the long-term unemployed tell an equally worrisome story.[15] The share of the labor force experiencing unemployment for a half year or more—the standard definition of long-term unemployment—has grown dramatically over the last fifty years. Indeed, from the late 1960s to the late 2000s, the share of workers who experience long-term unemployment during the peak of the business cycle more than quadrupled.[16] Mark McClellan's story of losing his job without a new one in sight sounds more familiar today because it is—even when the economy is roaring, there are more than four times as many people in the same boat.

The picture is even worse during recessions. Historically, the number of workers unemployed for more than six months—after which unemployment benefits run out in most states—peaks about six to eight months after the end of the recession. This seems unsurprising: a six-to-eight-month lag is what you would expect for a program that requires that workers be unemployed for at least six months. Yet the 1991 and the 2001 downturns saw a far different pattern. In 1991, long-term unemployment peaked nineteen months into the recovery, and in 2001, it peaked *twenty-nine months in*.[17] More than two years after the 2001 recession had "ended," the number of Jeff Martinellis and Lisa Casino-Schuetzes losing their jobs—and unlike Jeff and Lisa, unable to find other work—was still rising even as the official unemployment rate declined (the first time this has happened since statistics have been collected). And contrary to common perception, the long-term unemployed during the 2001 recession were older, better educated, and more likely to be professionals than the unemployed as a whole.[18]

This last point may come as a shock. After all, the general view—backed up by plenty of evidence—is that it is younger workers who've borne the brunt of the destabilizing changes in the labor market of the past two decades, especially younger workers without a college degree.[19] Compared with previous generations, today's young Americans are more likely to fall into poverty, are more indebted (in part because of the rising costs of education), and are experiencing much more variable and negative economic outcomes.

Yet the evidence is strong that established, educated workers have seen the most dramatic *increase* in the negative consequences of losing

their jobs. During the mid-1990s expansion, workers with a college degree or higher suffered an earnings loss of less than 5 percent when they
found another full-time job after being displaced from full-time employment. During the 2001–2003 period, the earnings loss was an astounding
20 percent—almost twice the loss experienced by workers with *less than
a high-school education.*[20] The share of the long-term unemployed who are
well educated—men and women with degrees that they thought would
secure their incomes forever—has risen dramatically, as has the share in
white-collar jobs.[21] Increasingly, workers who had it all are finding they
have little when their jobs disappear.

It's crucial to recognize that all this was true before the Great
Recession, which shattered the complacent consensus around long-term
unemployment—at least for a time. The 2008 downturn set a new post-
1930s standard for just how bad persistent joblessness could be. Never
before in the postwar era have long-term jobless workers constituted
more than 3 percent of the labor force. During the Great Recession, they
exceeded that share for *more than four years.* At its peak in April 2010, long-
term unemployment was so bad that almost half of all jobless Americans
had been out of work for more than half a year—more than twice the peak
reached in the last downturn. And long-term unemployment was just as
prevalent for highly educated workers as for those with only a high-school
diploma. Indeed, those with extensive education or advanced skills often
found themselves competing with less skilled workers for the same low-
wage positions.[22]

That was certainly the experience of Dennis Hansen, an aquatic biologist
with a masters degree who lost his job as an operations manager at a scien-
tific lab in late 2009. Hansen thought bouncing back would be easy, but he
was wrong. He applied to any job he could—an oil field hand, a chemist
working for a government contractor in Iraq. He even managed to get a few
temporary positions, including helping out at the post office one holiday
season. But it seemed as if everyone out of work was applying for anything
more permanent or well paid. After one interview that seemed promising,
the job went to an applicant with a PhD. "I was beat out by someone even
more overqualified than I was," he jokes. With the debt on his credit cards

mounting, he postponed his wedding. "It's definitely a roller coaster," Hansen says—a roller coaster that is especially unpleasant when he gets his hopes up, then faces rejection again. "That's when I'm frustrated, angry and wondering why I went to college for 10 years."[23]

The only truly unusual aspect of Hansen's experience is how common it is at a time when the share of those out of work has continued to fall. Look at it this way: at only three points in the last fifty years—1968–1969, 1999–2000, and 2017–2018—has the unemployment rate been in the vicinity of 4 percent, the milestone reached in early 2018. Yet the share of out-of-work Americans who had been searching for a job for six months or longer was just 5 percent in the late 1960s. By the late 1990s, it was up to 13 percent. In the most recent period, a full decade after the financial crisis, it remained stubbornly above 20 percent.

Why aren't employers scrambling for workers, and workers bidding up wages, when only one in twenty-five workers is out of a job? The answer is that many who find themselves, like Dennis Hansen, without a good job eventually give up looking for one. They're not irrational: the longer someone isn't employed the harder it is to get employed. For those who lost their jobs during the Great Recession, according to a Brookings Institution analysis, the odds of finding full-time employment was highest at the outset—though even then just one in five. After seven months without a job, the odds were one in ten; two years in, they were one in seventeen. Not surprisingly, more than a third of those unemployed for seven months or longer simply stopped looking for work.[24]

Jobless workers lose ground for several reasons. For one, they aren't using their skills—skills that may become increasingly misaligned with employers' needs in a rapidly changing economy. For another, even when long-term unemployment is pervasive, workers with significant gaps in their work history are often treated as damaged goods. (In 2012, a researcher sent a few thousand randomly varied resumes to employers: employers were more likely to request an interview with unqualified workers whose prior job had just ended than *qualified* workers who had been out of work for more than six months.)[25] And then there is the sheer strain of making ends meet while dealing with rejection after rejection. According to decades of research, long-term joblessness drags down emotional well-being and drives up suicide and mortality rates. Within families, it brings heightened risk of domestic violence, of kids having trouble in school, and of divorce—especially when it affects men. Dennis Hansen, for example, postponed his marriage because of his economic freefall. Yet he fears his relationship with his girlfriend may not survive: "We were watching the news when there was a report that the economy is getting better," he recounts. "She said, 'When is OUR economy going to get better?' That's just crushing for a guy."[26]

The federal government's definition of unemployment only counts workers who are still shaking the jobs tree: sending out resumes, contacting employers, working their networks. Those who've given up—however rational their resignation—are not considered part of the labor force. Neither are those who, when surveyed, report they would not have been able to have started a new job if they had been offered one the prior week, whatever the reason. These are the shadow unemployed: people who want to work, who would work, but who aren't counted as unemployed because, in the parlance of unemployment statistics, they're not "actively seeking work." And however you count them, the shadow unemployed have grown.

Despite low unemployment rates at the height of the business cycle, the labor force participation of working-age men has actually declined in the last generation. Meanwhile, after rising sharply in the 1970s and 1980s, the labor force participation of women has leveled off and, more recently, fallen—to an aggregate level substantially below that of men. The overall drop in male and female labor force participation doesn't reflect early retirement (in fact, workers older than fifty-five are the *only* age group whose labor force participation has increased), nor is it confined to the least-educated workers, though it is most severe among them.[27] Nor, perhaps most important, is it happening to the same degree in other rich democracies. Among its most similar peers—Canada, the United Kingdom, Spain, Sweden, Japan, France, and Germany—the United States is the *only* country to have seen labor force participation fall since the 1990s. In 1975, it had the second highest rate of participation among these nations; by 2013, it had the second lowest—ahead of France alone. This reversal of fortune indicates that structural changes in the economy do not dictate a shrinking workforce; how nations respond to these changes and other factors matter enormously, too.[28]

In any case, the decline in labor force participation has greatly masked the severity of the last few recessions—including the Great Recession—as well as the anemic "jobless" nature of the recoveries that followed. This is because most of those who have left the labor force, or opted not to enter it in the first place, are not "actively seeking work" and hence are not counted among the formally unemployed. There is good evidence, however, that many of these potential workers would be in the labor force were the employment opportunities for them better and were U.S. policies more supportive of skill-upgrading and workplace reentry. In the mid-2000s, for example, the total labor force "shortfall" compared with similar points in the business cycle in the past was as high as 5.1 million men and women.[29] This amount would have raised the official unemployment rate, then around 5 percent, to 8.7 percent. Much of the disconnect between Americans' pessimism about job security and America's rosy employment figures may reflect the simple reality that many potential workers have exited the labor force out of discouragement, not because they don't want to work.

JUST A MATTER OF DEGREES?

If you find these statistics surprising, you're not alone. Much of the writing on the American labor market suggests that the main place where workplace hardship and insecurity reign is among those who have failed to invest in the education and skills needed to succeed in a knowledge-based economy. This is certainly part of the story—the gap between workers with and without a college degree is large. Yet it misses an essential fact: high levels of education may be a prerequisite for success in today's economy, but they are by no means a guarantor of middle-class security.

Just a glance at the statistics makes this obvious. Over the last generation, average education levels have risen substantially, but middle-class incomes have not. Families in the middle of the economic ladder are headed by workers much better educated than their counterparts of thirty years ago, yet these families' incomes are not similarly higher. This surprising reality is most easily seen if we concentrate on workers just starting out in the labor market—today and in the past. Between 1973 and 2013, the earnings of entry-level male workers with just a high school diploma declined by 29 percent, while the earnings of equally educated entry-level female workers fell by 10 percent. Men and women with a college degree have done better, but mostly because less-educated workers have done so badly. In 1973, the average entry-level wage for a worker with a college degree was $21.10 an hour for men and $17.69 an hour for women. In 2013, it was—wait for it—$21.89 and $18.38, respectively.[30] Back in the days of my youth, a high school degree all but guaranteed a worker a stable, middle-class standard of living, but these days even a college degree is no guarantee.

You might think benefit costs are a big part of the explanation for stagnant wages. They're not. In fact, while health premiums went up, the chance of being covered by health insurance at work went down. Recently graduated workers with a high school degree had more than a 60 percent chance of getting a health plan at work in 1979. In 2010—the year the Affordable Care Act passed—less than 23 percent received health insurance. Similarly, the share of recent high-school graduates covered by a pension plan fell from 36 percent in 1979 to just over 16 percent in 2010. Again, college graduates fared better, but they didn't fare well. Between 1979 and 2010, their chance of receiving health insurance declined from almost 78 percent to slightly more than 61 percent, and of receiving a pension from around 51 percent to less than 46 percent.[31]

To be sure, these are just the averages. Some better-educated workers do splendidly, while others barely scrape by. But that's the whole point—education isn't a risk-free investment. Indeed, more than half of the rise in economic inequality in the United States involves the growing divergence of workers *with the same level of education and experience.*[32] In other words, people with the same number of years of schooling have much more disparate economic experiences than they used to—and that means investing in education, wise as it may be, is also increasingly risky.

Risky in part because the cost of such investments has skyrocketed. A generation ago, college meant modest loans and part-time work. Now it means big-time debt: between 1970 and 2013, as the number of students enrolled in college roughly doubled, the cash value of student loans rose by more than *1300* percent. In the fifteen years between 1993 and 2008, the percentage of students graduating from four-year public colleges with student loan debt increased from 25 percent to 63 percent. For those graduating from four-year private colleges, the proportion with debt rose from 40 percent to 73 percent. (These figures are for nonprofit colleges. For-profits were virtually unheard of fifteen years ago; they now enroll around a million students, virtually all of whom take out loans—often too big to repay.) In the aggregate, student loan debt substantially exceeds all the unpaid balances on Americans' credit cards.[33]

College students who borrow now graduate with almost $30,000 in debt on average, graduate students with more than twice that, and professional students with roughly five times that. Partly because college is so expensive, moreover, a large proportion of young adults who enter its gates don't exit them with a degree in hand, even though all the research suggests that a degree is necessary for the big economic premiums (what economists call "sheepskin effects"). Not surprisingly, students who drop out are more likely to come from less-privileged families and more likely to have taken on student loan burdens.[34] These students are caught in a double bind—after taking out loans for tens of thousands of dollars without crossing the finish line they have no chance to reap the substantial economic benefits the actual degree might confer.

What this suggests is that many of the skills needed to excel in the new world of work are risky investments—valuable (and costly) but frequently tied to jobs and lines of employment that can seemingly disappear in an instant. Vital to success in the new world of work, and difficult and expensive to gain, advanced skills nonetheless provide no sure guarantee of economic stability. For example, knowledge industries, such as telecommunications and electronics, pay handsomely. But they are also more volatile than traditional industries, expanding more quickly during expansions yet contracting more quickly during downturns.[35] And when the loss of skilled jobs is permanent—when layoffs are not responses to cyclical market demand but the consequence of permanent restructuring—workers who've invested in the skills needed to succeed find themselves without easy avenues for deploying those skills in alternative, high-paying ventures or maintaining their former benefits. The educated rise farther, but increasingly they fall farther, too.

WHO MOVED MY CHEESE?

Should all this worry us? Richard Cox and Michael Alm, in their cheerleading book *Myths of Rich and Poor,* think not. Yes, they concede, new economic realities have brought "sweeping changes in the way we live and work. At the same time, there's an unsettling shift from a national economy to an international one. Skills, technologies, and product lines can fall by the wayside in just a few years."[36] Yet, channeling the legions of self-help business books that tell anxious workers that change is their friend, from *Who Moved My Cheese?* to *We Got Fired! And It's the Best Thing That Ever Happened to Us!,* Cox and Alm offer this consoling advice: *"Be willing to retrain.* The average hourly wage for a computer programmer is $23.01. A typical textile worker makes only $8.25. What's more, the number of computer jobs is rising, while the opportunities in textiles are diminishing. Jobs come and go as the economy evolves, often benefiting those workers who learn new skills and keep up with economic changes."[37]

It seemed like such good advice in 1999, when Cox and Aim's book was published. Unfortunately, it looks much less sage today. In the five years after they urged laid-off workers to embrace their inner programmer, the profession lost more than 180,000 jobs, about a quarter of its total employment. The outlook for the future is bleak, even though more sophisticated computer jobs requiring more advanced skills are expanding.

The basic story isn't so different from what has happened in manufacturing. Automation and technological innovation have made it possible for fewer workers to do more. According to the Bureau of Labor Statistics' *Occupational Outlook Handbook,* "Sophisticated computer software now has the capability to write basic code, eliminating the need for many programmers to do this routine work." Outsourcing—the movement of jobs once performed within U.S. companies to overseas subsidiaries and contractors—is another issue: as the *Handbook* notes, "Computer programmers can perform their job function from anywhere in the world and can digitally transmit their programs to any location via e-mail."[38]

To add insult to injury, many programmers who received pink slips in the early 2000s were asked to train their replacements in return for more generous severance pay. "It was very callous," complained Stephen Gentry, a fifty-one-year-old father of three who was still unemployed when he spoke with *USA Today* in 2004, a year after his firing. "They asked us to make them feel at home while we trained them to take our jobs." Another former programmer, Myra Bronstein, described meeting workers from India flown in for an orientation before they took her job for one-sixteenth her salary. "I was staring hard at my shoes and trying not to cry," said Bronstein. "It was hideously awkward. I felt forced. It was very deflating and dehumanizing to train your replacement. I felt sucker-punched. It was as if they handed us a shovel and said, 'Here, dig your own grave.'" She, too, was still unemployed a year after being laid off.[39]

And remember: computer programmers are not poorly trained workers. More than 91 percent have gone to college and more than 67 percent have a degree (associate, bachelor's, or graduate). Back in the late 1990s, employers threw lavish offers and starting bonuses at young programmers just out of college: stock options, six-figure-salaries, even new cars. By the mid-2000s, as one disenchanted "tech" worker assessed the dismal scene, programmers were falling back to their modest status of the 1970s and 1980s, when they were "the basement cubicle geeks and they weren't very well off. They were making an honest living but weren't anything more than middle-class people just getting by."[40] Of course, those who were "just getting by" were the lucky ones—spared from the ax of automation and outsourcing, at least for now.

In the personal responsibility mantra, skills are the cornerstone of economic success. They certainly are. Yet skills—education, certification, on-the-job training—are not costless to obtain, nor do they come without risk. Skills are an investment, and often what economists call a "specific investment"—an investment that is tied to a particular line of work, industry, or technology. And the more specific the investment, the greater the cost and dislocation if that investment is left "stranded" by economic change.

Specific investments are the backbone of strong economies: they account for innovation; they bolster worker productivity; they allow countries to specialize in the highest-value work. But specific investments also create risk for workers, because they are investments whose return depends closely on the performance not just of the economy as the whole but of specific firms, industries, and occupations. When those firms, industries, or occupations go belly-up, workers cannot easily exploit the skills they have gained and they face inevitable costs—the costs of retraining, the costs of taking a job that does not require their skills, or, worst of all, the costs of leaving the workforce altogether.

I interviewed the wife of a laid-off textile worker for this book, so I was able to ask her about Cox and Aim's suggestion to retrain. Her name is Sandy Erksa, and she works as a physical therapist and is now the family's primary breadwinner. Her husband, Dennis, was fifty-six when the textile factory he worked for finally went under after a series of increasingly desperate shuffles from one parent company to another. A chemistry major in college, he now works at a Photoworks facility as a graphics finisher, earning $10 an hour without benefits—a third of what he used to make. Sandy laughed at the thought of him going back to school at nearly sixty, but she admitted he was not doing well where he was. "It's hard for a man," she says, "He was used to having a job with a certain amount of prestige. He was good at it, a perfectionist. He got along with everybody. For him, it's been hardest when he looks at the paycheck." Then, Sandy Erksa states the obvious: "This is not what we wanted. This is not what we planned."

SERVICE-SECTOR NATION

Dennis Erksa lost a high-paying job at Liberty Fabrics (which, as it was slowly divested of its American workers, changed names seemingly daily—from "Liberty Fabrics" to "Sara Lee" to "Hafner" to nothing). He ended up with a $10-an-hour job in which his college chemistry degree is about as useful as his detailed understanding of how lace is made. Dennis Erksa's descent was, of course, steeper than that of many job losers, and yet it captures one of the most profound risks that workers today face: the risk of moving across sectors of the economy. Today, as the service sector continues its steady expansion and manufacturing its ongoing decline, and as technological change sweeps through occupations as diverse as retailing and radiology, millions of Americans have recently experienced or are about to experience this unsettling transit.

The change might be called the "postindustrial revolution," in honor of Daniel Bell's famous 1973 prediction of a postindustrial society of knowledge and service industries that don't produce physical goods.[41] Yet, unlike the Industrial Revolution of more than a century ago, when the movement of Americans from rural farms to urban factories changed the face of our nation entirely, the postindustrial revolution is often hidden from view. Amid all the breathless talk about rising trade and financial integration, we too often forget that the most profound transformation is taking place within our own borders, driven by forces that have affected all rich societies, regardless of their openness to foreign trade and investment. This transformation is the rise of the service sector.

The shift is etched on our economic landscape: in the late 1960s, the nation's largest employer was General Motors, which paid its workers solidly middle-class incomes ($29,000 on average, in current dollars) and provided generous benefits. Today, the largest employer is Walmart, which pays its workers roughly $19,000 a year and has notoriously skimpy benefits.[42]

Walmart and GM, of course, represent extremes. But they give a sense of the scale and scope of the change. For decades U.S. manufacturing has been in steep decline, as an increasing share of employment has moved into the service sector—industries such as medical care and teaching that do not turn out physical products. In 1960 almost 40 percent of nonagricultural employment was in manufacturing. By 2015 only 9 percent was, and more than 80 percent of nonfarm work was in services. Manufacturing has not just fallen in relative terms but in absolute terms, too, with 7 million manufacturing jobs lost between 1979 and early 2017—well over half that total since 2000 alone.[43]

One of the main reasons the rise of the service sector is such a profound change is that the skills developed in manufacturing do not transfer easily to the frequently low-productivity world of service work, endangering the economic security of those who must make the perilous leap.[44] The shift of the economy toward services thus doesn't just affect those who work in the service sector. It also threatens the jobs of millions of workers in more traditional lines of employment, whose marketable skills and workplace benefits aren't likely to move with them if they are displaced. Like Jeff Martinelli, workers who had never envisioned doing anything other than factory jobs for their entire lives face the grim prospect of moving into service jobs, from retail trade to pest control, that not only don't pay as well as their old positions but also lack the benefits they had counted on to secure their families and finance their retirements.

That's what Scott Clark faced when, after working a quarter century in a circuit-board factory, he was laid off and, after a period of retraining, found himself working fifteen-hour days as a courier for four companies—none of which provided health or pension benefits, or even a simple vacation. Asked if he could bounce back, Clark was philosophical: "I really don't know. It's just too uncertain. It really is. There's nothing there. There's nothing you can just count on. I wish there was."[45]

At one point, the service sector seemed the last place where outsourcing and automation would occur. After all, many services require both proximity and so-called soft skills, the ability to interact with others in productive ways. But advances in artificial intelligence and robotics, as well as the increasing capacity of computers and telecommunications to make proximity less important, have swept through parts of the service sector once seen as immune to their dislocations. The business consulting group McKinsey has estimated that some service areas are more vulnerable to automation than manufacturing is—even without advances beyond current technology.[46] In accommodation and food services, for example, McKinsey estimates almost three-quarters of jobs are potentially at risk. In retail trade, just over half of jobs are at risk.

The changes are already taking place at Walmart. Locked in fierce competition with online retail giant Amazon, it is betting big on automation. The company is pioneering self-checkout software that allows shoppers to ring up their own groceries and bypass register lines. It is creating a grocery-delivery business that relies on personal shoppers paid like app-based drivers, who then hand off packages to actual app-based drivers for delivery. Assembly will also be farmed out to contingent workers whom Amazon hires online on a piece-rate basis to install televisions, build furniture, and the like. Increasingly, outsourcing doesn't mean moving jobs abroad; it means moving them online. "Wages are going to fall," predicts one economist. "It's interesting that Walmart is being so proactive in gig-ifying its own workforce. Retail is one of the sectors that you thought you couldn't really outsource, but maybe that was wrong."[47]

The service sector doesn't have to be gig-ified to be risky; much of it already is. Although service jobs are enormously diverse, ranging from mopping floors to managing investment plans, major segments of the service sector—retail trade, caregiving, customer relations—feature relatively low pay and limited benefits, with restricted opportunities for advancement. Many of these segments of the economy are also marked by seasonal employment and relatively high reliance on part-time and contingent workers and on employees who work unconventional shifts—many of whom are women.

Which brings us to another major transformation that the post-industrial revolution has wrought—the rise of a reserve army of part-time and contingent workers. In the 1950s, only about a tenth of workers were employed on a part-time basis, and formally temporary or contingent workers were virtually unheard of. By the 2010s, roughly 20 percent of workers were employed part-time, and as many as 4 percent were employed on a contingent basis.[48] The majority of part-time workers are female, so it might be thought that the rise is mostly due to the increasing workforce participation of women, who are often balancing child care and work. This pattern did indeed hold in the 1960s and 1970s, but since then the rise of part-time work does not seem to have been driven by growing female employment.[49]

Instead, the shift toward part-time and contingent work mostly reflects two other changes: the movement from manufacturing to services, where nearly all part-time and temporary jobs are found; and a marked increase in the reliance of key industries, such as retail shops, food establishments, and insurance and banking companies, on part-time work. Part-time and contingent work saves employers money for a variety of reasons, not least because these jobs generally feature low pay and low benefits (although for temporary workers, these gains may be eaten up by fees to temporary-help agencies, suggesting that here *flexibility* is the more important goal). A study comparing full-time and part-time workers *in the same industries doing exactly the same job* finds that "an individual can expect a lower wage rate if he or she decides to work part-time rather than full-time, and much lower benefits per hour."[50] As one expert on part-time employment trends observes, "The shift to part-time employment is neither a response to a technical imperative nor an outright antilabor measure. Rather, companies have shifted because they have decided cutting labor costs and enhancing staffing flexibility are more important—at least in some areas of work—than maintaining a stable workforce."[51]

At least part-timers are treated as employees, with the wage and hour protections and access to state and federal benefits such as unemployment insurance that come with this special legal status. Not so of contingent workers and independent contractors—which comprised around 20 percent of the workforce in 2010, according to the Government Accountability Office (a bit higher if self-employed workers are included in the count).[52]

At the moment, only a small minority of these workers are employed through online platforms, contrary to the common perception that contingent work is now mostly managed by digital apps or web sites. Yet those whose work *is* handled this way provide a glimpse of the future that should worry those whose isn't. Mechanical Turk is a task marketplace run by Amazon (and frequently used by my fellow political scientists as a cheap subject pool for surveys and behavioral experiments). "Turkers," as Amazon's online workers are called, do everything from verifying phone numbers and identifying images to data cleaning and even conducting missing person searches. They set their own hours, choose their tasks, and even rate their "clients"—the folks who hire them. What they don't do is make much money: one study estimated that median earnings for Turkers—about $1.75 an hour if they're quick, and, again, without pay or protections—equals about a fifth of what their work is actually worth to clients. Apparently, high flexibility comes at a high price.[53]

There is nothing wrong, of course, with the fundamental idea that workers should be able to work part time or on a temporary basis if they want to. Indeed, opportunities for such work for those who most value it—workers in school, parents of young children, older Americans who want to continue working after sixty-five—should surely be more extensive than they are. The problem is that in today's workplace, part-time and temporary work is set up for the convenience of employers, not workers. Companies get to pay less and provide fewer benefits to workers who too often end up at the mercy of employers' staffing needs and too often fall outside the protective scope of valued labor laws and benefits . The contingent workforce represents the purest form of the new employment contract—the culmination of the notion that workers are on their own, bearing all the risks and making all the investments necessary for economic success.

THE LOSER-TAKE-NONE ECONOMY

Work has always been at the core of the American Dream. When the great German sociologist Max Weber wrote *The Protestant Ethic and the Spirit of Capitalism,* it was the quintessential American, Benjamin Franklin, whom he took as representative of the Protestant ethic of work and thrift.[54] More than a century after Weber's landmark work, the ethic is alive and well—at least with regard to work. We work harder than citizens of other nations, and we value work more. We are also working more hours than in the past, because of the increased role of women in the workforce: 3,500 hours a year of paid labor for the average two-parent family in 2009, up from 2,800 hours a year in 1975. Indeed, our increased work hours are the main reason most Americans' incomes have continued to rise during a forty-year period in which workers' wages have been essentially flat.[55]

And yet, over the same generation in which we've come to work more and more, the nature of work in the United States has changed in ways that have challenged our vision of work as a guarantee of security and opportunity. The tightrope of work is higher, the winds of change that buffet us on it are stronger, but the safety net below us is tattered and incomplete.

America's program of unemployment protection has never been well equipped to deal with the risks that characterize the new world of work, and it has only grown less capable. In the original conception of the program, unemployment benefits were designed to ease workers in their transition between two jobs that paid relatively equally. Unemployment checks were meant to cope with temporary income loss, not to compensate workers for long-term earnings reductions, much less the loss of valued benefits.

The long-term unemployed weren't the central focus either. They would be enrolled in federal jobs programs or, as a last resort, given ongoing relief. In fact, under the terms of federal law, unemployment benefits have to be formally extended by Congress and the president to last longer than six months. And even though the long-term unemployed are far and away the group most disadvantaged by downturns and least capable of staying afloat, such extensions have become increasingly controversial.

In 2013, for example, Republican leaders refused to extend unemployment benefits despite the evidence of abnormally high long-term unemployment. (Workers whose benefits run out cannot reapply for benefits even if they are subsequently extended, and in 2013 nearly 5 million people faced a cutoff of benefits in the next year—at a time when long-term unemployment was higher than at the *worst point* of any prior post-WWII recession.)[56] The conservative argument against an extension was taken straight out of the personal responsibility playbook. According to Senator Rand Paul, Republican of Kentucky, extended unemployment benefits were "a disservice to these workers. When you allow people to be on unemployment insurance for 99 weeks, you're causing them to become part of this perpetual unemployed group in our economy."[57]

The critics had a point: simply providing unemployment benefits for longer periods, while necessary during downturns, is not an effective or attractive way of dealing with the main economic risk that structural unemployment represents—long-term downward mobility. There is no unemployment insurance that can help Lisa Casino-Schuetz save her house or Jeff Martinelli get his well-paying job back. There is no unemployment insurance that can deal with the permanent disappearance or erosion of benefits that can accompany job losses due to America's employment-based framework of social protection. There is no unemployment insurance that can retrain workers for new jobs, much less help them cope with crushed expectations. Unemployment insurance is vital. It is in dire need of upgrading. But it is clearly not enough to deal with the new workplace insecurity.

Tragically, our current system of unemployment insurance misses millions of the temporarily unemployed as well. Even as job insecurity has grown in recent decades, the unemployment insurance programs run by the states have contracted in reach and generosity. Between 1947 and 1995, the share of workers in covered employment who actually received benefits fell from 80 percent to 40 percent.[58] After rising during the Great Recession—thanks, in part, to the 2009 "stimulus" law, which boosted the program—the share fell even further to 27 percent in 2015, a historic low.[59] Low-wage workers are particularly ill-served. A 2007 federal report found that while they were more than twice as likely to be unemployed as were higher-wage workers, they were roughly half as likely to get benefits— even when they'd been on the job just as long. Many didn't earn enough to qualify for benefits. Others worked in contingent jobs not covered by unemployment insurance. Still others were fired or "quit" for reasons that rule out unemployment benefits—for example, because they had to leave work because child care was temporarily unavailable.[60]

All of these growing gaps hint at a deeper issue: even as the old model of employment has come undone, our government has not stepped into the breach. Even as corporations have abandoned the old contract, they have not forged a new contract that deals with the reality that workers constantly need to gain and upgrade skills, or the fact that women with children are now more likely to work than not. Companies are shedding or restructuring traditional workplace benefits at a dramatic rate, but few are helping American families cope with the new risks they face—the second part of our story of growing insecurity, and our next topic.

4

Risky Families

Julie and Jerry Pickett represent the very definition of the two-earner, middle-class family. They live in a suburban home with three young kids, and each has long believed that both parents should be in the workforce. Julie, unlike many women of her parents' generation, always expected to contribute to her family's security through employment. For a time (ironically, it would soon turn out), she worked as a debt collector. Then, she was the owner of a small retail business. Jerry Pickett works, too—as the owner of a modest plumbing and heating company. Given her debt-collection work, Julie never let the family run more than a small balance on their credit cards.

When the Picketts had twins, however, Julie stopped working, in part because good child care was hard to find in their community. Then, Jerry's business, always seasonal, slowed down. Suddenly, the family was in debt and had to enroll in Medicaid, the health program for the poor. Even though Julie went back to work as soon as the kids entered school, the debt remained. Now, the phone never stops ringing with calls from collectors—people in Julie's old line of work. "At this point, I don't know what to do," says Julie. "I'm still paying for groceries I bought for my family eight years ago."[1]

George and Vicki Yandle's financial woes were precipitated by a tragic event: the discovery that their daughter, Dixie, had an aggressive cancer that would soon take her leg and eventually her life. The toll on her parents was enormous. Vicki, who had juggled child care and work in order to help support the family, lost her job at a local furniture store after she took time off to care for her daughter. Meanwhile, George lost his $80,000-a-year job after his boss accused him of driving up the company's health premiums and of being disloyal to the firm because of his frequent trips to the hospital. After eighteen months without work, George found a new job. Yet the Yandles were still living on one-third of their previous income, caring for a dying child whose medical bills over the next six years would top $2 million. To avoid having their home foreclosed, George and Vicki even asked their grown kids to move back in and pay rent.[2]

Stories like these—and there are millions more—have become so familiar that we almost forget how distinctive they are to our times. Forty years ago, families' dependence on financial contributions from women like Julie and Vicki was relatively rare. The majority of married women with kids stayed at home while their husbands worked for pay. Today, almost all husbands still work, but married women—even married women with very young children—are much more likely to work than not. Roughly 6 in 10 married mothers of infant children work. In 1975, only 3 in 10 did.[3] At the same time, the contribution of women's earnings to household income has grown dramatically. In 1970, less than a third of married couples worked roughly equal numbers of hours a week, and in about half of families, men earned essentially all of the family's income.[4] By 2000 more than 60 percent of married couples worked approximately equal hours, and only about a fifth of families featured the *Leave It to Beaver* male-breadwinner model.[5] In the course of a single generation, the norm for married women with children shifted from staying home to care for children to working (often full time) in the paid labor force to bolster family finances.

And bolster family finances women have. Although real median wages have essentially remained flat over the last generation, middle-income families have seen stronger income growth, with their real median incomes rising around 13 percent between 1979 and 2013.[6] Yet the whole of this rise is due to the fact that women are working many more hours outside the home than they once did.[7] Indeed, without the increased work hours and pay of women, middle-class incomes would have *fallen* between 1979 and 2013.[8] In short, middle-class families have gotten richer only because women have started working for pay, stepped up their work hours, or earned higher salaries—and, paradoxically, this is a major reason these families' standard of living is now at greater risk.

As women with children have moved en masse from home into the workplace, average American families are working many more hours in paid labor, while still spending at least as much time with their children as they did in the past. But families are managing this difficult balancing act without some of the common supports that working families enjoy abroad, such as paid leave to have a child, or time off to care for sick children or elderly parents. To be sure, there have been some attempts to improve the situation. Two months before her daughter Dixie died in 1993, Vicki Yandle was invited to speak at the signing of the Family and Medical Leave Act—legislation that had been championed by feminist leaders for years as a way of helping working parents take time off from work after the birth or adoption of children (as well as to care for themselves or a family member in the case of serious illness). At the ceremony, Vicki spoke of the hardship that she and her husband had faced trying to care for their daughter and still work at their jobs. When Dixie died just weeks later, Vicki Yandle posted a short memorial online: "To my darling daughter Dixie, you touched the hearts . . . of friends and relatives [and] all who crossed your path while on this earth. I know that now you are flying free."[9]

Yet although the Family and Medical Leave Act makes unpaid family leave mandatory for larger employers, smaller employers aren't required to offer unpaid leave and *paid* family leave remains rare, even among large employers.[10] Indeed, the fierce struggle over the Family and Medical Leave

Act suggests that—for all the emphasis on family values in contemporary political debate, and for all the worry about declining birth rates and an aging population—U.S. public policy treats families almost entirely as a personal responsibility, rather than a social priority. Only two countries in the world fail to provide some kind of cash benefit during maternity leave, according to the International Labor Organization: the United States and New Guinea. Among forty-one developed nations surveyed by the Organization for Economic Cooperation and Development, the United States is the only one that doesn't mandate paid leave. Indeed, the guaranteed leave period for those covered by the Family and Medical Leave Act (12 weeks) is shorter than the *paid* leave period of all but one of these nations, too.[11] Although a handful of states have stepped into the breach (five as of July 2018: California, New Jersey, New York, Rhode Island, and Washington, D.C.) paid leave remains elusive for most middle-income families and virtually nonexistent for lower-income households.[12]

Much attention has been paid to the "time bind" that both men and women feel as they try to balance the heightened responsibilities of parenting and their increased work hours.[13] Much less attention, however, has been paid to what might be called the "risk bind," the ways in which the movement of women into the workforce during a period of relatively flat earnings and rising family expenses has increased the risks to families' expected standard of living, pushing families deeper and deeper into debt, and sometimes into financial ruin.[14] These rising risks have fallen disproportionately on women, but they are felt by nearly all Americans who've devoted themselves to marriage or taken on the responsibilities of parenthood—men as well as women, the solidly middle class as well as the working poor.

The risk bind is the major reason that American families are taking on more debt than ever before—debt that itself is becoming increasingly risky. And it is the major reason, in a generation in which millions of Americans have gained the ultimate in private risk sharing—two incomes under one roof—the security of middle-class families has steadily declined. The safety-net family has become the risky family.

TROUBLE IN TWO-EARNER PARADISE

The risky family is at odds with everything we've been told about the new world of work and family. Families are supposed to be islands of stability amid a sea of societal uncertainty. In fact, the conventional assumption about the new American family is that it serves as a form of private *risk sharing*, allowing families to deal with shocks to income that affect one spouse by increasing the work effort of the other.[15] The analogy here might be a stock portfolio. Rather than holding a single stock (the husband's earnings), the modern family holds two stocks (the husband's and wife's earnings)—and holding two stocks is never more risky than holding one. To paraphrase the old adage of investment, two-earner couples don't put all their eggs in one basket.

The evidence on family income instability bears this point out—to a point. Singles living alone and lone parents have always had more unstable incomes than married couples with children.[16] Yet married couples with children have nonetheless seen a dramatic increase in the instability of their incomes over the last two decades. Indeed, what's most striking when one delves beneath the surface of the statistics is how little the increased risk sharing inherent in the two-income family seems to have cushioned families, either against rising income volatility or other types of financial strain.

Consider personal bankruptcy. Before the rules for personal bankruptcy were tightened in 2005, people who were married and had kids were fully *twice* as likely to file for bankruptcy as single adults or childless couples. Divorced women with kids were almost three times as likely to file for bankruptcy as single women without kids.[17] Nor do the signs of strain end there: families with children are more likely to lose their homes than families without children or than single adults. They're also much more likely to report being behind on their credit-card bills.[18] And they are drowning in debt, with staggering levels of indebtedness not seen among other household types.

Clearly, something is financially amiss with the once rock-solid American family. But what? Why hasn't the rising number of two-earner families protected more Americans from the risks of financial disaster? Why are so many families going bankrupt, running up huge debts, losing their homes, or just barely making ends meet?

The answer lies ultimately in a simple fact. To most families, a second income is not a *luxury* but a *necessity* in a context in which wages are relatively flat and the cost of raising a family is high and rising. The world has not stood still, after all, as women have entered the workforce: wages have basically flatlined; the job market has become more uncertain; the difficulty of balancing work and family has increased; and the costs of housing, education, health care, and child care have exploded. It is families that have borne the brunt of these larger changes, and it is families that falter when, as is too often the case, the strain proves too much. The family used to be a refuge from risk. Today, it is the epicenter of risk. And increasingly, families are a source of risk all their own.

Families—or more precisely what goes on within a family, from childbirth to divorce, from sickness to disability—are a source of risk precisely because the extra work hours and income that families have gained are a necessity, not a luxury. Precisely because it takes more work and more income to maintain a middle-class standard of living, the questions that face families when financially threatening events occur are suddenly more stark. What happens when women leave the workforce to have children, as Julie Pickett did? What happens when a child, like Dixie Yandle, is chronically ill? What happens when one spouse loses his or her job? What happens when families themselves fall apart? And what happens to the substantial minority of parents who don't even enjoy the private risk sharing of marriage or cohabitation—who are trying to keep up with the married Joneses on a single income?[19] How can they expect to weather the growing shocks that families face?

There's another point about risk that often gets missed. Although having two workers in a family reduces the chance that family income will fall to zero, it increases the chance that one family worker will experience drops in or interruptions of earnings. Think about it: if every worker has an equal chance of experiencing a drop in his or her income, a family with two workers has a substantially greater chance of experiencing an income shock. You may never lose all the eggs when they are in more than one basket, but the likelihood of losing at least some of them is greater.

That was the story for the Grace family—an educated professional couple living in Somerville, Massachusetts. The family certainly benefited from having two earners. Peter Grace was a systems analyst; his wife, Joyce, a computer programmer working full time. But because they were both in the workforce, their expenses were high. Their youngest child was in day care, their oldest in a YMCA after-school program. Peter and Joyce had also stretched themselves thin to buy a 1,400-square-foot fixer-upper in one of the hottest real estate markets in the nation—which they now wondered if they could keep.

It's not as if they were living in the lap of luxury. They had two cars, yes, but the second—a 1972 Dodge Dart—had broken down and so they were canceling the insurance on it. When they moved into their turn-of-the-century home, they had to bathe the kids in a boat cooler because the plumbing was in such disrepair. The cost of fixing the leaky roof on the place, which still lacked a kitchen sink, had required that Peter liquidate part of his 401(k). Besides the house and the now-depleted 401(k)s, the family had no savings—a legacy of long years in college, with big bills and loans to pay off.

Then, Peter was let go by Fidelity Investments—a victim of major layoffs within the financial sector. Even with Joyce's full-time work, his unemployment check barely kept them afloat. (After months of frantic and fruitless searching, Peter was on the verge of taking a night shift at Home Depot or another low-wage service job.) And, frighteningly, Joyce's computer job was not secure either. "We don't talk about [me losing my job]," she explained, shooing her son away so he couldn't hear the conversation. "Even if they cut my hours, like they did for other people where I work, I don't know [if] I could take the eight-hour hit."[20]

The Graces are caught in the risk bind. Like millions of Americans—men and women with jobs and kids who are working hard and doing right by their families—they make up our nation's new class of highly leveraged investors. Yet what they are leveraging their futures for isn't anything grand or unusual. It is simply the dream of a good, middle-class life. Today's two-earner family tries to spread risk by drawing on two incomes rather than one. Yet, extended on credit and vulnerable to the increasingly uncertain job market, families find themselves constantly on the financial edge. If just one family member slips, the whole financial edifice of middle-class life can come crumbling in on itself, taking the simple American dream of economic advancement along with it.

THE INDEBTED FAMILY

Though bankruptcy and foreclosure are the most dramatic ruptures in the thinly stretched fabric of American family finances, the day-to-day strain is best captured by a simpler fact: *American families are drowning in debt.* Since the early 1970s, the personal savings rate has plummeted from around a tenth of disposable income to the low single digits (2.6 percent at the end of 2017—roughly where it was before the financial crisis).[21] Meanwhile, the total debt held by Americans has ballooned as a share of income, especially for families with children. As a share of income in 2007, total debt—including mortgages, credit-card debt, car loans, and other liabilities—was roughly 170 percent of income for the median couple with children that had debt (about 90 percent of such couples), higher than for any other family type. Although debt levels dropped and personal savings rates increased during the Great Recession, they have been trending the other way since 2010—and non-mortgage debt is actually higher now than in 2007.[22]

When it comes to economic security, this may be the most troubling aspect of the debt story: millions upon millions of families have virtually no accumulated wealth to tide them over when things go bad. The growing precariousness of family incomes would be one thing if families were building up large nest eggs to sustain them when their incomes went south.[23] Unfortunately, this isn't happening. According to the Survey of Income and Program Participation, more than 25 percent of families in 2016 couldn't maintain even a poverty-level standard of living for three months if they were forced to spend down their wealth.[24]

But even these estimates are optimistic, because they include housing, which is a difficult asset to turn into cash, at least if a family wants to have a place to live. If the focus is just highly "liquid" assets—checking and savings accounts, money market funds, and the like—the picture is considerably more grim. In 2013, the majority of households (55 percent) did not have enough liquid savings to replace a single month of their income.[25] Indeed, the typical middle-class family would have to liquidate not just its cash and checking accounts but all its investments, including all its retirement accounts, to cover a 25 percent loss in its annual income—a loss that we have seen is surprisingly common. The reality is that the assets of most families just aren't that liquid. Despite much talk about the democratization of the stock market, most families do not hold stocks outside of retirement accounts—which can only be accessed for a penalty, and by risking one's retirement income. In 2017, only around 14 percent of households held stocks directly; even if retirement accounts are included, the share is still less than half.[26]

The common response to this litany of statistics is to wonder exactly why Americans are so incapable of managing their finances. To most in the personal responsibility camp, the answer is simple: middle-class families have abandoned the old-fashioned virtue of thrift and embarked on a reckless spending spree, confident they will be bailed out by government when the day of reckoning arrives. As *Newsweek* columnist Robert Samuelson inveighed in 2004, Americans "like to spend what they earn— and they also compete compulsively to show how well they've done. As a result, anxiety and angst become a permanent way of life, even when the economy is doing fairly well. Enough is never enough."[27] During the debate over the 2005 bankruptcy bill, which greatly tightened the nation's laws for declaring bankruptcy, conservative advocates of the legislation painted a vivid picture of feckless families running up huge credit-card debts, then asking for others to bail them out. Senator Orrin Hatch, Republican from Utah, explained that millions of Americans are bankrupt or near-bankrupt because "they run up huge bills and then expect society to pay for them." Federal judge Edith Jones, a potential GOP Supreme Court appointee, contended that "[b]ankruptcy is increasingly seen as a big 'game,' with the losers being those who live within their means, while the bankrupts pursue more interesting and carefree lives."[28]

Yet Elizabeth Warren—the Democratic senator from Massachusetts who started out as a law professor studying bankruptcy law—has thrown cold water on this condescending chorus. As she and her daughter showed in their 2003 book, *The Two-Income Trap*, for many middle-class families the income gains of the past few decades have been eaten up by the rising cost of the biggest household expenses: housing, health care, education, and child care.[29] Families haven't been working more hours to get ahead, in Warren and Tyagi's telling; they've been working more hours just to break even.[30]

This problem is often called the "middle-class squeeze" (a term Warren coined). And while there are aspects of the squeeze argument that can be (and have been) disputed, the basic claim is certainly true: big-ticket family expenses such as housing, health care, and education have rapidly outpaced middle-class incomes—in part because these costs have risen much faster than general inflation, and in part because public and private protections have eroded. Health and housing costs and college tuition all weigh much more heavily on the typical family's budget than they used to, helping to fuel the massive explosion of household debt.[31]

But the squeeze by itself doesn't explain why families are at greater financial risk. Indeed, to the extent that the image of a squeeze suggests that families are caught in a static bind between costs and income, it directs our attention *away* from the mounting risks that families are facing. That's in part, ironically, because Warren and Tyagi treat family expenses in much the same way that critics of the middle class do—as "consumption" that gives no future reward.[32] This might make sense if middle-class families were spending most of their money on DVDs and designer shoes. Yet many of the big-ticket items that have come to represent more and more of family spending are best thought of not as consumption but as *investments*. They are not one-shot purchases but nest eggs that may give a big return down the line. That return, however, is risky, and precisely because families are so leveraged—both financially and in terms of work hours—they are bearing this risk with less financial flexibility than in the past.

Consider housing. Buying a good house in a good neighborhood with good schools is a wise investment in the future for most families. The children will benefit from a better education. Assuming property values stay high, families can sell their houses for more, or take advantage of the growing assortment of financial vehicles that allow homeowners to tap into rising home equity. As long as the market stays hot, families who go into debt to buy a home merely face a cash-flow problem—and one, moreover, that creditors have been creatively working to lessen through second mortgages and the like.

The problem is that there is no guarantee that a housing market will remain hot—as tens of millions of families discovered to their misfortune in the late 2010s.[33] And when the air goes out of housing markets, families are suddenly in serious trouble. What's at issue for families, in other words, isn't just the size of the monthly mortgage check; it's the increased economic risk they are assuming as housing comes to represent more and more of the typical family budget.

Or consider education, another classic investment in the future. Education is a lot more important than it used to be—and a lot more costly. Many of these higher costs have been covered by borrowing, by students as well as their families.[34] But not only is education a big investment, as we saw in the last chapter, it is also a surprisingly risky one. Returns to skills have gone up, but so too has the variability of those returns. All of which suggests that the investments that families are making in education are increasingly risky gambles.

Most of the increase in typical household wealth, moreover, has occurred among older Americans, not among younger families. Indeed, the pattern of wealth accumulation has changed in the last generation in ways that strongly reinforce the story of increasing financial risk for families. The economic life cycle that most of us think of as typical ensured economic security and upward mobility: workers emerged from the educational system with little debt, went modestly into hock to buy a home, but by middle-age were largely debt-free, allowing them to look forward to retirement without undue anxiety.

Today's middle-income families, however, follow a darker path: deeply in debt out of college, they pay a much larger share of income to finance a home (*if* they can finance a home), even though they're buying homes at later ages than in the past. Without savings, they often rely on high-interest credit cards—America's "plastic safety net"—to weather tough patches, or they tap into their home equity. And by middle age, today's families are at the peak of their indebtedness, rather than moving into the clear.

We can see this in the Panel Study of Income Dynamics, which has asked questions about wealth on a regular basis since the 1980s.[35] The typical family whose heads grew up in the 1940s and early 1950s entered middle age (age thirty-five to forty-four) in 1983 with a household wealth of more than $75,000 (including housing wealth). For young families whose heads grew up in the 1960s and early 1970s, by contrast, the middle-aged situation reached in 2002 was not nearly as bright: the median family held less than $42,000 (all wealth estimates in this chapter account for inflation).[36] And for those young families whose heads grew up in the 1970s and 1980s, median wealth at the same age (in 2014) was just $16,000. In short, the typical wealth holdings of middle-aged families today are less than one-fourth what the median middle-aged family had forty years ago.

At the same time, middle-aged Americans are piling up vastly more debt than their parents did at the same stage of life, particularly student loan and credit-card debt.[37] In 1989, according to the federal Survey of Consumer Finances, the typical household headed by someone aged thirty-five to forty-four had $56,100 in debt. By 2016—seven years after the Great Recession—the median middle-aged household had $93,700 in debt, down from a post-recession peak of $119,400 in 2010.[38]

Not surprisingly, the gap in wealth between young and old families has grown: in 1983, median household wealth of older families (whose heads were older than sixty-five) was more than six times the median for young families (age twenty-five to thirty-four), according to the PSID. By 2014 it was more than *thirty-six times* as great.[39]

And rising debt and falling wealth for younger Americans haven't been accompanied by higher consumer spending. To the contrary, young Americans in the 1990s (so-called Generation X) spent less than their parents (baby boomers) did in the 1970s. "With the possible exception of having a larger array of entertainment and other goods to purchase," write two economists, "members of Generation X appear to be worse off by every measure."[40]Today's young Americans, sometimes called "millennials," look even more frugal, spending less than baby boomers, and even Gen-Xers, on everything.[41] Everything, that is, besides housing, health care, pensions, and education: millennials spend 50 percent more on rent than did boomers at their age, 75 percent more on health care, and almost 150 percent more on education.[42]

The message, in short, is that middle-class families are not merely more in debt than they used to be, their debt is increasingly tied up in risky investments in education and housing. Families are facing greater insecurity not just because they have inflexible budgets but also because the things they are spending their budgets on entail more significant risk.

All this would be one thing if the only risks families faced came from the investments they made. But, of course, families also face risks to their earnings just like everyone else. Job loss does not distinguish between those who have children and those who do not. Skills are no less fragile just because you have decided to join in holy matrimony or take the plunge into parenthood. But there is a risk for which the distinction does matter—and this risk is a threat to families' increasingly rickety finances that few rarely think of in connection with economic insecurity: the birth of a child.

BABY BLUES

After Peter Grace lost his job at Fidelity and the family was struggling just to get by, Joyce Grace didn't want her son to hear about money troubles. But when it comes to two-earner families, money troubles and kids often go hand in hand. Two-earner moms and dads are not simply workers, after all. They are also parents. And because they are, the trade-offs posed by the new world of work and family become all the more stark. If both parents work, who stays home when a kid gets sick? If both parents work, what happens to family finances when one leaves the workforce to raise a new baby or care for young children or elderly parents? The answers to these questions often mean the difference between staying afloat or sinking for today's middle-class families.

The assumption of the economics literature is that all of the services that stay-at-home moms used to provide can be purchased privately—that a sick kid can be cared for by a babysitter, an elderly parent by a nursing home. But the love of a parent or child is not something that can be bought in the marketplace, and in many cases it is nearly impossible to arrange affordable and adequate substitutes for family care. When both parents work, events within the family that require the love and care of a parent produce special demands and strains that traditional one-earner families did not face.

At the root of the dilemma is the simple reality that raising children is long, hard (and, yes, terrifically rewarding) work—costly in terms of both time and money. Over the last generation, the expectations on parents have grown dramatically, even as the costs of parenthood have risen.[43] Parents are expected to devote eighteen years of their lives and tens of thousands of dollars to provide continuous guidance, love, education, and care to each of their offspring. Indeed, our society depends on these massive investments to flourish and grow. But most of the costs of raising children are not borne by the societies that reap the benefit; they are borne by parents. The result is a wholesale transformation of the economic effects of kids. In the not-so-distant past, children were an insurance policy for parents—an additional worker on the farm, a helping hand when parents grew older. Today, for all the joy and love children bring into a family, they are, in simple economic terms, a risk—and a risk that parents bear almost wholly on their own.

We are not used to thinking of children in this way (and thankfully so, or few of us would probably take the plunge into parenthood). The facts, however, are clear. According to the 2015 calculations of the U.S. Department of Agriculture, raising a single child to age eighteen will cost almost $284,570 for a middle-income family (taking inflation into account). For two children, this works out to around $27,000 a year, every year, from birth to age eighteen.[44] Children can be a blow to family *incomes* as well. Although many women continue to work through pregnancy, some cannot. And most mothers and fathers want to spend at least limited time away from work with their new children after birth—time that is almost always unpaid, when it is provided at all. Little surprise, then, that fully a quarter of "poverty spells" in the United States—periods in which family income drops below the federal poverty line—begin with the birth of a child, or that the presence of children in the household is the single best predictor that a woman will end up filing for bankruptcy.[45]

The strains are felt even by families that manage to stay afloat financially. Whatever the measure, families with kids are consistently closest to financial meltdown. Consider a deceptively simple question: "If you were to lose your job, how long could you go without a job before experiencing significant financial hardship?" The Gallup Poll has repeatedly asked a random national sample of employed Americans exactly this. Consistently, a substantial majority of Americans say they can last no more than *four months* with serious financial hardship. But here is an equally notable finding, based on a statistical analysis of the 2003 survey responses: those who had children were about 50 percent more likely than those who didn't to say they would experience financial hardship after only a *week*. Indeed, once basic demographic characteristics, such as age and education, are taken into account, people with kids were both significantly more likely to say they could make it no more than a month without their job and significantly *less* likely to say they could make it for a year or more. Financially speaking, parenting is no picnic.[46]

And, ultimately, parents *have* to do much of the vital task of raising kids on their own. Bluntly put, child-rearing is not easy to outsource. The core issue here is not the quality of day care—the best-quality day care is very good, if often prohibitively expensive—and what research has been done does not suggest that formal child care is itself harmful (bad child care is another matter, but formal caregivers do not have a monopoly on that).[47] The core issue is that raising kids requires serious parental investment even when high-quality child care is available, and high-quality child care is often financially out of reach for even middle-class families.

Parents recognize the value of this parental investment, and they act on this recognition. A striking finding of time-use research is that parents today spend at least as much time with their children as they did in the mid-1960s, when most families featured the stay-at-home-mom model. True, women are spending much less time on housework, but their overall time with their children has remained remarkably stable. Men, by contrast, are clearly spending *more* time with their children than they used to, though still substantially less than women. In balancing work and family, parents have largely preserved the precious time with their children that is so crucial. What they have sacrificed is time with each other and their communities, time spent doing other household chores, time for themselves, and time sleeping.[48]

Though children are always a serious commitment, they are an especially serious commitment when they are ill or disabled. Estimates range widely, but as many as 19 percent of American children are thought to have a chronic physical, behavioral, or developmental condition that requires special care and services.[49] The toll of caring for these children is great, as the Yandles will testify. Parents of such children are much more likely to earn incomes that leave them in poverty than are parents with healthy children, even when other factors that might affect household income are factored in. But families with ill or disabled children are doubly disadvantaged because they must spend more on health and social services for their children on their smaller incomes. "Families with exceptional children," one study concludes, "are at exceptional risk of economic hardship."[50]

Parents, of course, also have parents of their own, and they are getting older and more in need of care, too. Of the roughly 20 million Americans who are caring for elderly parents, around 40 percent have kids to care for themselves.[51] These are members of the so-called Sandwich Generation, caught between their duties as parents and their duties *to their* parents. In the early 2010s, nearly 16 million elderly Americans reported at least one disability that limited their ability to perform basic activities or live independently.[52] Most of the care these older Americans receive comes from family members, and the family members who are most likely to assume this caregiving role—more likely even than spouses—are daughters and daughters-in-law. According to a 2006 study by the Urban Institute, daughters who are caring for their frail parents spent on average nearly 100 hours per month providing assistance (215 hours if they are the primary caregivers). And, again, these numbers represent just the time commitment. Frail older Americans typically have relatively limited wealth and extremely low incomes, and Medicare and private health insurance do not cover most long-term health services. (Medicaid for the poor does cover some services, but only a very small share of frail older Americans who are not institutionalized are covered by it.) The financial and time costs of caring for older parents can thus be substantial, and they are costs that are rapidly rising for working families as the population ages.[53]

Linda Sylvester is a case in point. At the age of forty, she found herself caring for three elderly parents (her parents and her mother-in-law) and three teenage sons. Her mother, who is blind, lives in the Sylvesters' home. Her father, who has Alzheimer's disease, lives in a nursing home. Her mother-in-law, who still lives nominally on her own, is frequently bedridden with arthritis. When the stress and headaches began to be overwhelming, Linda quit her job as a dental hygienist, relying on her husband, Chuck, to earn the family's living. "I always feel guilty that I don't do enough," Linda says. "I don't go to the nursing home enough. I don't help my mother-in-law enough. But then I have my own kids, and I want to make sure I spend time with them."[54]

As Linda's story suggests, the unavoidable investment of time that raising children or caring for older parents entails does not come from both spouses equally. Although men are more involved in caregiving and housework than they once were, women still do the lion's share of both—and bear the greatest cost. For all their huge gains in status, education, and earnings, women today still remain much more financially at risk than men. The gap in earnings between working women who have kids and those who do not—what economists call the "wage penalty for motherhood"—remains stubbornly large.[55] Women are the ones most likely to have their incomes and careers disrupted, the ones most likely to work in jobs with low pay and few benefits, and the ones most likely to work part time or on a temporary basis. Not surprisingly, they are also the ones most disadvantaged when families themselves fall apart.

WHEN FAMILIES FAIL

Divorce is rarely discussed in connection with the shift of women from home to work—perhaps out of resistance to the suggestion that family breakup might be driven by simple economic calculations. Yet there is little doubt that the greater ability of women to support themselves and children outside of marriage (despite the endurance of a substantial gender gap in earnings) is a factor in the post-1960s increase in divorce rates. Across the Western world, divorce has become more common when and where women's participation in the labor force has expanded.[56] This is not to suggest that law and culture (much less love) are immaterial, only that the increased instability of American families over the last thirty years has an important connection to the expansion of female economic autonomy.

The probability of a first marriage ending in divorce or separation within ten years rose from about 14 percent in the early 1950s to roughly 30 percent by the mid-1970s, where it's largely stayed since.[57] This is not just an American problem—divorce rates have risen in all nations in which women have gained economic opportunities. Compared with a generation ago, the ability of women to sustain themselves economically outside of marriage has certainly increased; yet the financial effects of divorce on families, and especially women, are frequently devastating. In a world in which two earners are needed to live a middle-class life, parents working and raising kids mostly or entirely on their own face truly dire circumstances.

Those parents, of course, are overwhelmingly women, which is one reason women experience much more severe economic drops after divorce than do men. A wealth of studies has documented that women see a substantial drop in family income when they divorce, with the biggest drops occurring in high-income families and among women who had been married for many years before divorce.[58] This is not because women's earnings fall after divorce—women generally work longer and make more. Rather, it is for two obvious reasons: men usually contribute more to family incomes, which means divorce hurts women more than men, and women usually end up assuming the lion's share of child-rearing, which means they must bear these costs largely on their own. Spousal incomes are becoming more equal. So too, more slowly, are men's contribution to child-rearing after a divorce. Still, divorced parents who end up suffering major—and sometimes catastrophic—financial losses are overwhelmingly women.[59]

Ann Brash was the child of a divorce, but her own life had been relatively free of hardship—until, that is, she and her husband divorced, leaving her to take care of her two kids on her own. Ann had gone to college but, like two-fifths or so of college attendees, never received her degree (she eventually did by passing an exam to obtain extra credits). Ann scraped by, homeless for a time, working as an editor for a small-time publisher, yet always insistent that she would spend time with her children, who eventually got into prestigious colleges.

Yet things went from bad to worse. Her car broke down, and she bought a new one to get to work. The deal had seemed good, but it left her with unmanageable car payments. Ann quickly fell into debt, relying on credit cards to keep going. As her credit worsened, the interest rates offered became higher. Ann finally decided to declare bankruptcy, but found that she could not even afford the almost $1,000 worth of fees that she had to pay to get the process started. The financial counselor she went to told her she had no choice—she had to stop paying her credit-card bills altogether. After seven months, she had saved up enough money, and filed for bankruptcy. But even without her debts, she is barely scraping by. "One half of the biweekly check goes to rent," she explains. "The other half to the car. Then there are the utilities and transportation costs to get back and forth to work. We're not having Christmas this year, though we will try to have a meal. I'm sorry, I don't mean to complain."[60]

Men may not experience the large drops in income that women do when they divorce, but the costs of divorce for them are rising. The familiar assertion that men always do better after a divorce is simply false—true only among the dwindling minority of families in which men earned almost all the family's money before the marriage ended. When earnings within marriage are more even (as they are for an increasing share of families), and especially when fathers have at least partial custody of children, men also suffer economically from divorce, and these losses appear to be long-lived, rather than temporary.[61] One important reason for these losses is that mandatory child-support payments have become more common, meaning that divorced men cannot easily shirk their responsibilities for their children, as they once frequently did.

Still, despite all these changes, divorce still remains much more threatening financially for women than for men.[62] Moreover, women who work longer hours are actually more likely to divorce than women who work shorter hours or do not work at all.[63] This is a new—and striking—development: in the 1960s and 1970s, two-earner couples and one-earner couples were about equally likely to break up. By the 1990s, however, two-earner heterosexual couples were substantially more likely to break up than one-earner couples (two-earner homosexual couples are actually less likely to break up).[64] Once again, when it comes to divorce, the increased workforce participation of women has brought new risks as well as new opportunities—a reflection of the degree to which our public and private policies have failed to track long-overdue changes in women's roles.

THE RIGHT CHOICES ARE RISKY

Strong families are the backbone of strong societies. And yet, strong families do not magically emerge. They take hard work and commitment, and they require investments—of love, of course, but also of time and money. These investments are ingrained in our nature, but they are also ingrained in custom and common sense. We are told that we should raise children in strong and stable families, that we should commit to long and healthy marriages, that we should invest in good schools for our kids and good homes for our families.

These investments are crucial and increasingly costly. Yet they have also become more uncertain, and families have been left to cope with this uncertainty on their own. The response has been the greatest run-up of private debt in American history, as families have leveraged themselves ever more aggressively to maintain a middle-class standard of living, while working more hours than ever before.

This might seem like a simple story of bad choices, a morality tale about how we've placed work and material goods above family (or in rarer cases, the other way around). Yet at root it is an economic story. Children today are an economic risk rather than a reward, and the severity of that risk has increased. Two-earner families mark a great cultural shift, to be sure. But it is a shift that has been reinforced by an economic reality: the need for two incomes to live a middle-class life. For two-earner parents forced to pay more for basic household expenses while shelling out hard-earned income for services that stay-at-home moms once provided, the idea that choices are all that matter rings hollow.

To the Personal Responsibility Crusade, strong families are built on good personal decisions. If a family can't afford to have kids, it shouldn't. If it gets into hot water, it must be its own fault. But the stories and statistics we've explored show just how unrealistic this view is. People sometimes do make bad choices, but how can that explain the millions of middle-class families straining to make ends meet? How can it explain the dilemmas and hardship faced by the Picketts or the Graces or Ann Brash or Linda Sylvester? And what answers does it offer to those strained families when the bottom suddenly falls out?

Forming a family and having kids is indeed the most personal of decisions. Yet when Americans build strong families, it has profound benefits for society as a whole: stronger neighborhoods, more productive workers, new generations of leaders and scientists, explorers, and artists. These benefits, however, do not come without cost. They are paid for through the sacrifices that families must make, the risks that families must bear, usually without much compensation or assistance. As these risks and sacrifices grow, Americans increasingly find themselves forced to choose between economic security and having a family and children. This is a choice that truly deserves to be called "bad."

5

Risky Retirement

The images still haunt us: families holding folded flags, crying before open graves, processing the nightmare in the weeks after the tragic events of September 11, 2001. Ellen Saracini was among the mourners. Her husband, fifty-one-year-old Victor J. Saracini, was the captain of United Airlines Flight 175, the second plane that crashed into the World Trade Center. Victor was a former navy pilot and, according to one neighbor, "a great guy, a man's man," a fierce protector of his wife and two teenage daughters who surely "fought to the end."[1] Victor had protected his family even in their time of loss—through his life insurance and the generous widow's pension that Ellen received from United Airlines. For Ellen and the girls, the money was welcome. It would pay for college and support Ellen's parents, who lived in an assisted living facility.

Four years later, however, the value of the pension on which the Saracinis were now reliant was cut by more than half. After two years in bankruptcy,

United announced that it had reached a deal with the courts and the Pension Benefit Guaranty Corporation (the federally authorized agency that insures traditional pensions) to default on all its pension plans—a retreat from $7.4 billion in commitments. United's default in 2005 still represents the largest pension failure in American history.[2] (In 2012, American Airlines came close to terminating its retirement plans, but ended up freezing them instead: workers kept their plans but the company stopped making contributions to them.) Overnight, Ellen—and her family—saw the majority of her widow's pension disappear. Like most pilots (but unlike most workers whose pensions are insured by the Pension Benefit Guaranty Corporation), Victor had earned a pension larger than the amount fully insured by the agency. There was also the fact that his employment had been "terminated" at fifty-one—well before the agency's threshold of sixty-five for full benefits. Ellen Saracini describes her situation as "double jeopardy." Yet she talks mostly about the problems of other United workers. "My own situation is not a crisis," she says. "But a lot of other people have real hardship—medical costs they won't be able to afford, houses they won't be able to keep. . . . Everyone was affected by September 11, just to different degrees, and now everyone is affected by this decision . . . just to different degrees. Each one is drastic in the eyes of the person it touches."[3]

The collapse of United's pensions may have been drastic, but it was not without precedent. Just a few years earlier, Bethlehem Steel and U.S. Airways also dumped their cash-strapped plans on the Pension Benefit Guaranty Corporation (known in Washington as the PBGC). Since United's collapse, Delta (2006) and Delphi (2009) have joined the growing list of multibillion-dollar failures.[4] Yet the thought on almost everyone's mind back in 2005 was the collapse of Enron—a wildly celebrated energy conglomerate that, before its ignominious implosion in 2001, was America's seventh largest corporation.[5] By the time of United's collapse, the word *Enron* had become shorthand for the risks faced by workers holding a retirement account when a company goes under.

The basic problem at Enron was simple: more than 60 percent of Enron's pension assets were in the company's soaring stock, and when Enron went under, so too did workers' pensions. With Enron's share price plummeting seemingly overnight from $90 to just 26 cents per share, thousands of workers not only lost their jobs but most of their retirement savings as well.[6] One of these workers was Charles Weiss, a well-paid technical manager who saw almost all of the $300,000 in retirement savings he had built up vanish in an instant. "They ruined us," Weiss laments. "What Enron did was perpetrate financial terrorism on the employees and shareholders of the company." Another former employee, Tom Padgett—who, at age fifty-nine in 2001, was ten years Weiss's senior—lost even more. In late December 2000, his pension assets were more than $600,000. A year later, they were $11,000. "Betrayal is a good word for what Enron did to me," Padgett says. "There are other words, but you couldn't print them."[7]

The irony is thick: United and Enron—the old-economy transporter and the new-economy trader—were briefly fused as symbols of the increasingly precarious state of American retirement security. But the obvious analogies can mislead. Each company was mismanaged; each fell into bankruptcy; each saw its pension collapse. And yet the reasons for the collapse and the story of what happened next are starkly and revealingly different.

Despite the scale of United's default, most of the airline's employees will eventually receive all of the benefits they were promised at the time of the plan's disbandment. Highly paid workers and those who do not reach the age of sixty-five before benefits are paid—a group that, tragically, includes Victor Saracini—will receive less. Even so, historically, more than 8 out of 10 workers get full benefits when their plans are taken over by the PBGC.[8] Those pensions, moreover, are based on strict formulas that protect workers even if the stock market drops or they live longer than expected in retirement. And although United won the right to default on its plan, it only did so after a legal fight in which both sides—the corporation and its workers—were allowed to make their case.

Now look at the Enron debacle. Most workers caught in the company's implosion lost much more than even the most unfavorably treated United employee. It's easy to criticize employers for overinvesting in company stock—until one realizes that overinvesting in company stock is one of the most common errors that pension holders make, that Enron employees actually invested less in their own company stock than many workers do

today, that Enron matched employee contributions to the plan with company stock (and required that such matches be held till age fifty), and
that, when the end was near, it actually "locked down" its plan, preventing
workers from reshuffling their holdings—just one example of the plan's
mismanagement that would come to light.[9]

The most important difference, however, is the simplest: Enron's retirement plan was not a traditional defined-benefit pension of the sort
that United offered. It was a 401(k), and 401(k)s, like other defined-
contribution plans, are completely uninsured—for the simple reason that
they don't offer anything to insure. A 401(k) pension plan is akin to a private savings account. If it grows, all the money is yours. But if it dwindles,
all the losses are yours, too. There is no agency looking out for you. Nor is
there any guarantee that you will get an adequate benefit for your entire retired life. For all the pain and dashed expectations experienced by United's
employees, their plans were protected by a government-backed agency, and
the terms of their plans were defined in precise language with legal force.
The most highly paid of United's workers lost a great deal, to be sure; many
others had to cope with the reality that they would no longer be able to ac-
crue the large pensions they had come to expect. But Enron's unfortunate
employees got *nothing*—no insurance, no guarantees, no compensation.
They were on their own.

This contrast is fundamental, because American retirement security is
looking more and more like Enron. As recently as 1984, more than 80 percent of large and medium-sized firms offered a defined-benefit plan; today,
only around a quarter do, and the share continues to fall.[10] Companies
are rapidly "freezing" their defined-benefit plans (that is, preventing new
workers from joining the plan), and shifting them over to alternative
forms (such as the so-called cash-balance plan) that are more like 401(k)s.
Meanwhile, 401(k) plans have gone from nothing to a national obses-
sion, their total assets rising from zero to roughly a quarter of our nation's
economy.[11] If workers get a pension today, they get a 401(k). Three digits
and a letter spell the future of American retirement security.

And that is what is so worrisome. Traditional pension plans are hardly
risk free. Yet they have three essential elements that make them especially

vital for retirement planning for ordinary workers: they are mandatory for covered employees, making them a form of forced savings; they are professionally managed under rules that prevent common errors, such as overinvesting in company stock; and they pool the key risks to retirement income. Much ink has been spilled comparing the returns of 401(k)s and old-style pensions. (According to a study of returns between 1985 and 2001, the dinosaurs have actually won, earning returns that exceed those of their upstart competitors by about 1 percent a year.)[12] But the central issue for retirement security isn't the return, but the risk. Some people do well with 401(k)s; others—such as Charles Weiss, who saw most of his $300,000 in assets vanish, and Tom Padgett, who lost almost twice that—do poorly. The difference, in a word, is risk.

The difference is also who is bearing the risk—thousands, even millions of Americans jointly or each account-holder individually. The Personal Responsibility Crusade has had perhaps its greatest success in the area of retirement security, where responsibility for almost all the management and risk of private retirement planning has shifted onto workers and their families. Though added almost haphazardly in the late 1970s, little Section 401(k) of the tax code—and its siblings, from Individual Retirement Accounts to tax-free education savings plans to Health Savings Accounts—have become the guiding template for conservatives' grand plan for a privatized system of social protection.[13] Advocates of individualized retirement savings have not only worked to promote private plans; they have also sought legal and policy changes that undermine the security of traditional defined-benefit plans and the agency that insures them, the PBGC. The last guaranteed pillar, Social Security, would be their biggest prize in the campaign to shift from guaranteed benefits to individual accounts.[14]

The debate is momentous, and it is about more than when people should retire, or how they should invest, or even whether Social Security should be reformed. It is about risk. To understand the real debate, we need to understand why guaranteed private pensions and Social Security were created in the first place. Then we need to understand why—in an age of growing economic insecurity—such guarantees remain more vital than ever, and more at risk.

THE PROBLEM OF EXPECTATIONS

To grasp why pensions exist—and why 401(k)s work so poorly as guarantees of retirement security—it helps to talk with Susan Lemoine. In many ways, she seems an unlikely person to worry about retirement. Her husband, John Lemoine, used to work at AT&T making more than $70,000 a year. The Lemoines have four kids, now all teenagers. She is only forty-one—more than a decade younger than John—and she works as a paralegal. But Susan Lemoine says, "I will work until the day I die."[15]

Susan is not alone in her pessimistic thinking. After consistently falling for decades, the participation of older Americans in the workforce is rising, and many older Americans who are still working say they can't afford not to. Between 40 and 50 percent of adults, according to recent Gallup Polls, fear that they aren't prepared for retirement—the highest level of concern about any financial topic.[16] And like Susan, more and more think that they will have to postpone their retirement or, more rarely, forgo it altogether.

How can this be? Retiring without adequate income would seem the easiest risk of all to avoid. Virtually everyone but Supreme Court justices expects to retire at some point. Retirement does not, one would think, drop into people's lives unannounced. It creeps up slowly, usually with plenty of advance warning. And it is an event so common that the AARP has close to 38 million members.[17] So why are so many Americans unprepared and fearful?

The answer is *expectations*. As routine as retirement is, it actually involves a relatively complex set of calculations—ones that, unfortunately, intersect with serious biases in the way people think about risks and the future. Consider the variables that a relatively young worker has to consider: How much will I make in the coming years? How much of my pre-retirement income do I need to live in retirement? When will I retire, and how long will I live after I retire? Will I marry, will I have children, and how much will that affect my savings? What are the likely long-term trajectories of the stock and bond markets and the cost of living? Will I change or lose jobs? Will my health remain good? Will my employers offer me a pension, and of what sort? And what's going to happen to Social Security?

Importantly, most of these questions involve the long term—at times, the very long term. What's more, many of the variables we have to consider—future longevity, stock-market returns, the fate of Social Security—are inherently uncertain. Few workers in 1950 would have predicted that fifty years later people would routinely live into their eighties. Workers who cashed in stocks in August 1987 would not have known that those who did so four months later would be receiving back more than a quarter less, on average, than those who had cashed in earlier.[18] Four in ten retired workers report that they left their jobs earlier than planned because of layoffs, health problems, or sick family members.[19] These are precisely the sorts of considerations that, as behavioral economists have found, people both routinely and systematically misperceive and regularly fail to incorporate into their planning. Traditional pensions address this problem by pooling many of these uncertain risks under the auspices of employers, who promise a guaranteed pension in retirement based on years of work, pay, family size, and the like.

Traditional pensions also deal with another problem that behavioral economists have recently highlighted: *procrastination*. When sacrifices must be made in the present to ensure well-being in the relatively distant future, many people tend to be myopic—they act in ways that they end up regretting in the future. Myopia of this sort seems to be wired deeply into the human psyche, but it is an even greater problem when current resources are scarce. With today's families often cash strapped, it is understandable why short-term sacrifices are so hard to make, even if they have large long-term gains. This is one reason people so often "tie themselves to the mast"—as Ulysses did to resist the sirens in *The Odyssey*—constraining their short-term choices in order to do the right thing for the future.[20] Traditional pension plans do this: because the employer contributes on workers' behalf (in effect, paying workers in the form of future, rather than current, income), they essentially force workers to save.

All this is to explain why Susan Lemoine's story isn't as unusual as it might seem. Her plight reflects the problem of expectations—or rather, dashed expectations. Her husband, John, was forced to take early retirement at AT&T, and although in the years afterward he worked more than one job to supplement his pension (as a maintenance worker at Sam's Club, then a part-time X-ray technician and full-time security guard), he eventually had to stop working because of an auto accident. If Susan had known John would lose his well-paid job at AT&T, she might have acted differently. Maybe she would have gone back to school or spent less time with the kids. And John might have saved more if he had understood that he was going to have to leave the workforce prematurely, or that AT&T, along with other large companies, was going to cut back on retiree health coverage, or if he had anticipated just how costly health care was going to be when he hit his fifties. They might even have had fewer kids.

The fact that people with good incomes and good jobs face trouble planning privately for retirement suggests how serious the problem of expectations is. Traditional pension plans and Social Security developed as a means of dealing with the problem of expectations for middle-class and working-class Americans, who had always faced the greatest risk in planning for retirement. Now, with traditional plans nearly extinct and Social Security under siege, this uniquely American solution is in doubt. And the model that has rapidly replaced it—tax-free accounts that are not only heavily tilted toward the affluent but also transparently incapable of solving the problem of expectations—is putting more and more Americans at risk.

SECURING RETIREMENT

In 1875 a railroad freight-forwarder named American Express adopted a radical innovation in workplace benefits: the formal pension plan.[21] Before American Express's move, retirees did sometimes receive help in old age, but workers had no right to benefits, which were given (or withheld) solely at the discretion of the company. This was pretty much how it stood even after 1875. Although formal plans grew in number in the early twentieth century, most salaried and wage workers were still on their own when it came to retirement.

In the popular story of what happened next, these early pension plans were devastated by the Great Depression, making clear the need for a federal Social Security program. The truth is more complex—and crucial to grasp if we are to understand what is being lost today. Formal private plans actually weathered the Depression surprisingly well. Indeed, soon after Social Security was passed, most companies that operated private plans began to build their plans on top of Social Security, a practice known as "integration." In effect, integration meant that workers received pensions from their employers that took into account Social Security payments. If their Social Security benefits were higher, their private benefits were lower. If their Social Security benefits went up, their private benefits went down.

Over the following decades, Social Security expanded dramatically to become the primary source of retirement income for most workers. But for the better paid and the unionized, private pensions were a big supplement, boosting retirement income for these workers to European levels or higher. In return for working for a firm for a certain number of years, companies promised workers that they would add whatever was needed on top of Social Security to provide a generous guaranteed income for workers and their families throughout their retired lives.

The highpoint of this distinctly American system was 1974, the year that the Employee Retirement Income Security Act, or ERISA, was passed. ERISA was designed to make private pension plans a secure counterpart to Social Security, in part by creating the Pension Benefit Guaranty Corporation, the insurance program for private plans that bailed out United's pensions. The act put in place strict rules to ensure that workers would be guaranteed their full benefits, just as they were with Social Security. The law was, in the words of Jacob Javits—the Republican senator from New York who was the legislation's tireless champion—"the greatest development in the life of the American worker since Social Security." Under the law, Javits grandly predicted, "private plans will develop more rapidly than in the past because the Congress will have assured that pension promises are kept and reasonable expectations built on these promises are not disappointed."[22]

Soon after ERISA passed, however, it became clear that Javits's sunny proclamation had not foreseen a momentous shift in the world of private pensions—the unexpected emergence and explosion of the 401(k). The result was a transformation as profound as the one that Javits had confidently foreseen, yet ultimately far less happy for the cause of American retirement security.

TED BENNA'S REVOLUTION

Ted Benna is not an unassuming man. He is quick to tell reporters of his pivotal role in the development of the 401(k). He clearly relishes his familiar moniker, "father of the 401(k)." He is tireless in his defense of his cherished offspring, insisting that few 401(k) plans have any difficulties to speak of. Yet even Ted Benna admits that he had no idea he would spawn a revolution when in 1981—thanks to his friendship with a Reagan-administration cabinet secretary—he was able to petition the Reagan administration to rule on the legality of what we now know as the 401(k) plan.

Nor, it seems, did anyone else see the revolution coming. When Congress added Section 401(k) to the tax code in 1978 to resolve some long-standing disputes over profit-sharing plans offered by employers, no mention was made of the new tax provision, except a brief note in the congressional report on the 1978 legislation indicating that the effects of section 401(k) would be "negligible."[23] It is no overstatement to suggest that this may have been the least prescient prediction in the history of the American Congress.

The essence of the 401(k) is often thought to be investment in stock-market mutual funds, and indeed 401(k)s created the modern mutual-fund movement. But the hallmark of 401(k)s—the point on which Benna pressed for clarification in 1981—is that they let workers set aside *their own* earnings for retirement. This is what makes 401(k)s a world apart from traditional defined-benefit pension plans. The account is in an *employee's* name and under an *employee's* control. The *employee*, not the company, decides whether and how much to contribute, at least up to federal limits. Workers who leave a company take their accounts with them, either in the form of a single payment or by "rolling over" their holdings into an IRA or another 401(k). The money, with some important restrictions, is theirs, and it's still tax-free.

To American corporations—and American conservatives—the unexpected new possibilities of Section 401(k) were embraced with an enthusiasm not normally associated with obscure provisions of the tax code. Traditional defined-benefit plans were instigated by employers for two main reasons. First, by guaranteeing long-service workers that they would receive a generous pension, defined-benefit plans helped employers foster and retain loyal and skilled lifetime employees.[24] With the demise of the old employment contract, this rationale no longer carried the weight it once did. The second reason for traditional defined-benefit pensions was even less relevant as the 1980s rolled on—unions. Organized labor had always been a crucial force pressing for defined-benefit pensions. But as unions grew less common, employers had less reason to care what they thought. Thus went another motive for traditional pension plans.

If the old virtues of defined-benefit plans seemed less compelling to employers, the one singular virtue of 401(k) plans became all the more irresistible: 401(k)s are dirt cheap. In the late 1970s, private employers devoted more than 4 percent of workers' compensation to pensions. By the late 1980s, they were contributing around 2.5 percent.[25] Most 401(k) contributions, after all, are made by workers, not employers. And many workers offered 401(k) plans—roughly a third—contribute nothing to them, meaning that even those employers that match employee contributions are completely off the hook.[26] It is no secret, either, which workers are most likely to contribute: those with the highest earnings. But in contrast to traditional plans, employers don't have to worry much about how skewed their 401(k)s are toward the best-paid workers, because any skew is putatively the result of workers' choices.

If employers were the biggest beneficiaries of Section 401(k), they were hardly the only ones. Mutual funds and investment banks embraced 401(k)s as the Second Coming. One financial planning publication seemed unable to find sufficient praise: "A cultural icon, a measure of our financial well-being, and a symbol of democratic power—individuals of all walks of life own Corporate America through their 401(k)s."[27] In 1999 *Money* magazine offered up a breathless history of mutual funds and the 401(k). "Over the full sweep of time, mutual funds have shown that they are probably the greatest contribution to financial democracy ever devised," the review began. Then—in a sign of just how little understood the origins of 401(k)s are even among enthusiasts—*Money* placed the creation of 401(k)s in 1975 (they were created in 1978), said they were part of ERISA (they were not, and ERISA was passed in 1974), and stated that ERISA "passed after years of advocacy by Ted Benna" (poor Jacob Javits; he never stood a chance).[28]

Although the initial creation of 401(k)s in 1978 seems to have been mostly inadvertent, it did not take long for conservatives to see their potential. Conservatives had initially placed their faith in Individual Retirement Accounts, which dramatically expanded as part of Reagan's tax cuts in 1981—the same year that the Reagan IRS granted Ted Benna's petition to create the first 401(k). In the 1980s, with Democrats in control of the House of Representatives, conservatives had limited success expanding tax breaks for IRAs and 401(k)s. But after Republicans took both houses of Congress in 1994, IRAs were expanded, and the uses to which they could be put were loosened, making IRAs closer to all-purpose, tax-free savings accounts that could be tapped for favored big-ticket expenses, such as college and the purchase of a home. After George W. Bush captured the White House in 2000, Republicans also successfully pushed for a major expansion of 401(k)s, increasing how much could be put in the accounts and making sure that this amount would automatically rise in the future.

To be sure, not all enthusiasts had grand policy visions in mind. Tax-free accounts, after all, represented a big tax break especially valuable to the well off—and, hence, especially attractive to antitax conservatives, whatever the long-term effects. Yet the potential *political* benefits of the 401(k) and IRA revolution were never far from the minds of leading advocates. As early as 1983, Stuart Butler—the Waldo of the conservative policy movement we met earlier—had coauthored a strategy memo in which he called for expanding tax-free private accounts into "a small-scale private Social Security system," while mobilizing "banks, insurance companies, and other institutions that will gain from providing such plans to the public."[29] In the first Bush administration, officials described the expansion of 401(k)s as a strategy of "empowerment" that "would create a framework within which individuals are free to do the best they can do for themselves."[30] By the time the second President Bush was campaigning for Social Security privatization in 2005, he was speaking of a "401(k) culture."[31] Asked why conservatives should support 401(k)s, a Heritage Foundation economist said simply, "When citizens have a vested interest in the economy and own more property (or investment assets), the more . . . politically conservative your society will be."[32]

In the eyes of Wall Street and Washington, section 401(k) was the harbinger of a joyous new era. Unfortunately, it would be the first era since Social Security's creation when, instead of expanding, retirement security began to slip away.

THE 401(K) BAIT AND SWITCH

At the end of the 1990s, Americans could legitimately have many doubts about their retirement security. But one thing that nobody with a defined-contribution pension plan to his or her name could doubt was that the stock market had been beneficent.

Between 1994 and 1999, the Dow Jones Industrial Average increased from 3,600 to more than 11,000. Like the fortunate child born into wealth, the 401(k) was fathered at the beginning of almost two decades of unusually consistent and rapid stock-market growth. Surely there could not have been a more auspicious environment for Ted Benna's brainchild to take root and grow.

All the more remarkable, then, that as 401(k)s grew like Topsy, the retirement savings of most Americans hardly rose at all. In fact, the median American family headed by someone aged forty-seven to sixty-four saw its retirement wealth fall significantly during this period. So at odds with received wisdom is this fact that it must be repeated: *over the fifteen years between 1983 and 1998, the typical family approaching retirement saw the wealth earmarked for its retirement decline, not rise.* The stock market skyrocketed, 401(k)s exploded—and the typical family saw its retirement wealth drop.

To be sure, defined-contribution accounts grew handsomely during this period, especially in the 1990s. Yet, at the same time, the retirement wealth represented by defined-benefit plans declined as employers stopped offering them. So too did expected Social Security benefits, thanks to the cutbacks in Social Security passed in 1983. When all the gains and losses are added up, the median family approaching retirement—that is, the family exactly in the middle of the retirement wealth distribution—ended the 1990s with 11 percent *less* in retirement wealth than the median family had in 1983. And the story gets worse. The proportion of near-retirement families that are likely to live on less than *half* of their prior income in retirement increased substantially between 1989 and 1998—from less than 30 percent to more than 40 percent. In other words, more than two out of five families nearing retirement in 1998 were likely to be living on less than half of their present income—a sharp increase in less than a decade.[33]

If these results prompt incredulity, rest assured: this is a natural response. Throughout the bull markets of the 1990s, 2000s, and 2010s, commentators crowed that contemporary 401(k)-empowered Americans were the first to truly share in the fruits of the stock market's bounty. In one sense, the claims were true: more Americans than ever invested in the stock market through their retirement accounts, but what was often left out is how unequal the scale of these investments was.

We are told that the "average" American has tens of thousands of dollars socked away in a 401(k), but in fact roughly three-quarters of account holders have less than the widely cited average of around $80,000.[34] The median among account-holders—which is a better measure of what's typical—is less than $20,000.[35] And all these figures include only those who *have* 401(k)s, when nearly 40 percent of workers do not have access to a defined-contribution pension plan, and more than half of workers do not contribute to one.[36] Overall, around three-quarters of defined-contribution pension and IRA assets are held by the richest fifth of Americans.[37] And even those who do contribute adequately tend to make common investing errors, such as investing in funds with excessive management fees, putting their money in low-yield bonds, neglecting to rebalance their accounts periodically, and overinvesting in their own company's stock.

In the personal responsibility mantra, all these are failures of individual choice: failure to find an employer who offers a plan, failure to contribute, failure to contribute adequately, failure to manage accounts well. "It's kind of a severe doctrine," said one Treasury Department official during the first Bush administration when asked about the potential risks posed by 401(k)s. "It's rough, because you're not protecting people against themselves. They have the responsibility."[38]

But who ends up having the "responsibility" for bad outcomes under 401(k)s is not random: it is in fact lower-income workers who are least likely to receive a plan or contribute to it—in part because of the distorted way in which 401(k)s are subsidized. The tax breaks for 401(k)s are worth the most to high-income people. Unlike traditional pensions, moreover, 401(k)s can be used to save money for one's heirs. High-income workers also don't have much need for a guaranteed income in retirement, precisely the feature of old-style plans that most workers valued above all.

The all-too-common failure of workers to contribute to or properly manage 401(k)s also reflects well-understood biases in retirement planning that, we've seen, are deeply ingrained in the human psyche. Studies suggest, for instance, that simply automatically enrolling workers in 401(k)s, rather than requiring that they opt in, doubles initial enrollment in 401(k) plans, increasing it to nearly 90 percent.[39]

Yet most crucial of all, all these choices are simply not an issue with traditional defined-benefit pensions, which have essentially 100 percent participation rates for covered workers. Workers forced to save, save. Workers not forced to save, don't, or don't save enough. Yes, failure to save for retirement is a personal choice, at least for workers with access to 401(k) plans. But the structure of 401(k)s explains much of the choice: 401(k)s are almost tailor-made to produce insufficient retirement savings for ordinary workers—and, indeed, this is one reason they're so cheap for employers to run.

One lawyer active in pension litigation—a burgeoning field as more and more workers at companies such as Enron, WorldCom, and Global Crossing suddenly lose their pensions—told me about a trade association meeting at which 401(k) providers were, in his words, "enthusiastically peddling their wares." A panel at the conference focused on strategies to motivate workers to participate. After the standard hortatory presentations, a human resources manager stood up and asked a blunt question:

> Am I missing something? How am I supposed to get my workers to contribute more? A typical participant at my company is forty-five, has two kids, makes $60,000, has no defined-benefit pension, and has maybe $50,000 in his 401(k), tops. When I show him the fancy projections you're telling me about, suggesting he needs a million dollars to have anything like the life he's living now, he just says, "Forget it. What's the point?" So how am I supposed to get him to contribute more?

There was a long silence. Then, one panelist was brave enough to jump in. If the typical worker only had $50,000 at age forty-five, the panelist responded, that's his own fault—he can't retire. But, of course, $50,000 is more than most account-holders have in their 401(k)s. If this worker—who has a 401(k) and who's put away a substantial sum—can't retire on his 401(k), few workers can. The lawyer who told me the story described the conference as akin to "an auto show at which half the cars don't have engines."

The risks posed by 401(k)s go beyond the participation problem to encompass nearly all of the managerial and savings responsibilities imposed on workers. Consider one of the most distinctive features of defined-contribution plans: the ability of workers to take their pension as a "lump sum," that is, in the form of cash, when they leave an employer. As a means of protecting retirement wealth, this is of considerable benefit to workers who change jobs frequently—but only if they save the money. Unfortunately, the majority of those who receive a lump-sum distribution do not roll all of it into tax-favored accounts, such as IRAs and other 401(k)s.[40] They do not despite the fact that they must pay income taxes on all their benefits, as well as a penalty of 10 percent if they are younger than fifty-five.

How could people be so foolish? A clue is provided by research on what affects workers' use of lump sum distributions. Workers who are laid off are 47 percent less likely to roll over their pension distributions. Workers who relocate to obtain a new job are 50 percent less likely. And workers who leave work to care for a family member are 77 *percent* less likely. "Overall," as one economist concludes, "the evidence suggests that pension assets have been used to buffer economic shocks to the household."[41] Here, then, is another private response to economic insecurity—but one that leaves families more vulnerable to one of the greatest risks of all: retiring without adequate income.

Which brings us back to the crucial issue—risk. All of these faults of 401(k)s would be one thing if defined-contribution plans provided a secure guarantee of retirement income. Yet entirely the opposite is the case: 401(k)s put all the major risks and responsibilities—market risk, outliving one's savings, deciding how much to contribute and how to invest those contributions—onto workers themselves. As 401(k)s have expanded and traditional defined-benefit plans have eroded, the nation has in effect engaged in a vast experiment to see how Americans fare in a world in which retirement planning is an individual responsibility and in which families bear the resulting risks on their own. It is now clear that this experiment has failed.

After all, defined-contribution pensions did not simply add to the menu of options that workers already had. Some fortunate workers receive both defined-contribution and defined-benefit plans, but most workers—especially younger workers—have only one choice if they're lucky: a 401(k). In 1983 only about 6.6 percent of families' private pension wealth, on average, was in defined-contribution plans such as 401(k)s; in 2007 more than half was. For households headed by workers younger than forty-seven, the shift was even more stark, from around 10 percent of pension wealth in the defined-contribution system to more than 73 percent.[42] This means, in effect, that the private retirement fortunes of all but today's oldest workers are dependent on the fate of 401(k)s. And this means, in turn, that these retirement fortunes are dependent on the future of financial markets.

To be sure, there is nothing that requires that 401(k)s be invested in stocks. Workers are free to buy bonds or a conservative mix of stocks and bonds, and indeed a significant share of workers invest their 401(k)s too conservatively for their age.[43] Still, the investment gurus are right that stocks deliver a higher overall return. The problem is that this return comes with higher risk, and 401(k)s place all of this higher risk on workers, offering little of the investment guidance and none of the protections against economic loss that are inherent in defined-benefit pensions.

Sometimes, the losses can be staggering, as one unlucky employee of MCI discovered. Laid off after WorldCom acquired MCI in 2001, Jim Horner (not his real name) had worked for MCI for more than twenty years as a skilled technician, during which time he had built up $900,000 in his 401(k) retirement account. In his fifties, without a college degree, and with his skills no longer valued, he had had a rough time finding a new job and was now working behind the counter at a relative's ice-cream parlor. In 2003, a check for around $800 arrived from the now-bankrupt WorldCom. Jim feared the company was trying to buy him off, although he'd never thought of joining in the legal actions against the telecommunications giant, the "creative accounting" of which had destroyed the company's stock and thousands of jobs. But the check was something less sinister, and more tragic. It was his 401(k). The plan's policy was to send a lump-sum payment to all former workers when their plan balance fell below a minimal level. Jim's near-million-dollar pension—which, like the 401(k)s of many others in the company, was invested in company stock—was now his, all $767.14 of it. Although I can't use his real name, I have seen a copy of his 401(k) payout stub, and it is chilling:

Birth Date: xx/xx/48
Employment Date: xx/xx/79
Plan Entry Date: xx/xx/80
Reason: Termination xx/xx/01
Effective Date: xx/xx/03
Options: Lump Sum Payment
Total Shares/Units: 11,937.4735
Total Payment Amount: $950.93
Federal Income Tax Withheld: $191.79
Net Distribution Amount: $767.14

Jim's situation is, of course, extreme. But the risks posed by the stock market are much bigger than most 401(k) enthusiasts recognize. Even under highly favorable assumptions, workers who invest their private accounts in the stock market during their working lives will receive wildly divergent pensions, depending on whether they retire when the market is up or down. According to one analysis that stacks the deck in favor of private accounts (assuming, for example, that they have no administrative costs, that everyone who uses them invests in a broad stock-market index fund, and that it's possible to purchase a fairly priced "annuity" paying a lifetime income at retirement), the biggest pension received by a worker is *five* times as large as the smallest, with the rate of return varying from as low as 2 percent to as high as 10 percent—a highly risky basis for retirement planning.[44]

But, of course, in the real world, it is not so easy to turn a retirement account into a lifetime guaranteed income of the sort that Social Security and defined-benefit pensions provide—which brings us to the second big risk of defined-contribution plans: outliving one's assets. To protect against this risk requires purchasing an annuity, yet annuity markets are notoriously prone to failure. The main reason they're prone to failure is that those most likely to live a long time after retirement are also most likely to purchase annuities, so insurers generally charge very high rates for a guaranteed income (as much as 10 percent higher than what an "actuarially fair" cost would be).[45] Hard as it may be to believe, a 401(k) account with a balance of $65,000 will purchase an annual guaranteed benefit of only around $4,250 at age sixty-five.[46] Little surprise, then, that most people don't use their 401(k) accounts to buy an annuity—an understandable decision that nonetheless places them at serious risk of outliving their assets.

Again, the true effects of the 401(k) revolution have yet to be seen. We will know them with certainty only when today's younger workers start retiring. But the signs are already troubling. Building on decades of data and scholarship, researchers at Boston College have produced the "Retirement Risk Index," a comprehensive measure of retirement security that takes into account all sources of retirement wealth and estimates whether they are sufficient to finance a secure retirement. According to the index, the share of working-age households at risk of being financially unprepared at age sixty-five has jumped from 31 percent in 1983 to more than 53 percent in 2010. Younger Americans, who have borne the brunt of the transformation of retirement protections, are far more likely to be at risk than older Americans. Roughly *60 percent* of those born from the mid-1970s through the early 1980s are at risk of being financially unprepared.[47] In other words, 6 in 10 younger workers are slated to retire without the share of preretirement income they will need to support themselves in old age (generally, about 70 percent).

The situation is not as stark for today's retirees and those about to join their ranks. But all but the richest are facing much greater risks as well. According to a 2015 study by the Government Accountability Office, roughly half of households with heads fifty-five years of age or older had no retirement savings in a tax-favored account in 2013.[48] At the same time, debt is a rapidly growing among families with heads older than fifty-five. Between 1992 and 2010, the median debt level among older families with debt rose from $18,546 to $61,219 (in 2016 dollars) before falling back to $47,800 in 2016. The share of older families with debt also rose substantially—from 53.8 percent in 1992 to 68 percent in 2016. The sharpest increase actually occurred among the oldest elderly, those aged seventy-five or more: in 1992, less than a third were indebted; by 2016, almost half were.[49]

Older Americans are also much more likely to work than in the past, and they are working more. In 2016, almost 19 percent of Americans aged sixty-five and older were in the paid labor force, up from around 12 percent in in the early 1990s—making the elderly the fastest-growing age group in the workforce. Around two-thirds, moreover, are working full-time—a dramatic increase from two decades ago, when part-time work was more common than full-time employment.[50]

These trends suggest that while much attention has been paid to the accumulation of assets *for* retirement, far less has been devoted to the issue of how Americans manage their assets *in* retirement. Defined-benefit plans and Social Security ensure that workers receive a relatively stable income as long as they live. There are no such guarantees when it comes to IRAs and 401(k) plans, and every reason to think that many retirees will exhaust their accounts well before they die.[51]

That was Joanne Molnar's experience. Her 401(k) account at the day care she helped managed had contained around $40,000 when the stock market was booming. But by 2008, it was down to $2,000—decimated, she says, by poor investment guidance by the company's owner. Her husband, Mark, co-owned a small business, restoring pianos, and they had their own home in Connecticut. Neither the business or the home, however, weathered the Great Recession—they liquidated Mark's share of the business, sold the home, bought an RV, and drove to Maine to look for jobs near their son and his kids. Now, they live in their RV and work at a campground in Maine sometimes frequented by wealthier retirees: cleaning showers and toilets, mowing grass, emptying garbage cans. They may go to Texas or Wisconsin, where their two other sons live. Mark gets Social Security, but he still thinks he will be working for a decade or more. "Forget the government," he says, perhaps forgetting that the government sends him his only guaranteed monthly check. "We're on our own. You have to fend for yourself."[52]

SOCIAL INSECURITY

The transformation of private pensions from shared benefits into individualized accounts makes a guaranteed foundation of retirement savings all the more important. And as defined-benefit pensions vanish, Social Security is, for most Americans, the only guaranteed pension left. Yet the role of Social Security has actually declined in the last twenty years. The wealth represented by expected Social Security benefits fell in the 1980s and 1990s.[53] Looking forward, Social Security is expected to replace a smaller share of pre-retirement income than it did in the past.[54] And, of course, all these estimates assume that Social Security will pay promised benefits—an assumption that is safer than Social Security's doomsayers believe, but which still hinges on favorable economic and demographic trends and some adjustments in the program.

You would think that the greater risk of private retirement pensions would cause political leaders to embrace Social Security even more warmly. Of course, if you thought that, you would be wrong. At the same time that private pensions have grown more risky due to the rise of defined-contribution plans, critics of Social Security have argued that the program should be reformed to look more like, well, defined-contribution plans.

This is the essence of proposals for "privatizing" Social Security, which have moved from the radical fringe of American debate to the front row of personal responsibility crusaders' priorities. Back in the early 1980s, when Ronald Reagan was swept into power on a wave of dissatisfaction with the economy and its governance, the idea of privatizing Social Security was briefly raised but quickly beaten back. (One trial balloon was greeted with an unanimous no vote in the Senate.) After the rebuff, Stuart Butler declared ruefully to an audience of would-be privatizers, "if we are to achieve basic changes in the system, we must first prepare the political ground so that the fiasco of the last eighteen months is not repeated."[55] Preparing the ground, it turned out, meant not only expanding private retirement and savings accounts, but also mounting a major public campaign to decrease trust in the traditional Social Security program—by engaging in what Butler called "guerilla warfare against both the current Social Security system and the coalition that supports it."[56]

Guerilla warfare was a team sport. In what would become a standard cycle, trumped-up complaints against Social Security moved from conservative intellectual circles to policy experts in antigovernment think tanks into the mouths of Republican politicians—becoming, as in a childhood game of "telephone," more grandiose and inaccurate at each step of the journey. Thus the respected Harvard economist Martin Feldstein wrote a series of highly influential—and, it soon became clear, highly flawed—analyses arguing that Social Security was not only inherently unsound but a massive drag on the economy.[57] His complaints were picked up by anti–Social Security policy experts who dumbed them down for a broader audience and trumped them up for the press-release world of Washington. Within a matter of years, these talking points became the standard mantra of Republican leaders: Social Security was going broke; it was drastically reducing national savings; it was bad for widows and blacks; it was a form of fiscal child abuse that allowed greedy seniors to rob from the younger generation.[58]

The claims were often as preposterous as they were powerful. (How, for example, could Social Security so grievously disadvantage women when they received so much more back from the program relative to what they had paid in than did men? How could the program be running on empty when Republicans were calling for using the surplus in the program's trust fund to pay for new tax cuts?) But the plausibility of the Chicken Little chorus was less important than its overall impact. What Social Security had going for it, besides the fact that people liked its basic goal, was that millions of Americans had paid into it and expected to get back what they had been promised when they retired. Convincing Americans that the chance of getting full Social Security benefits was lower than the chance of aliens landing on Earth—as one humorous but completely bungled anti–Social Security survey suggested most younger workers felt—made the task of blowing up the present system that much easier.[59]

Still, the reality that workers expected to get back what they had paid in was the softest of soft underbellies of all plans for privatizing Social Security. The problem is this: since the late 1930s, Social Security has paid benefits with the revenue raised by current workers' contributions. Money from one generation of workers finances the retirement of their parents and grandparents. If, however, Social Security is to become a system of private IRA-style accounts, into which current workers put some or all of the money that they would have paid in taxes, the trillions needed to pay promised benefits have to come from somewhere else—or, more precisely, from new taxes, new benefit cuts, new borrowing, or some mix of the three. This fundamental dilemma is all the more acute because advocates of privatization know that the one thing they cannot do is threaten the benefits of the presently retired and those nearing retirement. Without a commitment to honor past contributions into the traditional system, Butler warned in 1983, "we can never overcome the political opposition to reform." Yet this commitment, he quickly added, "necessarily [places] constraints on the mechanisms that can be used to move the country towards a private system."[60]

What was completely swept under the rug in the campaign to sell the public and politically skittish leaders on privatization was how serious those "constraints" were. The costs of switching over to a private system came to be known as "transition costs," as if these were small and temporary hurdles to a win-win outcome. Yet these "transition costs" could run into the trillions and stretch out for decades into the future.[61]

And they were indeed real costs. Advocates of privatization could have simply said that benefits for retirees were too high and had to be cut, with the savings going into private accounts. But they knew all along that this was a losing strategy. Instead, they said private accounts would simply give all Americans the choice of obtaining higher returns in the stock market, without imposing serious burdens on anyone—a claim that was doubly false. The truth was that once the euphemistically labeled transition costs were taken into account and reasonable adjustments were made for the administrative costs of millions of new investment plans, Social Security provided a competitive rate of return. More important, the only way to pay the "transition costs" was to take something away from someone—either retirees in the form of lower benefits, all Americans in the form of higher taxes or reduced spending on other valued ends, or future generations in the form of new government debt. The free-lunch mantra simply denied basic rules of accounting.

More crucial still, the entire case for privatization bypassed the most fundamental issue of all: economic risk. Social Security, after all, is an insurance program, not a private investment account. It offers a guaranteed benefit in retirement that is more generous to families with low lifetime incomes, whose heads are disabled or pass away, and who have the good fortune to live a long time after retirement (elderly widows are the chief example). The program protects families not just against these risks but also against the risk of large drops in their assets due to stock-market or housing-price instability as well as the risk of unexpected inflation, which can devastate families on fixed incomes.

Virtually all of these protections would be undercut or eliminated by privatization. Workers would see their guaranteed benefits largely replaced by the returns on their accounts, which could vary greatly from person to person. Those disabled before retirement, those who end up living a long time after retirement, those with low incomes, those who retire when the stock market drops—all might end up with less than they would have enjoyed had they received the guaranteed benefit. In short, a social insurance program would be replaced by a system that shifted much more risk onto the shoulders of individual workers and their families.

Critics of Social Security sometimes scoff at this observation, noting that Social Security, too, is risky because it will need additional funds to pay promised benefits and because politicians can change the program at any time. The first point—about the program's potential funding problems—is valid but misguided as a basis for privatizing Social Security, because privatization will do nothing to help the program pay full benefits, and indeed will make it harder for it to do so.

The second point—about the risk of political intervention—is almost certainly wrong, as well as more than a little disingenuous. Social Security could be changed at any moment, but the popular view of the program as the "third rail" of American politics suggests that politicians don't wake up every morning eager to change it. Indeed, the only politicians trying to upend the program today are precisely the ones invoking the specter of politicians trying to upend the program. (It is like a mugger telling you to give up your wallet because someone might take it.) In any case, a system of private accounts would be open to similar sorts of political chicanery, because, as already noted, these accounts would be created by, funded by, and regulated by the federal government.

Social Security—because it pools risk across millions of citizens and uses the power of government to guarantee against the major threats to family income during (and, in some cases, before) retirement—simply does not have the kind of inherent uncertainty built into it that private accounts would. According to one reputable calculation done during the 2005 debate, based on historical and global stock returns, half of Americans who set up private accounts would fail to do better than they would under Social Security even if they used the conservative investment strategy (50 percent bonds/50 percent stocks) suggested by President Bush's Commission to Strengthen Social Security. Meanwhile, the least fortunate 10 percent of account-holders would each lose at least $49,980 in net retirement wealth. Losses like this are simply inconceivable under the present system.[62]

Given all this, it is remarkable how successful the Personal Responsibility Crusade has been in taking on the most popular and triumphant of America's bulwarks against insecurity. The reason for this success is clearly not the inherent appeal or plausibility of the case. Even after two decades of softening up the public, critics of Social Security fell flat in their most concerted attempt yet to convince Americans in 2005 that the program should be partially privatized. Intellectually, the case for reform is riddled with errors and non sequiturs that are so obvious and embarrassing that few nonbelievers would take the case seriously if it were not so influential among current political leaders. To be sure, Social Security has been weakened by its long-term funding gap, but, as we've seen, this would only be worsened by privatization plans.

The success of the Personal Responsibility Crusade in assaulting Social Security must instead be chalked up to the savvy, coordinated strategy of the crusaders themselves, who have boxed in the program by building up an alternative intellectual movement and programmatic infrastructure that covertly strikes at the heart of Social Security's insurance functions. In 1980 conservative policy advocate Peter Ferrara forthrightly said, in an anti–Social Security manifesto funded by the Cato Institute, that Social Security's insurance function should be handed over to the private sector and the rest of the program shunted off to the welfare system.[63] By 2005 when George W. Bush became the first president to take on Social Security, a frontal attack on America's most popular social program had come to be portrayed as the system's logical and costless continuation.

RECLAIMING RETIREMENT SECURITY

The argument of advocates of privatization is exactly the opposite of the notion that Social Security needs to remain a vital foundation of retirement security. It is that Social Security should jump on the 401(k) bandwagon and expose workers to even more of the risk that Social Security was originally designed to protect them from.

The plight of ordinary Americans such as Charles Weiss, Tom Padgett, Susan Lemoine, Jim Horner, and Joanne and Mark Molnar reminds us just how foolish such a move would be. Over the last forty years, the nation has shifted more and more of the risk and responsibility for retirement planning from employers and government onto workers and their families. Some Americans have done extremely well under this uncertain new system.

Many others, however, have barely budged upward, and the majority have basically stood still or fallen. All of us, however, are facing far greater risk in planning for our postwork years.

The promise of private pensions at their heyday was a secure retirement income that, when coupled with Social Security, would allow older Americans to spend their retired years in relative comfort. That promise, it is clear, will no longer be kept. But reforms to our private pension system could make private retirement accounts work far better as a source of secure retirement income. And the promise of Social Security *can* be kept—if we recognize and safeguard its vital role in providing economic security for American families.

Risky Health Care

Arnold Dorsett was an American success story. An air conditioner repairman, he earned more than his father ever did—almost $70,000 a year, thanks to a relentless schedule of eighty- to ninety-hour workweeks. He owned a good home in the suburbs. His young wife, Sharon—training to be a nurse when they met, and hoping to return to school soon—stayed home to care for their three kids. Arnold was driven, a striver. He was also, it turned out, the father of a young boy who was sick and getting sicker.

Zachary had not been healthy since his birth—one reason Sharon had never gotten that nursing degree and Arnold was working so hard to pay the bills. But it was not until Zachary was eight that he was diagnosed with an immune system disorder that promised even bigger medical costs down the road. By then, the bills had already crushed the family's finances. Despite having health insurance and refinancing their home, the Dorsetts had run up nearly $30,000 in outstanding credit-card balances and could no longer make their car or mortgage payments. In March 2005 they succumbed to the inevitable and filed for bankruptcy, becoming one of the 1 to 2 million Americans that year whose bankruptcies were medically related.[1] It was not an easy choice. Losing their house they could accept. Losing their pride was a different matter. "I make good money, and I work hard for it," Arnold Dorsett told the *New York Times*. "When I filed for bankruptcy, I felt I failed."[2]

Arnold Dorsett felt he had failed. He felt that he alone was somehow responsible for his plight. And, at the time, many of his fellow Americans seemed to share his view, confident that those who managed their finances well and searched out an employer offering good insurance would remain secure, however costly their care became. "My friends don't understand it," Sharon admits, describing her bankruptcy. "They think, how could it get so bad so quick? Unless you have a sick kid, you don't know what it's like."[3]

Even as Sharon was speaking, however, more and more Americans were finding out what it was like—from the parents of sick children to elderly Americans trying to afford prescription drugs to workers struggling to pay their health premiums (or finding their employers didn't offer health benefits at all). In 1993, a ferocious debate had been sparked by President Bill Clinton's ill-fated plan to create universal health insurance. The fourteen years that separated the plan's demise in 1994 and the financial crisis in 2008 proved to be a watershed, but not in the way Clinton had intended. The proportion of employers offering coverage to their workers fell by nearly 10 points.[4] The proportion of employers that financed the full cost of coverage—once the norm—plummeted.[5] Meanwhile, premiums shot up while most workers' wages barely increased at all. In just the four years between 2001 and 2005, the share of moderate-income Americans who lacked health coverage rose from just over one-quarter to more than 40 percent.[6] A system that was barely treading water was sinking fast.

Then, the national financial crisis hit—and the *personal* financial crisis engulfing families such as the Dorsetts moved from the back pages to the front pages. With the election of President Obama in November 2008, anxious conversations in corporate boardrooms and around kitchen tables exploded into a national debate about America's crumbling framework of health financing. The players in the discussion ranged from the giant old-economy manufacturer GM, which estimated it spends around $1,400 per finished vehicle on health costs, to the sprawling new-economy behemoth Walmart, which had come under increasing fire for its stingy health benefits even as its medical costs grew.[7] The players included state governments alarmed about the rising cost of Medicaid, and national officials sharply at odds about how to update Medicare and expand coverage for the uninsured. And they included families such as the Dorsetts, who never thought they'd be in the dark shadows of America's shiny high-tech system.

Roy and Patsy McKanna were among those families. They filed for bankruptcy around the same time as the Dorsetts did, after their adult daughter ran through her family's savings battling breast cancer. As Patsy McKanna recalled, "We were just trying to keep them from sinking until things got better. They took bankruptcy a little more than a year before we did. We managed our budget for 52 years. You never know what life's going to throw at you."[8]

Stories such as these—and there are literally millions more—infused the debate over the Affordable Care Act (ACA) in 2009 and helped ensure its narrow passage in Congress in 2010. Critics called the bill "Obamacare." Yet the basic outline had been laid down in Massachusetts in 2006 with a bipartisan reform plan that expanded Medicaid for low-income residents and provided regulated private plans to uninsured residents with higher incomes. Massachusetts had already banned such reviled insurance practices as charging exorbitantly high rates to the sick and explicitly excluding coverage for so-called preexisting conditions (the conditions patients already have and often most need insured). But Massachusetts strengthened these popular rules, and, more important, it helped pay for the premiums of this regulated private coverage, so that even those with high costs or low incomes could buy in. It also required that every resident show proof of coverage and penalized larger employers that didn't provide insurance (though the penalty was modest). A health policy star was born—one that disrupted the existing system to the minimum extent necessary to get almost everyone covered.

The ACA carried over nearly all these elements: new insurance rules, expanded Medicaid coverage, and tax credits to help people buy private plans through Massachusetts-style regulated markets. Initially, the legislation also included a proposal to allow the uninsured to buy into a program modeled after Medicare, the so-called public option. But the public option was dropped in the final desperate scramble to pass the bill, opposed by a few pivotal Senate Democrats who felt it was too governmental and by medical industry interests that feared it would be too effective at controlling prices. (Full disclosure: I helped develop the idea of the public option and, in fact, described it in the first edition of this book.)

The result was a plan that aimed to maintain what remained of America's crumbling employment-based system while filling in the growing gaps— without antagonizing the medical industry by proposing serious limits on America's astronomical pricing for drugs, medical technology, and health care services.

And it worked—sort of. The share of Americans younger than 65 without health insurance plummeted by almost half. Medical costs screeched to the lowest rate of growth in decades, though experts still debate how big a factor the law was in the slowdown. Yet the ACA has remained controversial since its inception. Many states have failed to expand their Medicaid programs as the ACA sought to require. The regulated marketplaces have had a rocky experience, with most offering far fewer plans to far fewer participants than expected. And health premiums and costs are again rising sharply.

Today, we are far closer to universal insurance than we were a few decades ago. Yet medical costs and insurance still lie at the epicenter of insecurity, and a growing number of Americans say more must be done. Unfortunately, the passage of the ACA has not chastened the Personal Responsibility Crusade. It has energized it, intensifying its call for risk-shifting reforms. At stake is not just the ACA, but the fate of America's embattled structure of health insurance itself.

SICK MARKETS

The best of American medical care is better than ever. Astounding advances in research and clinical practice have meant that diseases that once killed or hobbled almost everyone they struck can now be effectively treated and sometimes cured. Basic medical care is more refined and capable, if not always more available. Americans live longer than they used to (though life expectancy has been stagnant or falling for middle-aged white Americans without a college degree, and the United States ranks behind the rest of the rich democratic world on most basic health indicators). Americans are also less likely to spend their later years with debilitating conditions. And they have a much larger range of treatment options, at least when they have the money to pay for them.

The problem is, American medical care is also more expensive than ever, and this rising cost is creating pervasive insecurity. For all the wonders of advanced medicine, America's $3.5-trillion-a-year medical complex is enormously wasteful, ill-targeted, and inefficient. The United States spends more as a share of its economy on health care than any other nation.[9] Indeed, its public programs, which cover less than half the population, cost more per American than citizens in most other rich nations pay per person for their *universal* programs.[10] On top of this, nearly $250 billion a year is spent indirectly in the form of federal tax breaks for employer-provided health benefits.[11] And yet all this spending has not bought Americans the one thing that health insurance is supposed to provide: security.

Lack of health security is not confined to one part of the population. It is experienced by all Americans: those who are insured as well as those without coverage, those near the top of the economic ladder as well as those near the bottom, those who are healthy as well as those who are sick. What creates insecurity is the *possibility* of large shocks not covered by insurance. Those who lack insurance face insecurity, but so too do those who risk losing coverage when they change or lose jobs. Those who are impoverished face insecurity, but so too do those with higher incomes who experience catastrophic costs. Those who are sick face insecurity, but so too do healthy families who are just one sickness or injury away from financial calamity. As health costs have skyrocketed, health insecurity has become a problem faced by all Americans—fortunate and unfortunate alike.

At the root of the problem is the peculiar, and peculiarly flawed, character of health insurance markets. In many areas of economic life, we expect the free play of the competitive market to allocate resources in more or less efficient and productive ways—at least given basic limits and protections. Markets don't necessarily give us the outcomes that we consider just or fair. But when they function well, they give us outcomes that we can expect to be broadly efficient, ensuring that those with the desire and the means to purchase something get the best product at the lowest possible cost. Or so the argument goes when it comes to well-functioning markets. But the market for health insurance is anything but.

To start with the most fundamental issue, medical care is not like other goods. Most of us think it's fine that some people can't buy fancy clothing or fast cars, or have to eat at home instead of going out to splendid restaurants. But most of us draw the line at basic care. Someone who is gravely ill or injured needs treatment—period. This "rule of rescue" builds on a broader conviction: that everyone in an affluent society needs to have at least some protection against conditions and events that hinder their ability to partic-ipate as citizens and workers.[12]

And since medical care isn't an optional luxury, it's also an expense that almost everyone wants to have insurance against. Health insurance was once called "sickness insurance" for a simple reason: the main cost of health events used to be the time spent out of the workforce due to sickness. Today, however, the costs of medical treatment vastly dwarf the forgone earnings due to sickness, mostly because medicine can do so much more than it once did. In 2015, according to the Medical Expenditure Panel Survey, medical expenses for the year totaled $33,269 for the costliest 10 percent of patients; $50,572 for the costliest 5 percent; and $112,395 for the costliest 1 percent.[13] There is simply no way that families can finance expenses of this scale on their own. Insurance, like basic care, is not optional.

Yet, precisely because insurance is necessary and widespread, patients are not sensitive to the costs of medical care in the way that they are to the costs of other goods. Economists love the facetious example of restaurant insurance. If the cost of eating out was paid for by insurance, they note, we'd eat out a lot more often, pack a lot more in, and order the most ex-pensive items on the menu. The analogy is far from perfect, but the point is valid: health insurance greatly reduces the incentive to economize; it is *supposed* to. And this, in turn, drives up costs, making insurance all the more vital. When insurance is widespread, we can't expect the price of services to be the main constraint on spending. Cost control requires restraint through other means, whether private insurance policing, professional self-regulation, or public spending constraints.

All this would be less of a problem if the insurance market in medical care worked smoothly, but it does not. When insurance is for discrete, discernable risks that are easily assessed and not easily faked, private insurance performs splendidly. Unfortunately, the health insurance market isn't at all like this. Perhaps the biggest difference is that the likelihood of needing insurance and the magnitude of future costs are very difficult for insurers to estimate. As a result, insurers frequently know less—much less—about applicants' need for insurance than applicants themselves, and this gives rise to the great bugbear of private insurance markets: "adverse selection."[14]

Adverse selection is a fancy phrase for a simple fact—people who most need insurance are most likely to buy it. The problems begin when insurers try to protect themselves against adverse selection. One obvious response is to try to weed out or charge exorbitant rates to the highest-risk groups. Yet the ability of insurers to do this is limited by knowledge, by technology, and sometimes by law. And, of course, these practices undercut the ability of those who truly need insurance to obtain it. The other response is to raise premiums, but this simply reduces the number of people who have coverage. It cannot eliminate adverse selection, because at any premium, those most likely to need coverage are most likely to see it as in their interest to pay the premium.

The upshot is that insurance markets plagued by adverse selection tend to become highly fragmented and incomplete, or fail to function at all. Many people who want and need insurance can't buy it at a premium they're willing to pay, and exclusions and gaps in coverage are endemic. In the worst-case scenario, known to insurance aficionados as a "death spiral," insurers continually jack up rates to deal with adverse selection, driving healthier subscribers from the plan, which in turn sets off another round of rate hikes and another exodus of lower-risk patients, eventually sealing the insurance plan's doom.

Thankfully, American health insurance isn't in a death spiral of this sort. But it is experiencing a steady erosion—a death march—as Americans find it increasingly difficult to afford the ever-rising tab for health insurance and medical services. The ACA dramatically reversed the slide, but the erosion is beginning yet again.

Most of the current attention is directed at Medicaid—which critics want to scale back to pre-ACA levels—and at the troubled individual marketplaces created by the ACA, which, despite all the controversy, cover fewer than 12 million Americans.[15] The long-term story, however, is the crumbling of America's employment-based system of health financing. Employer-sponsored insurance arose in the mid-twentieth century as a distinctive response to the challenge of health insecurity in the United States. As medical costs have exploded and employers have retrenched, this old, odd bargain has come undone—and the Great Risk Shift has relentlessly played out.

THE NOT-SO-ACCIDENTAL SYSTEM

Americans don't think twice about the fact that, unless they're economically disadvantaged or older than sixty-five, they are expected to obtain health insurance through their employers. And yet, America's employment-based system is scarcely a natural market outcome. More important, this system is far from the norm. Indeed, the United States is the *only* rich capitalist nation that relies on employers to voluntarily provide health insurance to working-age citizens and their children.

The modern roots of America's distinctive system go back to the New Deal. Health insurance was a political issue at the state level before the 1930s, but efforts to create insurance programs on a state-by-state basis all foundered. The Great Depression, however, brought the issue to the national level, and in a new form. For the first time, the cost of medical care, not lost wages, was the concern, and President Roosevelt's top advisers believed strongly that some kind of government-backed insurance system was needed. As the Social Security Act was being finalized, one internal report to Roosevelt declared, "[T]he problem of medical care should not be regarded as being a third or fourth item in a general program for economic security.... [T]his part of the program is equally important ... and equally feasible."[16]

It may have been equally important, but it was not equally feasible. Doctors, insurers, and employers all were hostile to the idea, while organized labor expressed only tepid support. Many around Roosevelt believed the rest of the Social Security Act could be taken down by the fight and convinced him to put off pressing for action. Within a few years, however, Roosevelt was bogged down in Congress and leading a nation that was heading into the most fearsome war the world had ever seen. Government health insurance, as one account put it, was an "orphan" of the New Deal.[17]

But the orphan had siblings—in the private sector. Pressed to come up with an alternative to a public program, the American Medical Association softened its once-virulent opposition to voluntary insurance plans that would pay for doctor's care. Meanwhile, Baylor University Hospital in Texas became the big bang of modern health insurance when it pioneered the first Blue Cross plan for hospital care. Blue Cross was not really a normal commercial plan. It was instead a powerful example of private social activism, driven by true concern over the ability of workers of modest means to afford increasingly costly hospital care. For decades, in fact, Blue Cross plans did not even charge different rates to subscribers based on their likely medical costs. It pooled all risks on equal terms, just as Social Security did.

Employers were the crucial brokers in this emerging private system, for it was employers that soon became the virtually exclusive means by which workers obtained health benefits. The reasons for this were many. Employers provided a stable base for marketing and administering plans, and most firms had both healthy and unhealthy workers, allowing risks to be pooled within the workplace. By the 1950s, moreover, champions of the private sector in government had managed to ensure that health benefits received the same sort of favorable tax treatment that retirement pensions did. For employers, then, health insurance was an increasingly good deal: it bought them loyalty, healthier workers, and federal tax breaks.

It also bought them an insurance policy of their own—against national health insurance, which foundered in the fierce political debates of the

1940s in large part because private workplace insurance was so rapidly expanding. Between 1940 and 1950, enrollment in private health insurance rose from 12 million to 76.6 million, reaching for the first time a majority of Americans. To this day, we live with the legacy—a system in which most working Americans receive coverage from their employer, or not at all.

Yet we also live with another legacy, Medicare and Medicaid, which cover the three groups least capable of obtaining insurance in the private market—the aged, the disabled, and the poor. No other country in the world began its government insurance program with such vulnerable groups. The norm was to cover manual workers first, then move up the income ladder to reach all or most citizens. But focusing on the aged proved to be just the trick for frustrated American health reformers, allowing them to present their goals not as a radical break with the past but as a simple continuation of the expansion of private insurance.[18] In 1965, at the height of Lyndon Johnson's Great Society, the strategy paid off with the passage of Medicare and Medicaid. It was the first and last big expansion of federal health insurance in American history.

INSURANCE-SCLEROSIS

The years just after Medicare and Medicaid passed were the high-water mark of American health coverage. Already, however, signs of strain were showing, and the cracks only grew in the years to come.

First came the abandonment of broad risk pooling by private health plans. Charging similar rates to all subscribers had been a hallmark of the founding philosophy of Blue Cross. It was also a central reason Blue Cross plans received special state exemptions from normal insurance rules. Yet after World War II, commercial insurers moved into the workplace to poach Blue Cross customers, offering lower-risk groups reduced premiums. Under fierce competitive pressure, the Blues started doing the same—varying premiums based on the expected cost of enrollees, and thus ceasing to spread risk as widely as they once had.[19]

Another change was equally harmful to broad risk pooling. When Congress passed the Employee Retirement Income Security Act in

1974—the bill reshaping American pensions—it included a small provision that turned out to be a huge loophole. The provision essentially said that companies that paid directly for their workers' health costs (a practice known as "self-insurance"), could escape all state regulation of health insurance. What made the provision a loophole is that, unlike in pensions, ERISA didn't impose any new requirements on the health plans it freed from state control. Not surprisingly, larger corporations rushed to fill this regulatory vacuum by setting up their own self-insured health plans. Employers that self-insured continued to rely on private insurers to contract with medical providers and handle the payment of claims, but they no longer relied on those insurers to bear risk—the risk was now on them. By the early 1990s more than two-thirds of American companies—and essentially all the largest—self-insured.[20]

Smaller companies were less fortunate. For them, self-insurance posed big perils. Because they had so few workers, they couldn't spread risks easily within the firm, and they weren't as capable of managing the establishment and operation of self-insured plans. To make matters worse, when big firms self-insured, many of the most stable and lowest-risk working groups exited the insurance system, raising premiums for those firms too small or too cautious to self-insure—and helping to drive up the number of uninsured, which hit 38 million in 1992.[21]

The situation of Kerry Kennedy, the owner of a small furniture store in Titusville, Florida, showcases the growing dilemmas. Titusville, best known for the Space Center, is a historically conservative city, founded by a Confederate general. Yet Kennedy was supportive of government action to help the uninsured, and he was committed to providing insurance to his workers. In 1992, however, Kennedy was informed by his insurer that his premiums would ratchet up to a level he couldn't afford, because two of his workers were "high risk" owing to their advanced age. Those two workers were his mother and father, who founded the store and still worked in it.

If the story sounds familiar, it should. President Bill Clinton told it in a speech to a joint session of Congress in September 1993, on the eve of the introduction of his ill-fated Health Security Act. The plan—based on an intricate model known as "managed competition"—may not have been doomed from the start. But by the time legislation was submitted to Congress in late 1993, it was a hobbled creature dropped into the den of wolves that America's exorbitant medical system had created.

Advocates of the Clinton plan argued, rightly, that the American system of health insurance was at war with itself. Lack of broad coverage drove up costs, which reduced coverage, which in turn accelerated costs even more. But where the argument went terribly wrong was in assuming that the only outcome of this internal war was a victory for more extensive risk pooling. What the Health Security warriors missed, what would soon rise from the ashes of their defeat, was an alternative vision pointing to a very different endgame: the Personal Responsibility Crusade and its call for a system of individualized health insurance free of the entanglements of either government programs or workplace benefits.

HRC VERSUS PRC

The battle over the Clinton health plan marked the end of an era. It was not, of course, the end of the era of rising costs or declining coverage, as those who proclaimed that the system was healing itself so loudly insisted. It was the end of the era of conservative me-too-ism on health care.

In the 1970s, conservatives shifted from arguing against any government action in health care to claiming that it should be designed to support and bolster broad-reaching private insurance.[22] At the decade's opening, President Nixon called for mandating that all employers provide health benefits. By its closing, Stanford economist Alain Enthoven—a free-marketeer who advocated universal insurance—had come up with the notion of managed competition that eventually became the basis for Clinton's proposal. Even in the early 1990s, roughly half of Senate Republicans called for using tax breaks and regulations to extend existing private insurance to nearly all Americans.

What linked these proposals was a belief that broad risk pooling in health insurance was essential but needed to be achieved through private means. In essence, these proposals called for extending and improving America's existing system of private risk pooling, without too much government interference or intervention.

When President Clinton put Hillary Rodham Clinton in charge of formulating his reform plan, then, it wasn't completely far-fetched to expect that his effort would eventually attract moderate conservative allies. But what he hadn't counted on was the Personal Responsibility Crusade, emboldened by the opportunity to stake out a starkly different vision of the future of American health insurance. A debate that began as a dispute among differing proposals for expanded risk pooling quickly became an ideological battle over the idea of risk pooling itself. Round 1 of the battle— HRC versus PRC, if you will—saw the Personal Responsibility Crusade emerge not just victorious but with a powerful new alternative to private risk pooling: Health Savings Accounts.

At the center of the battle was a once-obscure congressman named Newt Gingrich. Entering the fight, Gingrich had only recently taken over the position of minority leader in the House. Yet, already, he was the undisputed leader of the increasingly powerful, vocal, and recalcitrant conservative wing of the GOP. But Gingrich didn't simply want Republicans in Congress to say no to the Clinton plan. As it became clear that the plan could be taken down—perhaps with the Democratic Party in tow—Gingrich began to outline an ambitious, antigovernment agenda, which moved to center stage when Republicans unexpectedly captured both houses of Congress in 1994.[23] And on this agenda was a bold new initiative that Gingrich was calling Medical Savings Accounts.

Newt Gingrich was not the father of Medical Savings Accounts. The basic idea had been around at least since the early 1970s, when economists first began to take a long hard look at America's insurance system. Economists were not of one mind about either problems or solutions, but most agreed that the widespread presence of health insurance in the medical sector was a, if not *the*, major cause of high and rising costs.[24] Some economists took this conclusion to indicate that health insurers need to exercise more vigilant oversight of patients and medical providers. Yet an influential wing argued quite the opposite: citing the problem of moral hazard, they argued that health insurance should be cut back to bare-bones catastrophic coverage, requiring that patients pay for care directly so as to encourage greater economy in treatment choices.

This position found its champion in the private sector in the person of J. Patrick Rooney, chairman of Golden Rule Insurance. Rooney was a huge donor to Gingrich and his causes.[25] Rooney was also a tireless advocate for Medical Savings Accounts and helped convince Gingrich and many conservatives in the House to press for them.[26] Meanwhile, conservative think tanks spewed out supportive ideas, ranging from souped-up accounts that would cover a whole range of consumer expenses to integrated plans for transforming American health insurance into a wholly individualized framework of tax breaks and individual accounts.[27] The ideas included a proposal eerily similar to plans for Social Security privatization, allowing workers to decide whether they wanted to contribute their payroll taxes to Medicare or put them in a medical IRA for their retirement (and, of course, go without Medicare).

Legislation was slower to come. Republicans held hostage a plan to improve the portability of health coverage in the mid-1990s until President Clinton gave in to their demands to create limited new tax breaks for Medical Savings Accounts. In 1997 a massive overhaul of Medicare created a pilot Medical Savings Account program for the elderly—which, like the rest of the legislation, proved an abject mess. Undaunted, enthusiasts recast Medical Savings Accounts as "Health Savings Accounts," and flexed their muscles again during the debate over a prescription drug benefit for Medicare beneficiaries. Indeed, the only way in which President Bush and Republican leaders were able to get conservatives to sign on to a prescription drug bill in 2003 was by throwing billions of dollars at such accounts—billions that, of course, could not be spent on the legislation's putative goal of providing prescription drug coverage to Medicare beneficiaries.

While Health Savings Accounts became a near-theological aspiration of the Right, most policy experts remained skeptical. They noted the obvious: Health Savings Accounts would be attractive mainly to healthy and well-off Americans who didn't fear exposing themselves to the risk of uncompensated costs. If adopted broadly, such accounts would undermine risk pooling in the private sector, because they would allow these workers to escape from group health plans, leaving their costlier colleagues behind. The exodus, if unchecked, could leave old-style group plans beset by a death spiral of adverse selection—as wave after wave of people jumped ship: first the healthiest, then the healthiest of those left behind, and so on.[28] Ultimately, Health Savings Accounts could tear apart the already tattered fabric of risk pooling in the private sector.

There was another big problem with Health Savings Accounts: nobody except their promoters really liked them. The 1996 demonstration project had authorized 750,000 Medical Savings Accounts—a cap that conservatives had complained would kill the goose that lay the golden egg of health insurance freedom. By 2004, however, fewer than a tenth that number of accounts had been established.[29]

The distinct lack of public enthusiasm for Health Savings Accounts was driven home to me when I interviewed a young woman who actually marketed HSAs for a large insurance company—let's call her Jane Doe. Jane admitted to me that while she loved the company for which she worked, she now led something of a double life. Her company had automatically enrolled all its workers in an HSA, and Jane—despite being young, healthy, and savvy—found the plan frustrating and inadequate. In other words, Jane spent her days selling a product to employers and individuals that she found awful and was convinced would hurt the traditional insurance that her company used to focus on.

Jane's story isn't all that unusual: despite the fact that the workers who choose HSAs are generally healthier and more financially savvy than the norm, customer satisfaction with such plans has remained low.[30] Nonetheless, the number of HSA enrollees has continued to rise, as more employers and workers have responded to the substantial federal encouragement. By 2016, roughly 26 million people were enrolled in HSAs. Perhaps more important, employers seem to be warming to HSAs. Between 2005 and 2016, the share of employers offering health benefits who provided an HSA skyrocketed from just 2 percent to over a quarter. After Republican Donald Trump unexpectedly won the 2016 presidential election, investors drove up the stock prices of companies managing HSAs, betting that unified GOP governance would create a boom market.[31]

The continued move toward HSAs would mean a major change in America's insurance system. It would also signal the culmination of a major shift in the strategies and arguments of conservatives. The Right once embraced private insurance precisely because it pooled risk without government intrusion. But as private insurance has grown less capable of spreading risk across America's working population—both because of the sharp decline in its reach and because of the dramatic change in employer and insurance practices—conservatives have not tried to save what they once championed. Instead, they have called for government intrusion to further fragment private risk pooling and undermine old-style workplace insurance. Just as defined-contribution pensions have upended the expectations of workers planning for retirement , HSAs are poised to make the increasingly risky world of private health insurance even more fragmented and frightening.

And not merely the world of private insurance, for the Personal Responsibility Crusade is also bringing its vision to an even more unlikely cause: turning America's successful insurance program for the aged and disabled into a privatized, defined-contribution approach.

MEDI-SCARE

The annals of American medical history are full of ironies, but few are as rich as the fact that HSAs have been pursued by their advocates mostly through Medicare reform. Actually, there is a greater irony: the most successful line of attack on the ACA—pivotal to Republicans' electoral success in the 2010 and 2014 midterm elections—has been that it cuts Medicare. (The claim is true only with the most tortured interpretation of the facts: the ACA did reduce some subsidies for private health plans that contract with Medicare, but it also expanded benefits and reduced out-of-pocket cost burdens.) In other words, the nation's one great source of health security—the only health plan that pools risk nationally not on the basis of work status or military service but essentially on the basis of citizenship—has become a battering ram for those bent on *reducing* health security.

When it was created in 1965, advocates of Medicare believed it would be the stepping-stone to universal coverage.[32] Medicare did expand to the disabled and people requiring dialysis, but it has otherwise been caught in a holding pattern—increasingly criticized as costly and outmoded, and increasingly insufficient as a source of health security for older Americans.

Which brings us to another dirty little secret of American medical care: despite Medicare, the aged are still at grave risk because of rising health costs. Built on the model of Blue Cross in the 1960s, Medicare has gradually fallen behind the private sector in the breadth and generosity of its coverage. No health plan designed today would fail to put limits on out-of-pocket costs paid by patients. Yet Medicare still does not include such across-the-board limits. No health plan designed today would exclude routine coverage for prescription drugs. Yet until recently Medicare did. And, as will be discussed, its faulty drug-coverage plan—enacted in 2003—still leaves gaping holes.

While Medicare coverage has remained largely unchanged, the cost of care for the elderly has exploded. Meanwhile, employers have increasingly sought to cut back their own provision of supplemental health insurance in retirement. (Between 1988 and 2016, the share of employers with 200 or more workers offering retiree health coverage fell from two-thirds to less than a quarter.)[33] And the private market for insurance to supplement Medicare—so-called Medigap insurance—has eroded as insurers find it harder and harder to maintain private risk pooling in the supplemental market. As a result, seniors are actually paying a larger share of their income on medical care today than they did at the time of Medicare's passage.[34]

Kathleen Frazier knows all about the medical problems facing older adults. She's only fifty-eight, but she qualifies for Medicare because she is disabled. So does her husband, a former IBM worker, who is seventy. Unfortunately, the couple realized a few years back that they could no longer afford the ever-more-expensive retiree health plan her husband had been guaranteed in return for agreeing to retire early during one of IBM's many restructuring efforts. Instead, they signed up for a new drug plan through a Medicare private HMO, which charges a higher premium than traditional Medicare. But Kathleen's costs quickly exceeded the spending limit in the plan, and the couple now has to pay for Kathleen's medication out of pocket. "We pay the rent because my seventy-year-old husband is working full time at $9 an hour," Kathleen says.

Still, Medicare is the most successful large-scale system of health insurance the United States has. It is not just overwhelmingly popular. It has been a pioneer in regulating medical prices in the only rich country in the world where such regulation is the exception rather than the rule. Closing its gaps and expanding its reach while continuing to use its purchasing power to hold down costs would seem a no-brainer. But as with so many other obvious ideas to improve economic security, Medicare has been pilloried as an out-of-control entitlement that needs to be reformed top-to-bottom so that senior citizens have greater incentives to choose care wisely—which means, it turns out, further undoing the broad risk pool that has been the program's greatest source of success.

After all, controlling Medicare spending can only be done in two ways. The first is controlling how much Medicare pays for services—which Medicare has actually done better than the private sector since the early 1980s.[35] The second is by shifting more of the costs and risks of care onto Medicare beneficiaries. Given that Medicare coverage is substantially less generous than the norm in the private sector and that most elderly and disabled Americans have modest incomes, shifting costs and risks would seem the very last option to embrace.[36] And yet, this is precisely what many critics of Medicare call for, under the guise of an innocuous-sounding idea known as "premium support."

Ironically, premium support—now a darling of the Right—is similar to the managed competition plan President Clinton advocated in 1993 (although Clinton's proposal covered all Americans, not just Medicare beneficiaries). In essence, people who are enrolled in Medicare would be given a fixed amount to either buy into traditional Medicare coverage or purchase a private alternative. (Some premium-support plans don't even preserve traditional Medicare; private plans are the only choice.) Much as in a defined-contribution pension plan, Medicare would cease to guarantee a specific benefit at a particular price but rather offer a guaranteed level of support ("premium support") for the purchase of private options or traditional Medicare coverage.[37] If a particular plan costs more than the premium-support amount, the remainder would be the responsibility of Medicare beneficiaries—even if those beneficiaries remained in the traditional Medicare program.

Like the Clinton health plan, the premium-support approach relies on a great number of heroic assumptions and delicate institutional choices, none of which is likely to come together well in practice. This is not just speculation: in 1997 a balanced budget deal between Clinton and congressional Republicans moved toward the premium-support idea by expanding the range of private health plans offered by Medicare and the incentives for seniors to enroll in them. The reforms were an unqualified bust. Overwhelmed by the confusing array of options in some regions, without any alternative options in others, seniors largely steered clear of the new plans. Meanwhile, despite attempts to sweeten the pot for private plans, many insurers pulled out of the program, leaving those seniors who had enrolled in private plans to obtain drug coverage stranded.

Less disastrous but no less indicative of the faith-based reliance on the private sector was the new Medicare drug benefit, passed by Republicans in 2003. The plan was full of contradictions from the outset. Its GOP advocates insisted that they could obtain drug coverage cheaply by relying on the private sector. But the costs of the program mushroomed as it made its way through the legislative process, even as the scope of the coverage came to look more and more limited. In the end, the bill had to be slammed through Congress in the dead of night, after holding the House vote open for an unprecedented three hours (most votes last only 15 minutes) so that Republican leaders could threaten and cajole.

The fundamental problem with the new law, however, was not its chaotic creation. It was its commitment to ensuring Medicare stay out of the business of providing drug coverage directly. Independent analyses based on the experience of other programs suggested that Medicare would likely obtain steep discounts on drugs if it purchased them directly. But the pharmaceutical industry went all out to head off the threat—even poaching the Republican who wrote the legislation in the House as its new lobbying chief upon his retirement (negotiations began while the bill was being written). The end result was a program that was much more confusing and much less generous than it could have been given its enormous price tag.[38] Perhaps most galling was the infamous "doughnut hole" in the new drug coverage, which required that seniors pay for all of their drug costs between $2,250 and $5,100 in a given year (the ACA gradually closed the gap, which is now slated to disappear in 2019).[39]

The premium-support approach replicates the misplaced fixation on the private sector that characterized these prior policy steps. Unlike them, however, it aims to shift more risk onto seniors' shoulders—which is why it is such a central challenge to the social insurance philosophy of Medicare.

To understand this, it helps to remember that the costs of medical care are extremely concentrated on the small portion of Americans who incur major health expenses in any given year.[40] As it is currently constructed, Medicare essentially pays for the high costs of these unfortunate Medicare beneficiaries by spreading the costs across all Medicare beneficiaries—and through taxes, across all Americans. Yet if Medicare were a system of multiple private plans competing with the traditional Medicare option, then it would be much harder to spread costs in this way. Some plans would get a healthy group of patients. Others, almost certainly including traditional Medicare, would not. Even with adjustments to account for this disparity, the premium-support approach would still create a substantial amount of sorting of patients that would undermine the ability of traditional Medicare to pool risks, and perhaps even to survive.

Again, these are not idle speculations. The entire history of private health insurance in the United States—from the abandonment of broad pooling by Blue Cross to the hypersegmentation of the market in the 1980s and 1990s because of the exodus of large employers from the private risk pool—illustrates the dangers. Advocates of premium support often point to the Federal Employees Health Benefit Program. But analyses suggest that there are huge discrepancies in the premiums of plans within the federal employee's program due simply to the health of the patients they enroll.[41] Such discrepancies would be much greater, and much more worrisome, in the context of Medicare, especially if they meant that senior citizens who wanted to have a free choice of doctor and a simple insurance plan—both hallmarks of Medicare—were not able to enroll in the program they once benefited from because of its higher cost.

At heart, then, proposals to "modernize" Medicare by introducing premium support are really about shifting the risk of rising health costs from the government onto senior citizens. And this shift will not be a one-time occurrence. If Medicare moves from a guaranteed package of benefits to a system that merely provides a fixed amount of support, then it will be much easier down the road to control Medicare costs by simply trimming the level of the fixed contribution. This is all the more true because Medicare beneficiaries would suddenly face very different premiums and enjoy very different benefit packages, undermining the unified constituency of beneficiaries that has made direct cuts in Medicare so difficult in the past. If these changes came to pass, traditional Medicare—the program in which most senior citizens are now enrolled and with which most are overwhelmingly satisfied—could well "wither on the vine," as Newt Gingrich famously predicted during the budget battles of the mid-1990s.[42]

THE MEDICAID MUDDLE

While Medicare has been caught in a holding pattern, America's other major health program, Medicaid, has significantly expanded over the past two decades—most recently and dramatically, with the enactment of the ACA. Along with its smaller and younger sibling, the State Children's Health Insurance Program (or S-CHIP), Medicaid covers almost 75 million Americans, including 44 percent of children under the age of six and 35 percent between the ages of six and eighteen. It pays the bills for half of all childbirths and for more than 3 in 5 elderly residents of nursing homes.[43] Along with the Earned Income Tax Credit—a refundable tax benefit for lower-income workers—Medicaid is now the leading example of a program that helps workers and families struggling to get ahead.

Shannon and Derek Combs are just such workers, and their family has benefited greatly from California's health programs for lower-income residents. Their daughter, Kelsey, is covered by the state's S-CHIP, and

Shannon herself has Medi-Cal coverage, because she's pregnant with the couple's second child. In a floral print dress, her blond hair hanging in ringlets around her shoulders, Shannon does not look like most Americans' stereotype of public-assistance recipients. And in a sense she isn't—because her assistance will last only as long as she's pregnant. She and Derek, resident managers of a storage-unit facility, have both been uninsured for as long as they can remember. Derek, thirty-one, has been healthy enough to pay for all his care out of pocket. But Shannon recently suffered from bleeding ulcers. Even though she was throwing up blood, she resisted regular checkups. Eventually she had to have emergency-room surgery, which left her with $9,000 in unpaid bills. Now, Derek is facing his own quandary. His teeth are decaying but he can't afford fillings, root canals, and crowns, so he will probably just have them pulled at $25 each.[44]

For all of Medicaid's value to struggling families such as the Combs's, Medicaid is still a bandage stretched thin over the festering wound of health insecurity, hamstrung by its structure from doing more and vulnerable to demands that it should do less. In the first place, most of Medicaid's spending does not do what most people think it does—provide health security to families like Shannon and Derek's. Instead, it funds care for the elderly poor in nursing homes, the blind, and the disabled. These three populations account for the lion's share of Medicaid spending. This spending is of course valuable, but it means that most of the debate about Medicaid misses the point. Cast as a dilemma concerning generosity toward the able-bodied poor, Medicaid's dilemma is more accurately a problem of letting every unmet health need fall on a single, cash-strapped program, straining its ability to provide basic health security to its original target population.[45]

Worse, Medicaid is limited in its ability to provide health security by its very structure. As a state-based program designed to reach populations without access to workplace health insurance, Medicaid faces two serious problems. The first is that despite its expansion over the last two decades, it is still viewed as a program for the indigent by many Americans. Not without justification: Medicaid pays medical providers low rates, so many shun Medicaid patients altogether. A great deal of Medicaid spending is funneled into crumbling community medical institutions. Applying for

Medicaid is often hopelessly complex. Partly as a result of this complexity, millions of Americans eligible for Medicaid do not enroll in the program. But even when enrolled in Medicaid, families often find themselves without coverage soon after they enroll, because they briefly lose official eligibility or more often, fail to follow cumbersome and frequent reapplication processes.

Shannon Combs had not known, for example, that Medicaid covers low-income pregnant women. She learned it only when she visited a doctor at the beginning of her pregnancy—not from the doctor, who had told her she would have to pay him $3,200 for a normal delivery (half of it up front), but from a pregnant receptionist who happened to be on the program. When Shannon went to sign up, she was shuffled from office to office—first a program for the medically indigent that turned her down, then four visits to the Medi-Cal office because, she says, "they kept asking me to bring new papers with me." "It seemed," Shannon recalled, "like obstacles were being put in front of me left and right."

The second reason Medicaid is vulnerable is that it is financed in substantial part at the state level. States are under competitive pressure to keep spending on social benefits modest so they can restrain taxes to recruit and keep businesses and invest in things that attract residents, such as high-quality schools. And unlike the federal government, a state generally cannot spend more during downturns to deal with the increased needs that accompany recessions. States therefore tend to cut back programs for the less advantaged precisely when the plight of the less advantaged is greatest. This further compromises health security during periods of economic hardship.

States also have widely different programs—as the political scientist Andrea Campbell discovered when her sister-in-law, Marcella, was suddenly thrust into California's program by a terrible car accident that left her a quadriplegic. (Miraculously, the pregnant Marcella was able to deliver her baby via a C-section. Medi-Cal financed the birth because Campbell's brother Dave worked for a small firm that lacked health insurance.) "I thought I knew a lot about these programs," Campbell admits. "Little did I know how useless I would be to Dave and Marcella as they tried to navigate the extraordinarily complex American system of social assistance."

What really stuck with Campbell was that Medicaid and other "social protections for low-income people vary tremendously from state to state, along every conceivable dimension, from the profound (can your baby get health care?) to the trivial (can you get cavities in your molars filled?). It all depends on where you live." In no other rich country, she concludes, "can your fate differ so much from one locale to another within the same country."[46]

The ACA was supposed to change that, closing the gap between generous and penurious states. It didn't, because in 2012 a majority of justices on the Supreme Court ruled that the Medicaid expansion had to be optional rather than mandatory. Although the ACA provided 100 percent federal support for the initial expansion, about half of states—all of them controlled by Republicans—refused to upgrade their programs to cover people with incomes up to around 140 percent of the federal poverty level. The number of holdouts has been declining. Yet as recently as September 2018, fourteen states had refused to increase their eligibility levels (three of these states were considering an expansion).[47] The typical state that hasn't expanded Medicaid only provides coverage to families with incomes below 43 percent of the poverty level (less than $9,000 for a family of three). Moreover, in these states childless adults generally have no access to Medicaid at all. As a result, roughly 2 million low-income Americans in these states don't qualify for Medicaid yet are too poor to get federal help under the ACA (since the federal law was written with the assumption that all states would expand Medicaid)—a social policy Catch-22 that bears some similarity to the Medicare donut hole.[48]

All this is more worrisome because the expansion of Medicaid and S-CHIP has become increasingly controversial. Criticism was often muted in the past. In recent years, however, state governors and Republicans in Washington have spearheaded efforts to scale back coverage. The most recent efforts have centered around so-called work requirements—state policies that mandate that able-bodied adult Medicaid beneficiaries show proof of employment or evidence they're in college or vocational training programs. Since most Medicaid beneficiaries who fit this description *are* working (and those who work, usually work full time), the likely effect of work requirements is to make it harder to qualify for and remain on Medicaid. In other words, work requirements shift even more risk onto these already highly insecure workers. As the Kaiser Family Foundation, a nonpartisan think tank, concluded in June 2018:

> Even among those working full-time, work can be fragile, unpredictable, and may not help people rise out of poverty. Even a temporary illness or emergency situation for those working in hourly jobs could result in failure to meet new hourly work requirements. The subsequent loss of health coverage could exacerbate financial insecurity. Finally, workers will need to verify work status regularly, and many Medicaid adults may face barriers in complying with reporting requirements due to limited experience with or access to computers.

After Republicans captured both Congress and the White House in 2016, the battle reached a fevered pitch. As part of their effort to roll back the ACA, Republican leaders in the House and Senate proposed dramatically cutting Medicaid—reducing its future funding by as much as $1 trillion over ten years. The method was familiar to those who had followed past GOP plans: Medicaid would be transformed into a federal "block grant" to the states that would be allowed to grow only at a constrained rate. Indeed, "repeal and replace Obamacare" mostly meant, in practice, "repeal" Medicaid as it had been known for decades and "replace" it with a program that was designed to shrink dramatically over time.

Critics of Medicaid have long wanted to limit the program's funding. But both the Republican Party's electorate and Medicaid have changed substantially in recent years. As the party's base has shifted toward rural and working-class voters and Medicaid has grown, the program has become a vital source of protection for many of the GOP's core constituents, including rural communities and small towns struggling with the scourge of opioid addiction. Thus, the 2017 bills threatened huge losses for families reliant on Medicaid—losses that would be particularly large for core Republican voters. Perhaps not surprisingly, it polled terribly—whether viewed on its own or in comparison with the ACA. In one survey taken on the eve of the House vote, just one in six Americans (17 percent) said they supported the Republicans' current bill. Other polls showed slightly higher support, but on average only around a quarter of Americans backed the GOP bills—the lowest number seen on any major piece of legislation with a real chance of passage in the past quarter century. By way of comparison, polls taken on the eve of ACA's passage—after a year of intense attacks on the law as a government takeover of medicine—showed 35 percent (Fox) to 47 percent (ABC-*Washington Post*) of voters in support.[49]

In the end, Republicans came up just shy of assembling the votes they needed to pass their health care bills in 2017. In a drama worthy of a Hollywood script, Senator John McCain—the Arizona Republican who had lost to Barack Obama in the 2008 presidential race and was now suffering from a deadly form of brain cancer—become the pivotal Republican vote against repealing President Obama's signature legislative achievement. Although Senate Majority Leader Mitch McConnell tried again with another bill a couple months later, the last few GOP votes proved just as elusive as they had before. President Trump vowed to use his executive authority to undermine the ACA, but congressional Republicans were forced to move on.

Still, the fight is hardly over. Republicans managed to include in their big 2018 tax bill a partial repeal of the ACA's unpopular requirement that individuals show proof of health insurance or pay a fine (the so-called individual mandate). Meanwhile, the Trump administration has done everything in its power to undermine the ACA and its Medicaid expansion. Top GOP officials have urged states to impose premiums on Medicaid beneficiaries and to make HSAs and high-deductible health plans available to them. They have pushed to make short-term policies with limited coverage more available and attractive, skirting existing consumer rules and potentially destabilizing insurance markets by siphoning off healthy patients. The Trump administration has even joined a multistate lawsuit against the requirement that insurers cover people with "pre-existing conditions"— the most popular provision of the ACA and one Trump has repeatedly vowed to preserve. Though the suit is unlikely to succeed, it's just part of a larger plan for constructing what two health policy experts called "parallel

insurance markets" that wouldn't be subject to the burdensome requirement that insurance plans actually provide health security.[50]

Eight years after the passage of the ACA, in short, the struggle over
risk pooling in American health insurance is as fierce as ever. Committed
to rolling back the legacies of the Obama presidency, contemporary
conservatives have also redoubled their commitment to shifting the risks
of health care onto individuals and their families.

A SIMPLE PLAN

American political leaders have long been convinced that any proposal that
would truly deliver affordable quality health care for all Americans would
be DOA. Yet Americans are more receptive to the idea than ever, and there
just might be the will today to bring back what we have lost—broad risk
pooling in American health insurance.

The solution is right under our noses: Medicare. As we've seen, Medicare
does need upgrading; Medicare *does* do too little to help the nonelderly.
But the answer isn't to tear down Medicare; it's to build up the program to make it a stable foundation for providing health insurance for all
Americans without access to good coverage. Making Medicare available to
all Americans without workplace insurance would, in a single stroke, help
Medicare *and* broaden health security. Though requiring new financing up
front, this solution would actually lessen Medicare's long-term cost problem
because it would make program spending less sensitive to the demographic
distribution of the population. By increasing the share of health spending
financed by Medicare, it would also give the government greater leverage
to control costs.

Perhaps most crucial, expanding coverage to the uninsured through
Medicare would powerfully link the health security of elderly and the
young—the fate of Kathleen Frazier and the fate of Shannon Combs. No
longer would young workers without insurance support elderly citizens
with good coverage. And no longer would advocates of expanded insurance coverage feel that improving Medicare was at odds with their ultimate
aims. Instead of simply making Medicare more like insurance for workers,

this Medicare reform strategy would also make insurance for workers more like Medicare: secure, affordable, and simple.

But wouldn't Americans reject a huge federal program called Medicare? The idea seems convincing—until one realizes that there already is such a program, it's called Medicare, and Americans absolutely love it. Indeed, many Americans don't even think of Medicare as a government program, as is suggested by the (perhaps apocryphal) story of an elderly constituent who jumped up at a congressional town-hall meeting and declared, "Keep government out of my Medicare."

We can preserve and improve Medicare for future generations, and we can finally make health insurance secure for all Americans. Or we can leave each bobbing separately in a sea of hostility to the ideal of insurance—an ideal that once fired enthusiasm for the goal of security for all Americans and could do so yet again.

CONCLUSION

Securing the Future

The Great Risk Shift has played out like a slow-motion car crash projected onto thousands of screens at once. There is the twisting steel, the acrid smell, the broken bodies, the lost dreams. But the time frame is extended, the fallout scattered. David Lamberger fights to keep his home in Michigan. Joanne and Mark Molnar drive their RV from job to job because they can't live on Social Security alone. The Combs family worries about what will happen when Medi-Cal coverage for Shannon ends. Julie and Jerry Pickett try to put out of their minds the endless phone calls from the debt collectors. The Dorsetts file their bankruptcy papers before taking Zachary to the doctor.

We can see the common thread that unites these stories only by looking at them through the lens of risk. Americans are richer than they once were—though most only modestly so. But they are also at much greater economic risk. Our incomes rise and fall more sharply. Our health care costs more and more. Our pensions put more risk and responsibility on us. Our jobs and our families are more financially perilous. Our workplace benefits have become less available and complete. All of these mounting risks add up to an ever more harrowing reality: increasingly, all of us—even those of us with good jobs and good pay, with children and spouses, with homes and college degrees—are riding the new economic roller coaster. And yet most of us seem to feel we are riding it alone.

The new insecurity doesn't look like the old insecurity—grainy Dorothea Lange photos of Depression-era men and women, their weathered faces projecting despair and helplessness. Those who experience it have homes, cars, families, degrees. They've usually tasted the fruits of success, if sometimes only fleetingly. They very rarely end up on the streets or in shelters. For most, insecurity is a private experience, hidden away behind closed doors, felt in quiet despair.

The Great Risk Shift has played out family by family, workplace by workplace, debate by debate. Only rarely has it resulted in common action, much less a serious policy response. Indeed, the strongest political movement that has emerged from an era of economic anxiety is dedicated *not* to reversing the slide toward ever greater insecurity, but accelerating it by shifting more risk onto Americans' fragile finances. With the flowering of the Tea Party in 2009, the paradox of contemporary national politics only became more glaring: as the floodwalls against economic risk crumble, a powerful set of activists and elites have argued with increasing fervor that many of the remaining protections should be swept away, too.

The victory of Donald Trump in the 2016 presidential election further intensified the contradiction. The Republican businessman's improbable ascendance was a wake-up call to those who believed economic insecurity would remain a sideshow in American public life. During the campaign, Trump bested his GOP rivals and then his Democratic opponent by tapping into the anxieties that many white working-class voters feel—anxieties not just about our changing economy but also about our changing society. Like right-wing populists in other nations, he had a blunt message for his insecure supporters: political leaders have abandoned you to help the powerful and the undeserving, and your security can only be restored by limiting immigration and trade and putting your faith in a strongman willing to act boldly and speak freely. Yet Trump did not call for tearing down existing programs of economic security. He said he would cover everyone with "far less expensive and far better" health insurance than that provided by the "virtually useless" Affordable Care Act.[1] He promised to "save Medicare, Medicaid, and Social Security without cuts."[2]

Once in office, however, Trump embraced the familiar platform of the Personal Responsibility Crusade. A "far less expensive and far better" health plan turned out to be a proposed massive reversal of the coverage gains under the Affordable Care Act.[3] Medicaid was not spared—to the contrary, it bore the brunt of the proposed reductions.[4] The signal legislative achievement of his first year in the White House was a tax cut that delivered more than three-quarters of its long-term benefits to the richest 1 percent of households.[5] By creating a big new budget hole, the tax law essentially guaranteed new fiscal pressures on popular social policies. And, indeed, his administration's budget blueprints proposed slashing the programs he had promised to "save . . . without cuts."[6] He staffed his administration with personal responsibility crusaders hostile to Medicare and Social Security. He did everything within his executive powers to sabotage the Affordable Care Act. He kneecapped the Consumer Financial Protection Bureau, appointing as its head a conservative deficit hawk who had described the financial watchdog agency for American families as a "sick, sad joke."[7] In short, he wrapped the anti-insurance campaign in a veneer of populism, but if anything intensified its extremism.

Say this for the Personal Responsibility Crusade: it has a vision and a goal. Critics of public and private programs of insurance know what they are against—the sharing of risk. And they know what they are for—greater personal responsibility and individual self-reliance, propelled by aggressive government policies that erode the bonds of shared fate and undermine the systems of social insurance that once linked Americans across lines of class and economic vulnerability.

There can be no turning back the clock on many of the changes that have swept through the American economy and American society. Employers are not going to provide the mini-welfare states of the past. Unions are not going to magically re-emerge to cover a third of the workforce. The competitive strains on American employers are not going to go away. And the tide of red ink facing government will not evaporate naturally.

But accepting these changes does not mean accepting the new economic insecurity, much less accepting the assumptions that lie behind the current assault on insurance. Personal responsibility has its place: Americans will need to do much to secure themselves in the new world of work and family. But they should be able to do so in a context in which government and employers act as a help, not a hindrance. And they should be protected by an improved framework of social protection that fills the most glaring gaps in the current patchwork, providing all Americans with the basic financial security they need to reach for the future—as workers, as parents, and as citizens.

That is the central message of this book: though driven by powerful forces, the Great Risk Shift is not inevitable, and we should demand better. We don't need to accept that we have to deal with risk all by ourselves. We can reshape our economy and policies to achieve the ideals we believe in, rather than letting our economy and policies reshape those ideals. Indeed, a basic foundation of insurance can provide huge economic and social gains. The long-term rewards of reversing the Great Risk Shift will vastly exceed the short-term costs.

The ideas are out there. The challenge is getting our political system to act. It will not be easy, but it can and must be done. In a nation as innovative and vibrant and wealthy as ours, people who work hard and do right by their families shouldn't live in constant fear of economic loss. They shouldn't feel that a single bad step means slipping from the ladder of advancement. The American Dream is about security and opportunity alike, and rebuilding it for the millions of middle-class families whose anxieties and struggles are reflected in the stories told in this book will require providing security and opportunity alike.

FROM PRIVATE ANXIETY TO PUBLIC ACTION

American politics has been roiled by the Great Risk Shift. Yet the dissatisfaction and anxiety that so many of us feel has often pushed us away from shared conversations rather than pulling us in. Part of the reason is that the shift of risk onto our shoulders has been steady and cumulative—at least until recently. Only now, in wake of the greatest financial crisis since the 1930s, are we starting to recognize the breadth and depth of the problem we face. What's more, economic risks are hard to perceive. They run headlong into the cognitive biases that we've developed over thousands of years to protect us against visible and immediate threats to our safety while keeping us from being overwhelmed by the buzzing, blooming confusion of our environment.[8] And even when we perceive risks, they often come at us as shots out of nowhere. Nobody slaps a label on our experiences of financial anxiety and loss that says, "Made in Washington, DC" or "Brought to you by your local employer." And few of us would know what to do with the information on the label anyway. Seeing economic risks as dropping from the sky is partly a way of protecting ourselves from our own sense of individual powerlessness.

Our reluctance to join together and voice our concerns also reflects the very nature of the new uncertainties we face. Once, we were protected from many of the most severe economic risks of modern capitalism by the combined energies of our employers and our government. In the last generation, however, all of us have increasingly come to perceive, rightly, that "it's up to us" to succeed in a highly individualized and uncertain economy.[9] Employers have cut back on the generous benefits they previously provided as a matter of course, and many government programs have become more threadbare. The job market has grown more uncertain, particularly for more educated workers who were once relatively insulated from employment insecurity. And as women have entered the workforce in record numbers, families also feel more strained and insecure than ever as they try to balance work and family.

These trends produce real anxiety and hardship, as we've learned. But they also produce a greater sense of self-credit for success—and a greater sense of self-blame for failure. When people feel they're on their own, they are less likely to think that risk pooling is possible (or even desirable) and more likely to settle for policies that help with the individual management of economic risks, whether in the form of private accounts in Social Security or HSAs or new tax breaks for savings and investment. In this sense, the Personal Responsibility Crusade is a self-fulfilling prophecy: shifting risks can encourage people to think that dealing with risks on their own is the best they can do.

When people put their own security first, they're also less likely to push for shared solutions. In a series of clever in-the-field experiments, the political scientist Adam Seth Levine has found that efforts to draw together citizens around the challenge of economic insecurity often backfire, because telling people about their economic insecurity drives them away from collective action by reminding them of the financial and time constraints they face.[10] Here is another self-reinforcing result of the Personal Responsibility Crusade: those who feel insecure also feel powerless—not because they lack resources or a willingness to engage but because messages that remind them of their insecurity cause them to put their own (declining) security first.

The Great Risk Shift has not merely caused Americans to turn inward. As Donald Trump's victory suggests, it has also led many to direct their anger outward: to search for scapegoats, to envy those who are perceived as still having a good deal, to see the problem in zero-sum terms (one person's gain is another's loss), when in fact increasing economic security would mostly be a win-win bargain. Popular support for the Personal Responsibility Crusade has always been fragile, because the ethos of individual risk management does not speak to the widespread desire for a basic foundation of economic security. But calling for such a foundation is not the only alternative to the individualistic mantra of personal responsibility. Darker alternatives loom as well—ones that substitute tribalism for individualism. If we are to avoid greater and greater balkanization of our increasingly diverse society, we must fight for solutions that reflect the reality that we are all in this together.

PROVIDING SECURITY TO EXPAND OPPORTUNITY

The starting point for a new vision is a simple but forgotten truth: economic security is a cornerstone of economic opportunity. Like businesses, people invest in the future when they have basic protection against the greatest downside risks of their choices.[11] The worker who fears being laid off at any moment may be more productive in the short run. But in the long run, insecure workers tend to underinvest in specialized training; they are more reluctant to change jobs; they try to minimize their sense of job commitment to protect themselves against psychological loss.[12]

Similarly, the family barely scraping by may work more hours; but in the long run insecure families are not going to be able to make the investments in education and other keys to their future that they should.[13] And, of course, none of these costs include the huge emotional, health, and economic losses absorbed by workers and their families when they lose their incomes, their homes, and their dreams.[14]

Students of U.S. public opinion have long marveled at our seemingly inconsistent embrace of government programs of insurance, on the one hand, and the ethic of rugged individualism, on the other. Americans are "operational liberals" and "philosophical conservatives," the political psychologists Lloyd Free and Hadley Cantril once argued.[15] They want to have their welfare state cake and eat their free-market capitalism, too. But why wouldn't they? If we are to be encouraged to invest in new skills, strong families, new jobs, and everything else that makes upward mobility possible, we need a broader umbrella of basic insurance, not a more tattered and narrow one.

The rewards of knowledge-economy capitalism are great, but so too are the risks. If we embrace its upsides, then we also have to accept that many Americans, at one point or another, will be hit with economic shocks they cannot cope with on their own.[16] More than that, we have to understand that protecting Americans against such risks is not just a necessary expense but an economic necessity—a way of ensuring that Americans feel secure enough to take the risks needed for them and their families to get ahead. Corporations enjoy limited liability, after all, precisely to encourage risk-taking. But while today we still have limited liability for American corporations, increasingly we have full liability for American families.

Just before losing his primary race to a Tea Party opponent in 2012, the Republican House Majority Leader Eric Cantor sent out a Labor Day tweet that read: "Today, we celebrate those who have taken a risk, worked hard, built a business and earned their own success."[17] Apparently, he thought the only folks "who have taken a risk" were the well off and corporations, not everyday Americans.

Providing economic security appears even more beneficial when considered against some of the leading alternatives that insecure citizens may otherwise back. Heavy-handed regulation of the economy, strict limits on cross-border trade and financial flows, restrictions on legal immigration that prevent talented workers from joining our economy, and similarly intrusive measures may gain widespread support from workers buffeted by economic turbulence. And yet these measures are likely to produce not greater economic security, but greater instability and slower growth.

There is a huge void in American politics just waiting to be filled by public leaders who can speak convincingly about the need to provide economic security to expand opportunity. During the debate over President Bush's ill-fated proposal for the privatization of Social Security, pollsters regularly reported ten to fifteen-point advantages for security-opportunity messages over various versions of President Bush's personal responsibility message.[18] Polls consistently show that Americans are overwhelmingly supportive of policies to provide economic security, with large majorities of Republicans as well as Democrats strongly backing them.[19] Above all, surveys show a pervasive and deepening public disquiet about the crumbling American Dream and a strong desire to right the balance—though little confidence today's leaders can do so.

Consider a revealing survey conducted in 2009 and then repeated in 2016. The Heartland Monitor Poll asked a representative sample of Americans whether, compared with their parents at the same age, the economy presented them "with more risks that endanger your standard of living." Even amid the relatively strong economy of 2016, more than 8 in 10 respondents said they faced more risks (57 percent) or the same level of risks (27 percent) relative to their parents. Just 11 percent said the economy presented them with fewer risks. These responses turned out to be strikingly similar to those provided at the height of the economic crisis in 2009, when 86 percent said more (64 percent) or the same risks (22 percent), and an identical 11 percent said fewer risks.

Meanwhile, the share of people who said they had "more opportunities to get ahead" than their parents had—a sentiment Americans have traditionally endorsed—actually fell between 2009 to 2016, from 54 percent to 44 percent. As Ronald Brownstein of the *National Journal* summarized the findings: "The 2008 downturn—and the slow, unevenly distributed recovery that has marked its aftermath—crystallized for many Americans a new normal, one that presents them with reduced economic security and heightened risk even while it provides them with new opportunities and flexibility."[20]

This sense of "heightened risk" is widespread. In a series of surveys I conducted with a research team in 2009, roughly half of Americans reported being "very" or "fairly" worried about their economic security. Across a range of economic risks, large majorities of Americans reported having at least some worries, with 4 in 10 or more expressing substantial worry about most risks. The greatest fears concerned retirement income adequacy (over 88 percent of respondents said they were worried), out-of-pocket medical costs and health insurance premiums (more than 70 percent), having to help out one's family financially (70 percent), keeping or finding a job (more than 69 percent), losing one's spouse or partner due to death or family separation (more than 66 percent), losing health insurance (65 percent), and getting out of debt (more than 64 percent).

The strains reported by middle-class Americans are staggering. In the 18 months covered by our survey, almost half of Americans said they had experienced at least one major employment dislocation within their family (involuntary unemployment or loss of more than a month of work due to sickness or injury). An even larger share experienced at least one major health dislocation (major out-of-pocket expenses, much higher insurance costs, or loss of insurance altogether).[21]

At the same time, Americans were—and continue to be—strikingly ill-prepared for major economic risks. In our survey, almost half said they could go less than two months without their current income before experiencing real hardship. And, indeed, households that experienced major economic shocks reported much higher levels of unmet basic needs: going without food because of the cost, losing one's house or rental, or going without health care because of the expense. Even within families in the third quartile of household income (annual income between $60,000 and $100,000), more than half of those who experienced job loss or medical disruptions reported being unable to meet at least one basic economic need.[22]

Perhaps it's no surprise, then, that when asked in June 2017, "Do you think the federal government should guarantee health insurance for all Americans, or isn't this the responsibility of the federal government?" a 3-in-5 majority of Americans said the federal government should provide this guarantee—the highest level since the divisive debate over the Affordable Care Act. Even among those who said guaranteeing health insurance wasn't a government responsibility, nearly 90 percent said that government should "continue programs like Medicare and Medicaid."[23] Most Americans today seem more worried about Big Insecurity than about Big Government.

FIRST, DO NO HARM

As we work to even out our nation's imbalanced priorities, our first priority should be Hippocrates's "Do no harm." Undoing what risk pooling remains in the private sector without putting something better in place does harm. Encouraging companies to drop or underfund their pension plans does harm. Piling tax break upon tax break permitting wealthy and healthy Americans to opt out of our tattered institutions of social insurance does harm. And though simplifying our tax code makes eminent sense, making it markedly less progressive or slashing future tax revenues that we need to finance social insurance does harm. A progressive income tax, after all, is effectively a form of insurance, reducing our contribution to public goods when income falls and raising it when income rises.

The acid test that major social policy reforms should have to meet is this: Do they substantially increase the risk on Americans' already burdened shoulders? If the answer is yes, then our response to these proposals should be no.

Most private account proposals fail this test. By putting "more skin in the game," they also make Americans more insecure. Accounts can help Americans manage their finances. But the incentives have to be right, and the incentives embodied in most existing tax-favored accounts are exactly backward, providing the most to those who are already most secure. Providing choice within public programs and giving people the tools they need to secure themselves are surely valuable goals. Yet these goals need to be achieved in ways that are consistent with providing basic financial security. Government can often "row, not steer"—but government should not be punching holes in families' financial lifeboats at the same time.[24]

Nor are private insurance markets going to emerge spontaneously to deal with the most pressing risks that we face. Although markets work splendidly in most areas of commerce, insurance markets often fail precisely when we need them most. The problem of adverse selection, for example, often makes it difficult for private insurers to provide good benefits at a premium that lower-risk people are willing to pay. (Adverse selection, it will be recalled, occurs because people who most need insurance are most likely to enroll in it.) Many of the risks that we most want to protect ourselves against—unemployment during severe downturns, for instance, or unexpected market changes that erode our retirement benefits—are hard to insure against because they are "systemic": they occur to many people at once and are thus particularly difficult for private insurers to effectively cover. And some risks, such as the cost of long-term care thirty or forty years down the line, are just too, well, risky for insurers to take on. As a result, insurance for these sorts of long-term, uncertain risks is usually incomplete and inadequate. To insist that we must wait for the private sector to deal with the Great Risk Shift is to hold Americans' security hostage to an unfounded hope, not a realistic aspiration.

Smart Modernization

Yet while we should work to preserve the best elements of existing policies, we should also recognize that the nature and causes of insecurity, and beliefs about how insecurity should be addressed, have all evolved considerably.

During the New Deal, economic insecurity was seen largely as a problem of drops in or interruptions of male earnings, whether due to unemployment, retirement, or other costly events. Even as working women became the norm, the special economic strains faced by two-earner families were largely neglected. So too were the distinctive unemployment patterns that became increasingly prevalent as industrial employment gave way to service work—for example, the shift of workers from one economic sector to another, which often leads to large cuts in pay and the need for specialized retraining.

Flaws in existing policies of risk protection have also become apparent. Our framework of social protection is overwhelmingly focused on the aged, even though young adults and families with children face the greatest economic strains. It emphasizes short-term exits from the workforce, even though long-term job losses and the displacement and obsolescence of skills have become more severe. It embodies, in places, the antiquated notion that family strains can be dealt with by a second earner—usually a woman—who can easily leave the workforce when there is a need for a parent at home. Above all, it is based on the idea that job-based private insurance can easily fill the gaps left by public programs—when it is ever more clear that it cannot.

This means the emphasis should be on portable insurance to help families deal with major interruptions to income and big blows to household wealth. It also means that these promises should be mostly separate from work for a particular employer—a commitment that moves seamlessly from job to job. If this sometimes means corporations are off the hook, so be it. Companies shouldn't decide whether their workers get fundamental risk protections, and a portable benefits system would be good for both employers and employees. By lowering and stabilizing costs for businesses that have already made a strong commitment to their workers' security, a portable benefits system would not only help workers, but also level the competitive playing field and improve the financial health of many now-embattled corporations.

By the same token, however, we should not let massive social risks be borne by institutions incapable of effectively carrying them. Bankruptcy should not be a backdoor social insurance system; private charity care should not be our primary medical safety net; credit cards should not be the main way that families get by when times are tight—and not just because these systems are prone to abuse and predation but also because they were not designed to bear the burden they now carry, much less to carry it effectively. To be sure, the principle of "do no harm" may dictate protecting even incomplete and inadequate safety nets when nothing better is possible. The ultimate goal, however, should be a new framework of social insurance that revitalizes the best elements of the present system while replacing those parts that work least effectively with stronger alternatives geared toward today's economy and society.

The place to begin is where this book began—with the new insecurity Americans face because of income volatility and job insecurity. Risky jobs lead to risky families, the second epicenter of insecurity where new approaches are badly needed. Risky retirement and risky health care are the final areas where solutions are both essential and available. Particularly important is a broader approach to health insurance that would finally provide all Americans health care they need at a price they can afford. A universal framework with the ability to restrain medical costs—a goal most rich democracies achieved long ago—would not only safeguard private budgets. It would also improve public budgets, reducing the threat posed by rising medical prices to our capacity to pursue other vital policy goals.

Dealing with Risks to Workers

Nowhere is the need for both restoration and reform more transparent than when it comes to our protections for the unemployed. Unemployment insurance has eroded dramatically in the last generation—state by state, recession by recession, worker by worker. Though it was expanded in 2008 (under President Bush) and 2009 (under President Obama), these gains have been more than reversed since. In 2016, only 27 percent of unemployed workers received benefits—the lowest level on record and a quarter below the pre-recession level of 36 percent. States have cut back the duration of benefits, traditionally set at twenty-six weeks, and made the filing process more difficult. Many workers in temporary or low-wage jobs are also not aware they are eligible for benefits, in part because states often make it difficult to find out who can apply and how.[25]

Yet ideas for restoring unemployment insurance are not hard to find, and the cost would be comparatively modest. In fact, there is evidence that unemployment insurance more than pays for itself in terms of higher economic productivity, because it encourages workers to take the time to match themselves to jobs for which they are truly suited.[26] During national downturns, moreover, unemployment insurance automatically boosts household incomes, preventing a downward spiral of business closings, housing foreclosures, and forgone educational investments.

Restoring strong national standards that require all states to cover workers for at least twenty-six weeks would go a long way toward filling the gaps in the present program. So too would an automatic trigger that extends benefits beyond their usual six-month cutoff when long-term unemployment makes up a substantial share of total unemployment. Long-term unemployment benefits could also be provided in the form of vouchers for retraining to use for the purchase of educational services. Workers who opt for retraining vouchers would receive more support than those who simply want cash, which would encourage the long-term unemployed to invest in new skills.

Unemployment insurance could also be an important platform for dealing with instability in earnings. Already, all states offer what is called "partial unemployment benefits" to covered workers who have their hours reduced through no fault of their own, including workers who have to take part-time jobs when laid off. Yet these programs vary enormously across the states in accessibility and generosity, and in many states, workers simply aren't aware they might qualify for partial benefits. Any new federal standards should seek to "level up" all states toward the most successful approaches.[27]

Ultimately, if unemployment insurance is to remain a source of economic security for workers in today's turbulent job market, it will need to be made a truly national program. Unlike the federal government, states generally cannot run deficits during downturns, and they face much fiercer competition to attract and retain businesses, which encourages them to keep the taxes that fund the program too low to ensure they have adequate reserves to deal with economic shocks. States also do not have the authority to set nationwide rules that govern who is counted as a covered worker—rules that will need to be broadened to include the growing ranks of contingent workers to ensure unemployment protection is more than a hollow promise. Even if financing and rules became federal, states could still administer their programs, and they could be allowed to experiment with new outreach and application processes that were shown to increase benefit receipt among eligible workers. But it makes little sense to allow states to be the first line of defense against a problem, unemployment, that is overwhelmingly determined by national economic trends. Federal unemployment insurance would be a much more reliable approach.

Unemployment insurance, however, isn't designed to deal with the most serious risk of losing a job—not temporary interruptions in income, but long-term declines in earnings power and standard of living. There is now broad agreement among economists that some form of wage insurance is needed for workers displaced by trade or re-engineering within an industry who end up not being able to find a new job with pay or benefits comparable to their old one.[28] These proposals are vastly superior to blunt restrictions on company hiring and firing. They are also vastly superior to placing heavy restraints on trade and financial flows in our dynamic, open economy—which is why even the most ardent free marketeers often support wage insurance.

The details of wage insurance proposals differ, but they have in common that they would provide a supplement to wages to encourage workers to take new jobs even if those jobs pay less than previous ones. The United States already has an extremely limited program of wage insurance for workers specifically displaced by foreign competition. But wage insurance should be available for all workers, not just those affected by trade. The experience of losing a job is just as devastating if your job is given to a machine rather than a low-wage worker in another country—and your wages should be protected in either case.

Dealing with risks to workers also means figuring out how to provide protections to the growing share of workers outside traditional employment arrangements. Sometimes the answer is simple: a very large share of workers labeled "independent contractors" are really just employees, and we should update our labor laws to define them as such. But when workers are truly independent—setting their own hours and fees, managing their own expenses, working for large numbers of clients—traditional approaches to unemployment and wage insurance may indeed fall short, since it's harder to collect regular contributions from such workers or to know whether job and earnings losses are beyond their control. The challenges are real, but not insuperable: California has long provided unemployment protections to qualified self-employed workers, and the U.S. Department of Labor has frequently used pilot programs to test out ways to adapt unemployment insurance to a changing workforce.[29] Indeed, the digital advances that make the gig economy possible could open up new possibilities for collecting regular contributions from and validating claims for independent workers—if our economic policies were finally brought in line with economic realities.

There is a final risk to earnings that most Americans prefer not to think about: disability. But over the past generation—as the population has aged, more women have moved into the paid workforce, our understanding of disability has broadened, and labor-market prospects for less educated workers have declined—the federal disability insurance program has grown substantially.[30] Today, around 9 million Americans receive disability benefits. More than two-thirds are over age fifty, and their benefits average roughly $1,100 a month. Most beneficiaries are severely disabled. But experts generally believe that a significant minority—a tenth to a quarter—would be able to do some paid work with proper accommodation. Still, a range of evidence suggests that earnings aren't likely to be a major source of income for most of them. People on disability insurance are allowed to earn up to around $1,000 a month and still be classified as unable to engage in "substantial gainful activity"—the standard for eligibility. And yet fewer than 1 in 8 beneficiaries had any earnings in 2007.[31]

To be sure, some beneficiaries would have worked more if they hadn't received disability checks. How much more is the difficult question.

One clever study looked at the officials who determine eligibility, called "examiners."[32] Overall, disability benefits are granted to roughly 1 in 3 of those who apply for disability—who, in addition to having a clinically verified disability that precludes paid employment, must have a minimum work history and wait five months to be eligible. The study found, however, that getting a different examiner could have resulted in a different eligibility decision in as many as a quarter of applications. In other words, lenient examiners might have said yes to applicants who were denied benefits, whereas tougher examiners might have said no to applicants who were granted benefits. Since whether an applicant gets a lenient or tough disability examiner is essentially random, the study was able to compare those who received benefits and those who didn't in those 1 in 4 cases that could have gone either way. What they found was that receiving disability benefits reduced earnings by an average of around $4,000 a year—a modest effect, given that these are the cases where disability is most ambiguous.

Still, it would make sense to test out program changes that would allow workers to receive partial or temporary benefits if their disability was not so severe or enduring to prevent them from working. Indeed, the fact that some disabled workers might be able to continue working under the right conditions is a strong argument for strengthening other sources of support for displaced workers—otherwise, these workers are much more likely to turn to disability insurance. It is also a strong argument for universal health insurance: those who are permanently disabled are eligible for Medicare, which encourages applications for workers with serious medical conditions. Improved disability insurance should be part of a stronger safety net for workers. But it shouldn't be a substitute for programs such as wage and unemployment insurance that help able-bodied Americans deal with heightened job insecurity.

Dealing with Risks to Families

Families were once a refuge from risk. Stay-at-home moms served as what Heather Boushey calls "silent partners."[33] They made it possible for American (male) workers to devote their time to paid employment, without needing flexible schedules or reliable child care or paid time off to care for sick kids or ailing parents. These vital supports didn't show up directly in productivity statistics, but make no mistake: they were a fundamental reason that businesses prospered, incomes rose, the old and the young were properly cared for, and the next generation of workers—and caregivers—were brought up to be responsible, educated adults.

Today, families are the epicenter of risk. The silent partners are now at work, too, and the vital supports they once provided are falling on other people: child care workers, retired parents or other nonworking relatives, and the vast range of service providers whose paid labor substitutes for the unpaid labor once done by women. Or these crucial tasks are failing to get done at all, or done only with significant personal sacrifices, from sleepless nights and forgone pay to part-time work and job losses caused by family crises.

Like many of the other risks discussed in this book, those that arise because of work-family conflict haven't been—and won't be—solved by employers acting on their own. Farsighted employers have found that providing paid sick days or paid family leave can increase productivity and reduce turnover. But for the most part these benefits are only available to the highly paid. More important, employers taking on these responsibilities will always be vulnerable to competition from those who do not, especially in areas of the labor market where workers have low wages and limited bargaining power. Nor, for much the same reason, will all states naturally move forward to address these risks. Some will and have, but creating a level playing field across workplaces and across the nation requires a simple federal framework.

Fortunately, the United States already has a popular platform for a national solution. The Family and Medical Leave Act was greeted with derision by personal responsibility crusaders when it was first proposed. Congressman John Boehner, who would later serve as Speaker of the House from 2011 to 2015, declared, "We don't need the federal government further strangling the free enterprise system in this country."[34] But the free-enterprise system clearly survived. In 2000, 90 percent of employers covered by the law said that it had had a positive or neutral effect on their profitability, and many said they experienced gains, mainly due to better employee retention and productivity.[35] Yet the act still does not apply to more than 4 in 10 workers in the United States, and there is little reason that it should not be extended to the vast majority of those now outside its protections.[36]

Nor is there any reason such leave should not provide a reasonable share of workers' former compensation. For most Americans, *unpaid* leave is simply not an option—they need the regular income that a job requires. Guaranteeing paid time off to care for a new child or a sick family member or to recover from a serious personal illness is a well-tested, affordable policy with a range of social and economic benefits (remember: the United States is the only advanced industrial nation without it). Moreover, it's popular with business in those U.S. states where it has been tried. Even better, it can be paid for by workers themselves through a simple payroll deduction that spreads the cost across people and over time—the essence of risk pooling. Since benefits for workers should be universal, contributions should be universal, too.

Paid sick days are another low-cost way to lessen work-family conflict. And here again states—and some cities—are paving the path toward national legislation. Unlike paid leave, however, paid sick days are probably best implemented as a legally required benefit, as health insurance now is for larger employers. Similarly, federal wage and hour laws could be updated to reflect changes in the workforce and in employers' scheduling practices that leave too many workers with little or no control over their own schedules. These laws should include a "right to request" that allows parents with young children to petition for altered work hours from their employer without fear of retaliation—to be granted at their employer's discretion. In the United Kingdom, simply creating a formalized process for such requests has led to a large increase in flexible work options, such as part-time or flexible working hours, working from home, and splitting a job across two workers. Under the U.K. policy—which only requires that employers considers workers' applications for flexible arrangements, not that they grant it—both men and women make requests (though women more often), virtually all are granted by employers, and the law has been enthusiastically expanded by governments of differing partisan orientations since its introduction nearly two decades ago.[37]

Finally, if workers need assurances to raise the next generation of Americans, they also need assurances to plan for their own future. Even the best-insured households need a personal safety net of relatively liquid savings to deal with the economic risks they face. As we've seen, however, most households lack sufficient savings to cushion even relatively modest financial blows. This is, in part, because our incentives for savings are "upside down."[38] The incentives for higher-income Americans to save have ballooned with the expansion of tax-favored investment vehicles. Yet most Americans receive relatively modest benefits from these ever-more-costly state and federal tax breaks. Keep in mind: Americans of all income levels help finance these savings incentives (after all, at a given level of federal spending and borrowing, cutting taxes on one household necessarily means raising them on another). So our current system essentially transfers resources from those who most need to save to those who least need to—and who are therefore most likely to simply shift their savings around to avoid taxes, rather than to save more.

According to the best research, if an account is going to actually boost savings among those not saving much now, it must be automatically established and automatically seeded with regular contributions. [38] Thus, all Americans should have a general savings account automatically established in their name (presumably linked to their Social Security number). It might even make sense to set up such accounts at birth with an initial allotment, as in proposals for "baby bonds" that aim to give children born into less affluent households a seed grant of wealth. Once accounts are established, lower-income account holders should regularly receive a modest federal contribution regardless of whether they put in their own dollars. On top of this, workers holding such accounts should have a default amount—again, modest—deducted from their paycheck. In turn, these contributions should be matched progressively (lower income, higher match)—again with federal funds. Finally, such accounts should be available but unsubsidized for high-income households. After all, the goal is to replace the current welter of upside-down tax breaks for nonretirement savings with a single tax-subsidized rainy-day account that is most generous for Americans of ordinary means.

Insuring Higher Education

There is one big expense, however, that such accounts are very poorly suited for: education. A personal safety net is built for temporary economic drops, such as unexpected earnings losses and sudden household expenses. It cannot and should not bear the enormous weight of four or more years of higher education. A college degree has become the equivalent of a high-school degree a half century ago—a prerequisite for a well-paying job. Yet we treat high school and college fundamentally differently. The former is treated as a public good; the latter as a personal responsibility. Almost uniquely among rich countries, in the United States the rising cost of higher education since the 1980s has been borne substantially by students and their parents through borrowing—one reason we've fallen farther and farther behind our rich peers in college completion.

This costly system doesn't just exacerbate profound inequalities of opportunity that already exist between children raised in less affluent households and those with the good fortune to be born into more affluent ones. Because the returns of a college education have become more vari-able, borrowing to finance that education is akin to buying stocks on the margin—going into debt to make an increasingly risky investment. The risks of this vital investment are only partly revealed by the growing risk of default (which isn't an escape valve, since the federal government can garnish wages and keep tax refunds when loans are in arrears, not to men-tion that defaulting on a loan destroys credit-worthiness for years to come). Precisely when young workers are trying to establish a career, buy a home, and perhaps start a family, our broken system imposes on them pervasive risk, constrains their credit, and engenders anxieties corrosive to future investments and opportunities. The costs of this system affect those who end up able to pay back their loans as well as the growing share who do not.

That share is much higher than commonly thought. You may have heard that "only" around 10 percent of student-loan borrowers default. That's true—if you follow those borrowers for just three years, the standard metric. Delve deeper into the federal data, however, and the numbers are more troubling. For borrowers who started repaying in 2012, fully 16 percent (841,000) had defaulted within five years, and roughly as many were severely delinquent or had stopped paying their loans altogether. In other words, the total share of those facing severe financial distress within five years had risen to 30 percent. In monetary terms, these distressed borrowers owed more than $23 billion.[39] And the problem is much worse at for-profit colleges, which rely much more than other private institutions—and, indeed, much more than public institutions—on federal dollars. (Among the eleven largest for-profits, five received more than 90 percent of their revenue from the federal government in 2013–2014, and *all* received more than 70 percent.[40]) If all this isn't a sign of a troubled system, it's not clear what would be.

Many steps must be taken to increase the ability of talented young people from all backgrounds to both pursue *and* complete a college degree, and thankfully our nation is now debating some of them. But one obvious advance would build on current policy to provide a vital new form of insurance. All federally backed student loans should be "income-contingent," with repayment based on future earnings. Moreover, these income-contingent loans should be fully forgiven after a reasonable period of repayment, such as twenty years. A young college student should know what share of their income they will pay after graduation and for how long, and know that, even if their income is low or drops or even disappears, they will be student debt free by middle age.

Income-contingent loans are essentially an insurance plan, providing greater support for past education if one's earnings turn out to be lower than expected. As a bonus, they also provide a nudge in favor of less lucrative degree-dependent positions that our society desparately needs filled, such as schoolteachers, nurses, and mental health counselers. And expanding income-contingent loans for higher education would hardly be a radical change. They are already embedded in federal policy, though they currently fall well short of the degree of risk-cushioning that would guarantee not just greater security but also broader opportunity.

The biggest problem is that income-contingent loans are currently not universal, which means that students who expect to have high earnings or who have family and social networks that can bail them out are least likely to participate. But for risk-spreading to work, it has to include all risk levels, not just students with the highest chance of defaulting. Nor should a universal framework of income-contingent loans be self-financing: society benefits enormously from higher education, and thus society should write off some of the costs of forgiving loans from those who end up with low lifetime incomes.

It might be feared that borrowers will deliberately hold down their incomes to minimize their payments. But that's not a real concern if the level of repayment is modest. Economists have searched in vain for evidence that households' work and earnings are highly sensitive to tax rates; there's little reason to think an income-based repayment plan would have much effect either [41] (More specifically, what people *earn* doesn't appear highly responsive to tax rates, according to recent studies. By contrast, what taxpayers report as their total income—which reflects not only earnings, but also the use of deductions and credits and the timing of capital gains— *does* appear highly responsive. So recent studies simultaneously suggest that income-contingent loans aren't likely to reduce borrowers' work effort *and* that we should focus our worries about distortionary tax policies on the scores of costly provisions enacted in the name of economic security that are mostly used by affluent households to lower their tax bills.

Income-contingent loans exemplify the ways in which providing insurance can increase opportunity. Although hardly a full response to the risks associated with ever-more-costly higher education, they would deliver benefits far larger than their minimal costs.

Social Security Plus

The biggest challenge today when it comes to personal savings concerns neither short-term shocks nor education costs. It is the daunting task of restoring a system of broad, guaranteed retirement pensions. For workers who expect to retire in thirty or forty years, defined-benefit pensions are already a thing of the past. But defined-contribution plans, such as 401(k)s, are failing miserably to provide a secure foundation for workers' retirement. The account value of a typical 401(k) is around $20,000, well below the savings a retired worker needs to live on.[42] Meanwhile, Social Security is set to replace less than 30 percent of pre-retirement income by 2035—down from nearly 40 percent today and almost 50 percent in 1980.[43] As a result, the share of working-age households at risk of being financially unprepared for retirement at age sixty-five has jumped from less than a third in 1983 to half in 2016.[44] In other words, half of younger workers are slated to retire without saving enough to maintain their standard of living in old age.

So far, the ideas on the table mostly look like Band-Aids. New credits for retirement savings or exhortations to workers and employers to do the right thing aren't going to change much, especially for those whose retirement savings are least adequate. Instead, what's needed is a fundamental rebalancing of risk. And that, in turn, requires bold solutions that go well beyond anything discussed in Washington or state capitals today.

Policy experts need to tell the truth: Americans won't save enough unless they are required to do so. The biggest problem with 401(k)s is not that their returns are uncertain, serious as that problem is. It is that half of workers don't have a 401(k), and almost nobody contributes enough to his or her account. We need to require that workers save adequately to fund their retirement. But we cannot do that unless those workers are given the protections against risk only government can provide. This is the bargain embodied in Social Security, and it's the bargain we need to extend to the whole system going forward.

Of course, many workers don't make enough to contribute very much, and some don't make enough to contribute anything. Fortunately, we have plenty of money to help these workers save more. Currently, the Treasury gives up roughly $200 billion in revenue a year subsidizing tax-favored plans such as 401(k)s.[45] Yet the vast majority of these tax benefits go to the richest Americans, with only a small share (around a tenth) going to the bottom half.[46] What if we instead took the money the government is

using to encourage rich people to save for retirement and spent it to encourage more retirement saving by the bottom half? What would that
system look like?

First, it would feature a stronger Social Security system. In the first edition of this book, I argued that Social Security may have to be moderately
pared back in the near future. After the financial crisis and more than a
decade of continuing declines in retirement security in the private sector,
I am now convinced we should close its financing gap almost entirely by
raising additional revenues—mainly by lifting or eliminating the cap on
earnings subject to its payroll tax and extending that tax to investment
earnings. In fact, we need to *boost* Social Security payouts for some vulnerable populations, such as women who were caregivers during their working
lives, not scale them back.

Certainly, we should not raise the retirement age. This once seemed
a commonsense idea in a nation with lengthening life spans. In the past
decade, however, a wave of startling studies have shown that workers in
the bottom half of the wage distribution have experienced essentially *no* increase in life expectancy over the past two decades.[47] Instead of subjecting
these workers to ever more penurious postwork years, we should maintain
earlier retirement as an option but increase the incentives for later retirement by boosting benefits for those who are able and willing to wait.

Second, we need to fix 401(k)s. Too few workers are offered them, enroll in them, or put enough in them—a reflection of perverse incentives
built into their very structure. Although it makes sense to build on what
people are familiar with, 401(k)s need a major overhaul, not modest
tweaks.

Step No. 1 of that overhaul is to make a 401(k)-style plan available to
all workers, whether or not their employer offers one. Step No. 2 is to automatically enroll workers and set a default contribution rate (I would
advocate around 6 percent). In turn, employers would be encouraged to
match worker contributions to these plans, and government would offer
additional matching funds for less affluent workers. These government
matches could and should be funded by scaling back the highly regressive
tax subsidies for retirement savings now offered. In other words, tax breaks

for higher-income workers should be capped to provide greater support for lower-income workers.

Universal 401(k)s with required contributions and government matching for low- and middle-income Americans would represent a fundamental change for the better. Everyone would be covered; people would save much more. Because the accounts would be universal, moreover, workers wouldn't have to roll their benefits over when they lost or changed jobs; they could just keep the account. (Not surprisingly, many workers don't roll over balances today—faced with a job change, they spend rather than save the often-modest sums in their accounts.)

Finally, I would take one more step—well, leap—toward a guaranteed benefit. Under the system I'm advocating, 401(k) accounts would be converted into a lifetime guaranteed income at retirement, with these new annuities provided directly by Social Security. Today, 401(k)s cannot offer a simple defined benefit, because private employers don't want to take on this task and private insurers lack the ability to spread risks over time and across large numbers of people. But that is something the federal government can easily do. If Social Security allowed people to convert some or all of their 401(k) accounts into a defined benefit, then 401(k)s could provide the same reliable monthly check that Social Security does.

Yale legal scholar Ian Ayres and I call this new public option "Social Security Plus."[48] It would allow all Americans to convert their retirement savings into additional Social Security benefits merely by rolling over their IRA or 401(k) account into their Social Security account. Social Security Plus wouldn't require the creation of a new government bureaucracy. The Social Security Administration already has an account set up for every American—a guaranteed benefit in their name funded by Social Security taxpayers and protected by law. It already has well-developed mechanisms for receiving and paying out billions of dollars. Social Security Plus would just represent a new source of inflows and outflows to the accounts of participating members.

Indeed, the program could be completely costless to the federal treasury: Social Security would simply calculate how much money would have to be rolled over for a given boost in benefits for people of different ages and characteristics (although I would argue that the federal government might kick in a little to make the deal sweeter, so that people don't run out of their retirement savings and fall back on other public benefits). And because these new annuities would be provided directly by the federal government to nearly all Americans at retirement, there would be little worry about the problems of adverse selection and high administrative costs that plague annuity markets today.

Interestingly, this proposal is not so different from an idea that was seriously considered by the developers of the Social Security Act in 1935, who argued that the post office should sell low-cost annuities to those who needed them.[49] In essence, Social Security Plus would bring back something close to a guaranteed private pension, with the federal government, rather than employers, pooling the risk. In the meantime, states and cities can spearhead the movement by offering their own default 401(k)-style plans, as several states are already considering or beginning to do. State accounts that automatically enrolled workers without a retirement plan could help vulnerable families plan for retirement and test out new policy approaches in advance of a federal response.

Americans know the current system isn't working, and they want it to become more like Social Security: simple, guaranteed, secure. Employers are not going back to their traditional role. Americans will not magically become supersavers. A generation of risk-shifting has failed. We shouldn't slash Social Security. We should make it the model for a transformed private system that actually provides retirement security.

Medicare Part E (for Everyone)

Just as Social Security should be the model for retirement security, Medicare should be the model for health security. Despite the Affordable Care Act, our patchwork quilt of health insurance costs way too much, and it leaves way too many Americans without adequate protection. Although the ACA dramatically improved things, roughly 30 million Americans still remain uninsured, average spending per person is still extremely high, and both numbers are rising again.

There is enormous diversity in how other rich democracies pay for health care. Some countries have a single government program, or "single payer," while others rely on regulated nonprofit insurers. What they all have in common, however, is universality and cost control. First, these nations guarantee all citizens coverage and then figure out how to pay for it. Only in the United States is the responsibility to get and pay for coverage largely left up to individuals and their employers, leaving tens of millions to fall through the cracks. Second, these systems use government's bargaining power to restrain medical costs. The major reason that U.S. spending is so high is that we pay such high prices for medical goods and services and prescription drugs, and the major reason we pay such high prices is that we don't regulate them as every other rich nation does.[50]

Indeed, the experience of other rich nations suggests that universality and cost control go together. When a nation's leaders commit themselves to providing insurance to everyone, they become much more aware of bill-padding and price-gouging. They also discover that government has a unique capacity to do something about it: it can require that providers charge uniform prices to everyone. Access and affordability are not in conflict. Done right, broadening coverage allows government to gain control over costs.

America's national health program, Medicare, is a case in point. If it weren't limited to Americans older than sixty-five or permanently disabled—admittedly, a big if—Medicare would fit comfortably into the spectrum of international models of health financing. For qualifying citizens, coverage is basically automatic. It's also affordable, with costs per beneficiary much lower than the expense of similar benefits in the private sector.

The reason for this cost advantage can be summed up in one word: prices. My Yale colleague Zack Cooper has gained access to the claims records of some of the biggest commercial insurers. What he's found is that the prices they pay are much higher than Medicare's. They also vary enormously across providers.[51] Moreover, the gap between Medicare and private insurance has been growing, as doctors and hospitals increasingly consolidate into large medical systems demanding premium prices. In recent years, Medicare's overall tab has risen with the retirement of the baby boom generation. Yet its spending per enrollee, which is what really matters, has been essentially flat and, indeed, has even fallen in some recent years.[52]

So why not just extend Medicare to everyone? The big problem, as should be clear by now, is that roughly half the population continues to be covered by employment-based health plans.[53] These plans have become less common, more expensive, and more restrictive. Still, these 150-plus million people with workplace coverage are generally satisfied (though beneficiaries of Medicare are even happier). Quickly shifting all these people from private plans into Medicare would be a huge lift. Even the extremely modest dislocations caused by the ACA precipitated a bipartisan scramble to ensure people could keep their current plans, however ill-designed or inadequate. And it's not as if everyone would be cheering the change on: throughout the history of American health insurance, deep-pocketed defenders of the status quo have repeatedly frightened those with private protections that their coverage will be taken away or undermined.

Financing the shift would also be a formidable challenge. We don't know exactly how much a universal Medicare program would cost. But whatever the precise number, there's no way to move a significant share of America's exorbitant spending onto the federal ledger without seriously hiking taxes.[54] To be sure, these taxes would replace private sources of financing, such as premiums. Unfortunately, most well-insured Americans have no idea how much they're now paying. What they see is their portion of their premium and their out-of-pocket spending. What they're actually paying is much greater. It includes the lower wages they receive because they get health benefits instead of cash and all the other hidden ways we finance health care—from the enormous cost of tax breaks for employer-provided health insurance to the higher prices that well-insured patients pay to cover the costs of uninsured and underinsured patients.

In short, immediately expanding Medicare to all Americans would achieve universal health care at a price our nation can afford—but only if we can overcome enormous political and fiscal hurdles. And trying and failing to enact "Medicare for All" might leave us even worse off than we are now. Not only will health reformers have squandered a window of political opportunity; they will also have invited a political backlash that could undermine existing protections.

What's needed, in short, is a step-by-step approach that achieves many of the positive results of Medicare for All yet still has a realistic chance of passage and real potential to move us toward broader and better risk sharing over time. For almost twenty years, I have been advocating such a policy (though, like any idea developed while young, it's required plenty of refinement since then). I call it "Medicare for Everyone," or Medicare Part E for short.

In concept, Medicare Part E is simple. Medicare would be made available—on generous terms—to able-bodied Americans younger than sixty-five. Thus, the centerpiece of Medicare Part E is the same as that of Medicare for All: a guarantee that a single national program is there for everyone. Under my proposal, coverage would be automatic and guaranteed— just as it in every other rich nation, and just as it is for Medicare beneficiaries today. People wouldn't need to go through complicated eligibility processes or hunt down coverage that qualified for public support, and they wouldn't have to re-enroll on an annual basis.

Unlike Medicare for All, however, Medicare Part E wouldn't seek to displace all existing coverage overnight. Instead, it would make Medicare the default source of coverage for everyone, but then allow people to obtain insurance through employment-based insurance and state Medicaid programs if those coverage sources met high (and rising) standards.

To make this work, employers would be given a choice: either provide insurance that was at least as generous as Medicare Part E's or contribute to the cost of Medicare Part E, which would automatically enroll their workers. Health policy wonks call this "play-or-pay." Employers would either *play* by offering qualified coverage to their workers (and their workers' families) or *pay* the federal government to cover their workers (and their workers' families) through Medicare Part E. Those without any direct or family tie to the workforce—a very small share of Americans not already covered by Medicare—could be signed up if and when they visited doctors and hospitals without insurance. Once people were in Medicare

Part E, however, they would remain in it no matter how their circumstancs changed, so long as they didn't have qualified coverage from an employer.

What about those eligible for Medicaid? Though the program has dramatically improved since its establishment—from a marginal program of welfare medicine into the nation's largest insurer—it remains highly variable in quality and breadth from state to state, is facing severe political and fiscal pressures, and pays doctors and hospitals so little that many providers refuse to accept it. The biggest problem is the continuing unwillingness of many Republican-controlled states to expand their programs as envisioned by the Affordable Care Act. But there are also millions of Americans who are eligible for the program but fall through its cracks, deterred by complex and burdensome eligibility rules and the stigma that still attaches to the program.

A basic test for any serious reform plan, therefore, is whether it ensures that all lower-income Americans are automatically enrolled in good health insurance. Medicare Part E meets that test. Once Medicare opened up to all Americans, the federal government would necessarily assume much of the job of guaranteeing enrollment for everyone without employment-based insurance. In practice, this approach could take one of two forms. If state Medicaid programs were left in place, then the federal government would simply facilitate enrollment in them. When lower-income Americans became eligible for Medicare Part E—say, when their employers reported they didn't provide coverage—the federal government would check to see if they qualified for Medicaid. If they did, it would transfer their coverage to the states. States, in turn, would be required to tell the federal government whenever someone's Medicaid coverage lapsed for whatever reason, so they could be covered by Medicare Part E instead.

A second alternative would be to fold Medicaid *into* Medicare (with special protections for its most vulnerable enrollees), which would further reduce the chance that lower-income people fell through the cracks. Merging Medicare and Medicaid would ensure all Americans without employment-based coverage received insurance automatically and on more or less equal terms. But even the first option of federally administered enrollment in state Medicaid programs would address the most serious problem with Medicaid today: that millions who are eligible don't get covered.

In short, opening up Medicare to everyone would deliver what's most inspiring about Medicare for All: guaranteed universal health care. But it would do so without trying to replace all existing insurance in one fell swoop. It would also begin to deliver on Medicare for All's second promise: lower prices. For one, more people covered by Medicare would mean more goods and services financed at Medicare rates (including prescription drugs—the prices of which Medicare should be allowed to negotiate, too). For another, private plans would face competitive pressure to demand better prices so they could keep their private-sector customers.

Indeed, insurers might even gain some leverage. Today, private plans provide insurance to a significant share of Medicare beneficiaries (roughly a third) through what's called Medicare Advantage. These regulated plans actually pay lower prices than do private plans that cover nonelderly Americans, because they can drive a harder bargain. When treating patients covered by Medicare, doctors and hospitals either get what private Medicare Advantage plans pay or they get Medicare's rates, so it's easier for private plans covering these patients to strike a tough deal. If Medicare Advantage plans covered younger Americans, too—and I'd argue they should—then private plans would be able to use the same "take our prices or take Medicare's" argument to drive a better bargain for younger patients as well.

Of course, even with these savings, Medicare Part E would require additional financing. Some of that would come from the contributions that employers make when they choose to "pay" rather than "play" (that is, pay a tax rather than provide insurance themselves). Just as with Medicare today, those enrolled in Medicare Part E would also pay an additional premium that varies by income, with lower-income enrollees paying a minimal amount. The remaining gap could be bridged with a range of sources, such as expanded payroll taxes for traditional Medicare, repeal of costly tax provisions that benefit only high-income Americans, and various "sin" taxes on alcohol, tobacco, and sugary drinks.

Medicare Part E is an ambitious proposal, I realize. Providers, drug manufacturers, and insurers will resist it, and they will surely win some fights. But every step toward a bigger Medicare program increases government's capacity to resist such special pleading in the future. And once in place, Medicare Part E could evolve in different directions, depending on how employers and the federal government fared in controlling costs. If employers came under greater strain, they would have the option of paying the play-or-pay tax to enroll their workers in Medicare Part E. If, however, they improved their ability to control costs, they would be more inclined to provide coverage on their own. Rather than a constant tug-of-war, then, Medicare Part E would create a constructive public-private dynamic that would result in the sector best able to control costs enrolling the largest share of Americans—without the security and care of those citizens held in the balance.

A TIME FOR VISION

Like all the proposals I have laid out, Medicare Part E is a big idea guided by a simple ideal: if you work hard and do right by your families, you shouldn't be insecure. You shouldn't have to depend on the goodwill of your employer, or on jerry-rigged private arrangements that are inadequate, inefficient, and unequal. You shouldn't have to live with crumbling institutions of risk sharing that can no longer carry the load, or struggle with policies grounded in assumptions that are no longer realistic or acceptable. A society that truly believes in economic opportunity must provide economic security, too.

Of course, these changes will not come without costs, and they certainly won't come without struggle. Yet against the costs, one must balance the savings. Billions in hidden taxes are currently imposed by laws that facilitate bankruptcy, mandate emergency-room care, and provide humanitarian relief to families allowed to fall so far that nobody can expect them to get back up on their own. At the same time, hundreds of billions of dollars in indirect spending flow from the federal government to well-off Americans who are already relatively secure. The reduction of these expenses must be accounted for when tallying up the bill, as should the huge drain that our current system imposes when people don't change jobs, don't have kids, don't invest in new skills because they fear the downside risks.

The costs of change are real, but so too are the costs of inaction. The status quo is not politically (or morally) tenable, and insecure citizens are demanding a response. They are not simply willing to "shake it off" and accept the rapid and frequent disruptions endemic to a global knowledge economy. If we do not provide security to increase opportunity, political leaders will find other ways to reassure anxious Americans, including ones that further rend our tattered social contract.

New ideas and proposals are essential, but they are not enough. More than anything else, I hope that the facts and ideas in this book will help spark a broad debate about how we as a nation should deal with the pressing economic risks of the twenty-first century. Today, Americans feel a loss of control over the circumstances that govern and shape their lives, and they are turning inward as a result, taking to heart the clear message of recent trends that they are on their own in the insecure new world of work and family. This is a threat to our nation's future, and to the vision of America that generations of Americans have held dear.

The philosophy behind the reforms that we need is one of constructive change guided by an abiding spirit, the spirit of shared fate. Today, when our fates are often joined more in fear than hope, when our society often seems riven by political and social divisions, it's hard to remember how much we all have in common when it comes to our economic hopes and values. Indeed, we are more linked than ever, because the Great Risk Shift has increasingly reached into the lives of all Americans—from those in the upper middle class such as Lisa Casino-Schuetz to those among the working poor such as David Lamberger. What the ever-present risk of falling from grace reminds us of is that, in a very real sense, all of us are in this together. The Great Risk Shift is not "their" problem; it is our problem, and it is ours to fix.

ACKNOWLEDGMENTS

In writing a book about risk, the big risk is getting lost. Risk appears in an enormous range of places, from the minutia of pension funding to some of the biggest trends in our society. It cuts not just across topics but also across disciplines, touching on political science, sociology, economics, law, psychology, history, policy analysis, and many other fields. Discussions of risk range from the philosophical to the hypertechnical, from the broadest-brush histories to the most fine-grained investigations, from the most public speeches to the most private conversations. Anyone who seeks to take in this huge vista in anything close to its full scope had better have a lot of help.

Fortunately, I have. Pride of place on my long list of able guides goes to the countless people who spoke with me about their own experience as I was writing this book. As I collected these stories (not all of which, I realized with a heavy heart, could make it into print), I was constantly amazed by and grateful for the willingness of people to speak with me about their own often-painful strains. For these Americans, I hope that I have added a sharp cry to the soft chorus of despair embodied in their stories.

Another invaluable source of guidance has been my colleagues, whose generosity provided a heartening reminder that the pursuit of knowledge is, at its best, a cooperative enterprise. So many fine thinkers have shared their work and their insights that I cannot possibly list them all. But I would be remiss if I did not thank the many participants in workshops, seminars, and private conversations who set me on new paths or set me straight. I want to give thanks to George Akerlof, Lily Batchelder, Jared Bernstein, Richard Burkhauser, Karen Dynan, Nicholas Eberstadt, Doug Elmendorf,

Sandy Jencks, Ron Haskins, Ron Kilgard, Jeffrey Liebman, Dean Lillard, Larry Mishel, Mark Rank, and Belle Sawhill for offering helpful guidance or providing me with specific evidence from their own analyses.

Writing this book would not have been possible were it not for the generous support of Yale University. While I was working on the first edition, Yale's Institution for Social and Policy Studies (ISPS) and Center for the Study of American Politics placed research funds at my disposal. I am grateful to Don Green and Alan Gerber for this assistance, as well as to the amazing staff who make ISPS what it is, especially the administrative wizard on whom I most rely, Pam Lamonaca. Now that I direct ISPS myself, I recognize just how rare it is to have an academic institution with the mission of using high-quality social science to inform pressing policy debates. ISPS gives public intellectualism a good name.

Eight thinkers who give public intellectualism a good name also gave the first edition of manuscript a close and conscientious reading, and I want to thank deeply Anne Alstott, Jonathan Cohn, John Langbein, Michael Graetz, Jerry Mashaw, Paul Pierson, Gene Sperling, and Elizabeth Warren. Honesty compels me to admit that they saved me from many errors, but they of course bear no responsibility for any that remain.

In preparing the second edition, I relied heavily on the theoretical insights and methodological skills of Philipp Rehm, a frequent coauthor and good friend whose pioneering work on the politics of economic risk has deeply influenced my own. In addition to partnering with me on a range of writings, Philipp was one of five original members of the Economic Security Index (ESI) project, which was generously supported by the Rockefeller Foundation. Besides Philipp, the ESI project included Gregory Huber, Mark Schlesinger, and Rob Valetta. Later, Austin Nichols joined the team, and we gained the assistance of an up-and-coming young economist, Stuart Craig. Victoria Bilski both managed the project and read and edited the entire first edition of this book. I want to thank all of them for their hard work and deep thinking, which has made this second edition much more encompassing and complete than it could have been otherwise. I also want to thank Janice Nittoli, who, as a program officer at Rockefeller, was the person most responsible for getting the ESI project off the ground. She died in 2017 at the age of fifty-six. Our small project is a tiny part of her legacy, but I like to think it captured her lifelong belief in the ability of policy expertise to improve the lives of working Americans.

Another group of academics also deserves special thanks: the participants in the Social Science Research Council's project on the "Privatization of Risk," which produced several reports as well as a series of books for NYU Press. The founding members of the project—Graciela Chichilnisky, Dalton Conley, Peter Diamond, Melissa Jacoby, William Janeway, Paul Krugman, Leslie McCall, David Moss, Katherine Newman, Robert Shiller, and Elizabeth Warren—represent the ultimate all-star team of public intellectuals (now, in at least one case, *very* public), and each of them has had considerable influence on my thinking. I am grateful to Craig Calhoun, former president of the Social Science Research Council, for envisioning and supporting this project.

I have also been fortunate to have the assistance of a stellar group of researchers. Nigar Nargis started helping me with this project when she was a graduate student at Cornell, and I have benefited from her counsel and friendship ever since. (She is now the chief economist studying tobacco policy at the American Cancer Society.) I also want to express my deep gratitude to Elisabeth Jacobs, who not only helped me in my reanalysis but also forged ahead on her own important work on economic insecurity. My amazing research assistants represent another all-star team: Biruktawit Assefa ("Birdy" to her friends), Marlon Castillo, Mario Chacon, Zahreen Ghaznavi, Annie Harper, Sandy Henderson, Nicole Kazee, Nancy Hite, Zachary Lawrence, Frank Limbrock, Neeraj Patel, Hans Christian Siller, and Alexandra Suich.

This book would not have come into being were it not for the faith and hard work of everyone at Oxford University Press, who believed in this book even when it was just a hazy gleam in my eye. The amazing editor of the first edition, Dedi Felman, was involved in every aspect of this book, and her gentle but insistent questions and skillful but sharp editorial pen have pressed me to produce a book that I hope lives up to her intelligent, exacting standards. My editor on the second edition, David McBride, saw both the potential and the pitfalls of producing a new version of a book about economic insecurity that first appeared prior to the financial crisis. He and his assistant, Emily Mackenzie, have been everything an author could want: thoughtful, responsive, and above all patient. So too has the wonderful production team for the second edition, including Liz Davey, Holly Mitchell, and Narmada Thangavelu.

My agent, Sydelle Kramer, deserves a special thanks. She didn't just help me figure out what I wanted to do with this book and guide me as I went; she also taught me almost everything I know about the world of publishing.

My greatest debt, as always, goes to my family. My wife, Oona Hathaway, has been my best friend and my most trusted guide for all of my adult life (amazingly, she saw potential in the seventeen-year-old version of me). So it is understandable why I can't fathom a world in which she isn't there helping me and teaching me and lifting me up. She has shaped who I am in the deepest sense, and I treasure what we have created together—above all, the two young lives sharing her beauty, intelligence, and humanity: Ava and Owen Hathaway Hacker.

Finally, I dedicate this book to my parents, Thomas and Margaret Hacker, who taught me the value of both love and learning, and to my mother-in-law, Anneke Hathaway, whose unfailing support has made it possible for me to be a husband, father, *and* scholar.

NOTES

Introduction: On the Edge

1. Jacob S. Hacker, "Call It the Family Risk Factor," *New York Times,* January 11, 2004, sec. 4, 15. These estimates, like the other calculations based on the Panel Study of Income Dynamics (PSID) that appear in chapter 1, were carried out in cooperation with Philipp Rehm, Nigar Nargis, Elisabeth Jacobs, Frank Limbrock, Nancy Hite, and Mario Chacon.

   Figure I.1 differs somewhat in presentation and content from the one that appeared in *The Times,* though not in basic substance or conclusion. First, the analysis is updated through 2014. Second, to avoid some apparent data inconsistencies that have become apparent in the Cross-National Equivalent File (CNEF) prepared by researchers at Cornell University from the PSID—which I used to obtain estimates of post-tax family income in my previous estimates—I have shifted to using only the PSID's own reported data, which does not consistently include information on taxes. Hence, all these analyses look only at *pretax* family income. Third, I have made some changes to the data analysis as described in note 27 to chapter 1 to deal with some apparent underreporting of family income in the early 1990s. Finally, to make the results more intelligible, I have switched to showing the *percentage increase* in volatility since the baseline year of 1972, rather than the raw volatility levels (expressed in terms of variance of log income). For a further description of the model used to calculate transitory variance of family income, as well as a comprehensive review of research on income and earnings volatility prior to 2008, see Jacob S. Hacker and Elisabeth Jacobs, "The Rising Instability of American Family Incomes, 1969–2004: Evidence from the Panel Study of Income Dynamics," Economic Policy Institute Briefing Paper #213, May 28, 2008, available online at https://www.epi.org/publication/bp213/.

2. For a thoughtful analysis of the ways in which advocates of public insurance constructed a link between natural and economic disasters, see Michele L. Landis, "Fate, Responsibility, and 'Natural' Disaster Relief; Narrating the American Welfare State," *Law & Society Review* 33:2 (1999): 257–318.

3. Franklin D. Roosevelt, "Second Inaugural Address," *Inaugural Addresses of the Presidents* (Washington, DC: U.S. Government Printing Office, 1989).

4. J. Bradford DeLong, "The Greater Depression," *Project Syndicate*, August 28, 2014, available online at https://www.project-syndicate.org/commentary/j--bradford-delong-argues-that-it-is-time-to-call-what-is-happening-in-europe-and-the-us-by-its-true-name.
5. Edward N. Wolff, "The Asset Price Meltdown and the Wealth of the Middle Class," *US2010 Project*, May 2013, available online at https://s4.ad.brown.edu/Projects/Diversity/Data/Report/report05012013.pdf.
6. Jacob S. Hacker et al., "The Economic Security Index: A New Measure for Research and Policy Analysis," *Review of Income and Wealth* 60:51 (May 2014): S5–S32.
7. Jacob S. Hacker, Philipp Rehm, and Mark Schlesinger, "The Insecure American: Economic Experiences, Financial Worries, and Policy Attitudes," *Perspectives on Politics* 11:1 (2013): 23–49.
8. Jacob S. Hacker, *The Divided Welfare State: The Battle over Public and Private Social Benefits in the United States* (New York: Cambridge University Press, 2002), 14–15.

Chapter 1

1. Calculated using data supplement to Congressional Budget Office, "The Distribution of Household Income and Federal Taxes, 2013," June 2016, available online at http://cbo.gov/publication/51361. "Middle class" is defined here as the middle three quintiles of the household income distribution.
2. American Bankruptcy Institute, "Annual Business and Non-business Filings by Year (1980–2017)," available online at http://www.abi.org/newsroom/bankruptcy-statistics. The numbers here are for non-business filings, which have risen as a share of total filings from 87 percent in 1980 to 97 percent in 2017.
3. Elizabeth Warren, "Financial Collapse and Class Status: Who Goes Bankrupt?" *Osgoode Hall Law Journal* 41:1 (2003): 115–46.
4. Calculated from Peter J. Elmer and Steven A. Seelig, "The Rising Long-Term Trend of Single-Family Mortgage Foreclosure Rates" (Federal Deposit Insurance Corporation Working Paper 98-2, n.d.), available online at www.fdic.gov/bank/analytical/working/98-2.pdf. Supplemented with data from U.S. Census Bureau, *Statistical Abstract of the United States: 2007* (Washington, DC: Census Bureau, 2007), 742.
5. Christian E. Weller, *Middle-Class Turmoil: High Risks Reflect Middle-Class Anxieties* (Washington, DC: Center for American Progress, December 2005), available online at https://www.americanprogress.org/issues/economy/news/2005/12/20/1742/middle-class-turmoil-high-risks-reflect-middle-class-anxieties/.
6. Janine Aron and John Muellbauer, "Modelling and Forecasting Mortgage Delinquency and Foreclosure in the UK," *VoxEU*, August 31, 2016, available online at https://voxeu.org/article/mortgage-delinquency-and-foreclosure-uk.
7. Suzette Hackney, "Michigan Families Struggling with Foreclosure," *Chicago Tribune*, October 23, 2005, available online at https://www.chicagotribune.com/news/ct-xpm-2005-10-23-0510230331-story.html.
8. Remarks by Julie L. Williams, Acting Comptroller of the Currency, New York, NY, May 3, 2005, available online at https://www.occ.treas.gov/news-issuances/speeches/2005/pub-speech-2005-44.pdf.

9. Matthew Desmond, *Evicted: Poverty and Profit in the American City* (New York: Crown, 2016); data are from https://evictionlab.org/help-faq/#us-stats.

10. *Americans at Risk: One in Three Uninsured* (Washington, DC: Families USA Foundation, 2009).

11. *The Newshour with Jim Lehrer*, "Coping without Health Insurance," November 28, 2005, available online at http://pbs.org/newshour/bb/health/july-dec05/insurance_ll-28.html.

12. Kaiser Family Foundation, "Key Facts about the Uninsured Population," November 29, 2017, available online at https://www.kff.org/uninsured/fact-sheet/key-facts-about-the-uninsured-population/.

13. Employee Benefits Research Institute, *EBRI Databook on Employe Benefits* (Washington, D.C.: EBRI, October 2015), Chap. 5.

14. Alicia H. Munnell, Anthony Webb, and Francesca Golub-Sass, *The National Retirement Risk Index: An Update* (Boston: Boston College Center for Retirement Research, October 2012), availableonline at http://crr.bc.edu/wp-content/uploads/2012/11/IB_12-20-508.pdf. See also Alicia H. Munnell, Wenliang Hou, and Anthony Webb, *NRRI Update Shows Half Still Falling Short* (Boston: Boston College Center for Retirement Research, December 2014), available online at http://crr.bc.edu/wp-content/uploads/2014/12/IB_14-20-508.pdf.

15. Pew Charitable Trusts, "The Precarious State of Family Balance Sheets," January 2015, available online at http://www.pewtrusts.org/~/media/assets/2015/01/fsm_balance_sheet_report.pdf.

16. Raj Chetty et al., "The Fading American Dream: Trends in Absolute Income Mobility since 1940," *Science* 24 (April 2017), available online at http://science.sciencemag.org/content/early/2017/04/21/science.aal4617/tab-pdf.

17. Hackney, "Families Fight for Their Homes."

18. This is the core theme of Ulrich Beck, *Risk Society: Towards a New Modernity*, trans. Mark Ritter (London: Sage, 1992).

19. Thomas Piketty, Emmanuel Saez, and Gabriel Zucman, "Distributional National Accounts: Methods and Estimates for the United States," *Quarterly Journal of Economics* 133:2 (May 2018): 553–609.

20. Katherine McGonagle and Narayan Sastry, "Using the Panel Study of Income Dynamics to Analyze Housing Decisions, Dynamics, and Effects," *Cityscape* 18:1 (2016): 185.

21. The PSID contains several survey groups, most notably, an original sample that was chosen to be nationally representative (but has become less so over time) and a supplementary sample of low-income respondents. I aggregate these samples and weight the analyses to ensure representative results. To avoid confusion, I label the results according to the year for which family income is reported, which is one year prior to the year the survey was conducted. So the survey conducted in 2015—the most recent survey year—is reported as 2014 data, as it measures 2014 incomes.

    The main measure used throughout this chapter is total pretax family income, defined as the sum of labor income, asset income, and public and private transfer income—for example, government cash benefits and alimony—for all members of a family. Unless otherwise noted, family income is adjusted for family size by dividing by the square root of family size, a common equivalence scale, reflecting the lesser costs per person of maintaining a larger family. I adjust for inflation using the Consumer Price Index for urban consumers, and drop people younger than 25 and older than 61 from the analysis, so as to leave out college students and retirees.

Since I completed the first hardcover edition of this book, some problems have come to light with the PSID's income measures, concentrated in the 1990s. During roughly five years in the early to mid-1990s, the lowest income categories in the PSID report lower incomes than seen in other data sets and the overall variance of family income jumps. Because these problems appear to be limited to the early to mid-1990s, they do not affect my estimates of how much income instability has risen from the late 1960s to the early 2000s. Nonetheless, in the analyses of volatility to follow, I correct for the potential underreporting of income in two ways. First, I drop all observations with family income of $1 or less—the lowest level recorded for much of the PSID's history (reported income can be lower than zero when families suffer business losses). Second, I trim an additional two percentiles of the income distribution from the bottom and top of the remaining observations. This not only brings the PSID income distribution closely in line with that of other respected datasets, but it also has the effect of eliminating concern about the inconsistent treatment of very high incomes in the PSID.

It is important to emphasize that the data issues just mentioned are quite limited in both duration (the early to mid-1990s) and scope (a relatively small number of cases in a huge data set). The PSID remains the sole income series that allows for the analysis of long-term income dynamics across a sample of the entire U.S. population over the full span of the last generation. My own detailed benchmarking tests suggest that except for the rise in low-income observations in the early 1990s that I seek to address in my estimates, the PSID tracks closely the Census Bureau's March Current Population Survey (CPS), which relies on larger samples than the PSID and is generally considered highly reliable for analysis of all but the highest-income Americans. My findings are also consistent with other recent analyses that use the PSID, including Peter Gottschalk and Robert Moffitt, "The Rising Instability of US Earnings," *Journal of Economic Perspectives* 23:4 (2009): 3–24; and Olga Gorbachev, "Did Household Consumption Become More Volatile?" *The American Economic Review* 101:5 (2011): 2248–70, available online at https://www.aeaweb.org/articles?id=10.1257/aer.101.5.2248. The latter finds not just that income volatility increased, but that so too has the unexplained instability of household spending—with "consumption volatility" rising most sharply among those with little or no household wealth to draw on during income downturns.

Although the PSID data are the gold standard for long-term longitudinal analysis of income, other data sources can supplement and refine its findings. As part of the Economic Security Index project, which I headed, my research team analyzed trends in the Survey of Income and Program Participation (SIPP), a series of short panels that begins in the mid-1980s. One virtue of the SIPP is that it tracks income on a monthly, rather than annual, basis, so it is much better suited to analyses of *short-term* income volatility than the PSID. What these analyses have found is that income has become highly variable from month to month for many workers. For example, one study found that three out of five prime earners (the highest-earning worker within a household) experienced at least one drop of 50 percent or more in their month-to-month earnings between 2008 and 2013, and that instability was greatest for workers in contingent arrangements, such as freelance jobs, platform work such as driving for Uber, and temporary employment. Andrew Stettner, Michael Cassidy, and George Wentworth, "A New Safety Net for An Era of Unstable Earnings," The Century Foundation, December 15, 2016, available online at https://tcf.org/content/report/new-safety-net-for-an-era-of-unstable-earnings. Similar findings have emerged from the "Financial Diaries Project," an intensive study of the financial lives of roughly 230 families in select communities in Ohio, Kentucky, California, Mississippi, and New York. Though not necessarily nationally representative, the Diaries provide a unique and valuable look at the interaction among income, spending, work, and family changes among families of diverse economic and demographic characteristics—and find, once again, enormous instability for even solidly middle-class households. Jonathan Morduch and Rachel Schneider, *The Financial Diaries: How American Families Cope in a World of Uncertainty* (Princeton, NJ: Princeton University Press, 2017).

In addition to the SIPP, my research team and I looked at patterns of year-to-year income drops in the CPS, matching observations across two-year intervals. Although the CPS is not a true panel data set, it recontacts roughly half of households and thus can be used for two-year analyses through statistical matching of households that do not move between surveys. Matching is imperfect, however, and only households that do not move are included, biasing the sample. Although weights can be used to make the sample demographically representative, they obviously cannot control for the unobserved differences between households that move and those that do not.

In any case, we found nearly identical patterns of income instability across the PSID, the SIPP, and the matched CPS data (see Jacob S. Hacker et al., "The Economic Security Index: A New Measure for Research and Policy Analysis," *Review of Income and Wealth* 60 (2014): S5–S32, available online at http://www.roiw.org/2014/s1/s2.pdf). The best available panel surveys of income all show a marked rise in the volatility of American family incomes.

Finally, in addition to panel surveys, *administrative* data also hold promise for examining income instability. Such data—collected in the course of enumerating, regulating, taxing, or providing benefits to people—have become much more common in economic analyses in the last decade, though use of them for examining household income volatility has been limited. Administrative data are often considered more accurate than survey-based data. But because obtaining and maintaining a representative sample over time and ensuring a full and consistent definition of income are so fundamental to analyses of income instability, administrative data may not be superior to panel data for volatility studies, especially when these data are based on tax filings or other public reporting that may themselves be restricted in the scope of the population covered and the types of income reported. That said, a 2013 study using tax data finds a 15 percent increase in "transitory variance" of household income between 1989 and 2007, though it notably fails to include self-employment income and cannot, by design, include those who do not file tax returns. Jason Debacker et al. "Rising Inequality: Transitory or Persistent? New Evidence from a Panel of U.S. Tax Returns," *Brookings Papers on Economic Activity* (Spring 2013): 67–142.

Another source of administrative data comes from commercial sources, such as AC Nielsen and JP Morgan Chase. These sources have the advantage that they can look at both income and spending patterns, often at very high levels of granularity. These data sets are limited to recent periods, however, and they cannot by definition include the unbanked or those whose transactions are not handled by the financial institution collecting the data. Diana Farrell and Fiona Greig, "Paychecks, Paydays, and the Online Platform Economy: Big Data on Income Volatility," JP Morgan Chase, February 2016, available online at https://www.jpmorganchase.com/corporate/institute/document/jpmc-institute-volatility-2-report.pdf; and "Coping with Costs: Big Data on Expense Volatility and Medical Payments," February 2017, available online at https://www.jpmorganchase.com/corporate/institute/document/institute-coping-with-costs-report.pdf.

22. The precise number is 43 percent (lowest income as a percentage of highest income). Like all the other figures and tables reported in this chapter, these numbers follow the real, weighted, family-size-adjusted family incomes of individuals aged 25–61. As in my other analyses, I drop observations with income of less than $1 and trim 2 percent of observations from both the top and bottom of the distribution to reduce the effect of outliers. Because of the PSID's switch to a biennial survey in 1997, which may skew comparisons of ten-year intervals between earlier and later periods due to the differing number of observations, the ratio is calculated for the ten-year window ending in 1997, including only individuals who appear at least four times in this ten-year interval.

23. See, for example, Andrew J. Rettenmaier and Donald R. Deere, "Climbing the Economic Ladder" (Washington, DC: The National Center for Policy Analysis, 2003), 17–18. Though the overall tone of the report is cheerful, a closer look at the data tells a less sunny story. While in a given year almost half of people in the middle three quintiles are likely to move to a different quintile, they are more likely to move to the quartile below the one they're in than to the one above. Those in the bottom quartile, who by definition cannot fall to a lower quartile, are much less likely to move. Only 31 percent are likely to change quartiles, and most of these move up by only a single quartile.

24. "Ever Higher, Ever Harder to Ascend," *Economist,* December 29, 2004, available online at http://www.economist.com/world/na/displayStory.cfm?story_id=3518560.

25. Miles Corak, "Income Inequality, Equality of Opportunity, and Intergenerational Mobility," *Journal of Economic Perspectives* 27:3 (Summer 2013), 79–102; Raj Chetty, "Improving Opportunities for Economic Mobility: New Evidence and Policy Lessons," *St. Louis Fed,* 2016, available online at https://www.stlouisfed.org/

~/media/files/pdfs/community-development/econmobilitypapers/section1/
econmobility_1-1chetty_508.pdf.

26. Raj Chetty, et al. "The Fading American Dream: Trends in Absolute Income Mobility since 1940," *Science* 356:6336 (2017): 398-406.

27. Daniel Kahneman and Amos Tversky, "Prospect Theory: An Analysis of Decisions under Risk," *Econometrica* 47:2 (1979): 263–91.

28. Organization for Economic Cooperation and Development (OECD), "Social Expenditure Update 2016: Social Spending Stays at Historically High Levels in Most OECD Countries" (Paris: OECD, October 2016), available online at http://www.oecd.org/els/soc/OECD2016-Social-Expenditure-Update.pdf.

29. Pew Charitable Trusts, *Americans' Financial Security: Perception and Reality* (Philadelphia: Pew, March 5, 2015), available online at https://www.pewtrusts.org/en/research-and-analysis/issue-briefs/2015/02/americans-financial-security-perceptions-and-reality.

30. International Labor Office (ILO), *Economic Security for a Better World* (Washington, DC: ILO, 2004).

31. For a description of the model used to calculate over-time income variance, see Robert A. Moffitt and Peter Gottschalk, "Trends in the Transitory Variance of Earnings in the United States," *Economic Journal* 112 (March 2002): 68–73. An alternative approach is to examine some measure of the dispersion of percentage changes in income over short periods of time, such as the standard deviation of percentage changes in family income from one year to the next or one year to two years later. This approach cannot distinguish between persistent and short-term changes. Nor does it exploit the long-term panel structure of the PSID data— the fact that we can look at income dynamics across multiple years, not just two. Nonetheless, the technique chosen does not change the finding of rising income volatility, which is highly robust to alternative models. In particular, Karen Dynan, Douglas Elmendorf, and Daniel Sichel ("The Evolution of Household Income Volatility," *The B.E. Journal of Economic Analysis & Policy* 12:2 (2012), available online at https://www.degruyter.com/view/j/bejeap.2012.12.issue-2/1935-1682.3347/1935-1682.3347.xml) look at the standard deviation of percentage changes and also finds a notable increase in family income volatility. The Dynan, Elmendorf, and Sichel analysis does find a smaller increase in volatility than I do over the period we both analyze. But this likely reflects their different definition of volatility as well as defensible but debatable analytic choices that the authors make that have the effect of reducing the trend—for example, their decision to use only the original non-low-income sample of the PSID. The authors also provide a trenchant discussion of the shortcomings of combining survey and administrative data as an alternative to the PSID, noting the risks of incomplete matching (when a person in one dataset can't be reliably identified in another and thus gets dropped). I would go further. Analyses that include only those whose data are most complete and continuous are most likely to *exclude* those who experience instability.

32. Not surprisingly, volatility is also higher for lower-income Americans. For a smart discussion of the implications of this for tax policy, see Lily Batchelder, "Taxing

the Poor: Income Averaging Reconsidered," *Harvard Journal on Legislation* 40 (2003): 395–452.

33. Elmer and Seelig, "The Rising Long-Term Trend of Single-Family Mortgage Foreclosure Rates," 31.

34. All my volatility results are based on analyses that transform income so that it is what statisticians call "mean-independent." This is just a fancy way of saying that the level of a family's income doesn't directly affect the measure of volatility. Take two families—each of whose income drops by 20 percent between two years. If family one has twice the income as family two, that 20 percent drop is going to be twice as large in dollar terms, even though the two families are experiencing exactly the same size change relative to their prior income. Using mean-independent measures fixes that, making it possible to compare volatility across people with different income levels and across years with different average income levels. All these analyses also use inflation-adjusted dollars, so year-to-year changes in the inflation rate don't show up as instability either.

35. Katherine S. Newman, *Falling from Grace: The Experience of Downward Mobility in the American Middle Class* (New York: Free Press, 1988).

36. As in all the analyses, I focus on the family-size-adjusted household income of individuals aged 25 to 61, aggregate the main PSID samples and weight accordingly, drop observations with income values less than $1, and trim an additional 2 percent from the top and bottom of the income distribution. Because the PSID switched to a biennial survey in 1997, these drops are measured by comparing income in a given year with its level two years prior. The PSID's first wave was in 1968 (surveying 1967 income), so the first year for which a measure of income drops is available is 1969 (1967–1969). For these calculations, the "early 1970s" is defined as 1967–1969, 1969–1971, and 1970–1972; the "early 2010s" is defined as 2008–2010 and 2010–2012.

37. U.S. Department of Health and Human Services 2018 Poverty Guidelines, available online at http://aspe.hhs.gov/poverty-guidelines.

38. Mark Rank, *One Nation, Underprivileged: Why American Poverty Affects Us All* (New York: Oxford University Press, 2004), 94.

39. UNICEF, *Child Well-Being in Rich Countries* (UNICEF Office of Research: Florence, 2013), 7, available online at https://www.unicef-irc.org/publications/pdf/rc11_eng.pdf; this analysis defines children as living in poverty when their family-size-adjusted incomes are less than 50 percent of the national median income.

40. Caroline Ratcliffe, "Child Poverty and Adult Success," Urban Institute, September 15, 2015, available online at https://www.urban.org/sites/default/files/publication/65766/2000369-Child-Poverty-and-Adult-Success.pdf.

41. Mark R. Rank and Thomas A. Hirschl, "The Likelihood of Experiencing Relative Poverty over the Life Course," *PLoS ONE* 10:7 (2015): e0133513.

42. Daniel Sandoval, Mark R. Rank, and Thomas A. Hirschl, "The Increasing Risk of Poverty across the American Life Course," *Demography* 46:4 (2009): 717–37.

Chapter 2

1. Economic Policy Institute, *State of Working America Data Library*, "Health Insurance Coverage," 2018 (data for 2016), available online at https://www.epi.org/data; Kaiser Family Foundation, "2016 Employer Health Benefits Survey," September

14, 2016, 6, available online at http://files.kff.org/attachment/Report-Employer-Health-Benefits-2016-Annual-Survey.

2. Kaiser Family Foundation, "2016 Employer Health Benefits Survey," 75, Cybele Weisser, "A Health Revolution in Slo-Mo," *Money* 34:7 (July 2005): 28.

3. White House Press Release, "President Signs Bankruptcy Abuse Prevention, Consumer Protection Act," April 20, 2005, available online at https://georgewbush-whitehouse.archives.gov/news/releases/2005/04/20050420-5.html.

4. Department of the Treasury, "Health Savings Accounts Frequently Asked Questions," downloaded from www.treasury.gov 2005.

5. "Santelli's Rant Heard Round the World," *CNBC*, March 2, 2016. Video available at https://youtu.be/bEZB4taSEoA.

6. Christopher S. Parker and Matt A. Barreto, *Change They Can't Believe In: The Tea Party and Reactionary Politics in America* (Princeton, NJ: Princeton University Press, 2013), 1.

7. David Korn, "Secret Video: Romney Tells Millionaire Donors What He REALLY Thinks of Obama Voters," Mother Jones Blog, September 17, 2012, http://www.motherjones.com/politics/2012/09/secret-video-romney-private-fundraiser.

8. Brian Beutler, "Joni Ernst: Poor People Aren't Entitled to Food, Clothing, or Health Care," *The New Republic*, October 17, 2014, available online at https://newrepublic.com/article/119892/ernst-health-care-food-clothes-too-generous-poor.

9. Derek Thompson, "The Worst Part of Paul Ryan's Budget," *Atlantic*, March 21, 2012, available online at http://www.theatlantic.com/business/archive/2012/03/the-worst-part-of-paul-ryans-budget/254845/

10. Arthur Delaney and Michael McAuliff, "Paul Ryan Wants 'Welfare Reform Round 2,'" *Huffington Post*, March 20, 2012, https://www.huffingtonpost.com/2012/03/20/paul-ryan-welfare-reform_n_1368277.html.

11. "House Speaker Weekly Briefing," *C-Span*, March 9, 2017, available online at https://www.c-span.org/video/?425131-1/speaker-ryan-explains-gop-health-care-plan-amid-growing-opposition.

12. Peter H. Wehner, "Some Thoughts on Social Security," January 3, 2005, available online at https://www.wsj.com/articles/SB110496995612018199.

13. Matthew Yglesias, "Paul Ryan Says He's Been 'Dreaming' of Medicaid Cuts since He Was 'Drinking out of Kegs,'" *Vox*, March 17, 2017, available online at https://www.vox.com/policy-and-politics/2017/3/17/14960358/paul-ryan-medicaid-keg.

14. Edwin E. Witte, *The Development of the Social Security Act* (Madison: University of Wisconsin Press, 1962), 21.

15. Ibid., 96.

16. Jacob S. Hacker, *The Divided Welfare State* (New York: Cambridge University Press, 2002); Robert Lieberman, *Shifting the Color Line: Race and the American Welfare State* (Cambridge, MA: Harvard University Press, 1998); Paul Starr, *The Social Transformation of American Medicine* (New York: Basic Books, 1982); Bartholomew H. Sparrow, *From the Outside In* (Princeton, NJ: Princeton University Press, 1996).

17. Roy Lubove, *The Struggle for Social Security* (Cambridge, MA: Harvard University Press, 1968), 174.

18. David Moss, *When All Else Fails: Government as the Ultimate Risk Manager* (Cambridge, MA: Harvard University Press), chaps. 3–5.

19. Franklin Roosevelt, "A Social Security Program Must Include All Those Who Need Its Protection," August 15, 1938, available online at https://www.ssa.gov/history/fdrstmts.html.

20. Ibid.

21. Franklin D. Roosevelt, "Message to Congress on Social Security," January 17, 1935, available online at http.ssa.gov/history/fdrstmts.html.

22. Michael K. Brown, *Race, Money, and the American Welfare State* (Ithaca, NY: Cornell University Press, 1999); Colin Gordon, *Dead on Arrival: The Politics of Health Care in Twentieth-Century America* (Princeton, NJ: Princeton University Press, 2003); Hacker, *Divided Welfare State;* Jennifer Klein, *For All These Rights: Business, Labor, and the Shaping of America's Public-Private Welfare State* (Princeton, NJ: Princeton University Press, 2003).

23. Thomas Hopkinson Elliot, interview, *Social Security Administration Project,* pt. 3, no. 154, tape recorded in 1965 (New York: Columbia University Oral History Collection, 1976), 51–52. Elliot was the key Roosevelt lawyer charged with working out an acceptable compromise regarding the opt-out proposal after the Social Security Act passed.

24. Hacker, *Divided Welfare State,* 214.

25. Fredric R. Heidinger, *The Social Role of Blue Cross as a Device for Financing the Costs of Hospital Care: An Evaluation* (Iowa City: Graduate Program in Hospital and Health Administration, University of Iowa, 1966), 20–21.

26. Gordon, *Dead on Arrival,* 76.

27. Jacoby, *Modern Manors,* 57.

28. Marion B. Folsom, *Social Administration Project,* part 3, no. 158, tape recorded in 1965 (New York: Columbia University Oral History Collection, 1976).

29. Hacker, *Divided Welfare State,* 142.

30. Tom Baker, "On the Genealogy of Moral Hazard," *Texas Law Review* 75: 2 (1996): 237–93.

31. Kenneth J. Arrow, "Uncertainty and the Welfare Economics of Medical Care," *American Economic Review* 53 (1963): 941–73.

32. Ibid., 961.

33. John Nyman, University of Minnesota health economist, quoted in Malcolm Gladwell, "The Moral-Hazard Myth," *New Yorker,* August 29, 2005, available online at https://www.newyorker.com/magazine/2005/08/29/the-moral-hazard-myth.

34. Mark V. Pauly, "The Economics of Moral Hazard: Comment" *American Economic Review* 58:1 (June 1968): 531–37.

35. See, for example, Martin S. Feldstein, "An Econometric Model of the Medicare System," *Quarterly Journal of Economics* 85:1 (February 1971): 1–20; "The Welfare Loss of Excess Health Insurance," *Journal of Political Economy* 8:2 (March–April 1973):251–80 "Economics of the New Unemployment," *Public Interest* 33 (Fall 1973): 3–42; "Social Security and Private Savings: Reply to Barro," *Journal of Political Economy* 90:3 (June 1982): 630–42.

36. This is a core theme of Mark A. Smith, *The Right Talk: How Conservatives Transformed the Great Society into the Economic Society* (Princeton, NJ: Princeton University Press, 2007).

37. Ronald Reagan, "First Inaugural Address," January 20, 1981, Ronald Reagan Presidential Foundation and Library, available online at https://www.reagan-foundation.org/ronald-reagan/reagan-quotes-speeches/inaugural-address/.

38. George L. Priest, "Rethinking the New Deal: The Role of the Government as an Insurer," *AEI Bradley Lecture Series,* February 12, 1996, available online at http://www.aei.org/publication/rethinking-the-new-deal/.

39. Charles Murray, *Losing Ground: American Social Policy, 1950–1980* (New York: Basic Books, 1994), 212.

40. The details about Reagan and his budget director and the *Times* quote are from Jonathan Chait, "Feast of the Wingnuts," *New Republic,* September 10, 2007, 29.

41. George Gilder, *Wealth and Poverty* (New York: Basic Books, 1981), 157.

42. Quoted in Baker, "On the Genealogy of Moral Hazard," 238.

43. Yascha Mounk, *The Age of Responsibility: Luck, Choice, and the Welfare State* (Cambridge, MA: Harvard University Press, 2017), 3.

44. The term is from Stuart Butler and Peter Germanis's blueprint for privatizing Social Security (discussed in chapter 5), "Achieving a 'Leninist' Strategy," *Cato Journal* 3:2 (Fall 1993): 547–56.

45. Stuart Butler, *Privatizing Federal Spending: A Strategy to Reduce the Deficit* (New York: Universe Books, 1985). See also the perceptive analysis of Steve Teles and Martha Derthick, "From Third Rail to Presidential Commitment—And Back? The Conservative Campaign for Social Security Privatization and the Limits of Long-Term Political Strategy" (paper prepared for Conference on Conservatives and American Political Development, Institution for Social and Policy Studies, Yale University, February 24, 2006).

46. Interview with Stuart Butler, Vice President for Domestic and Economic Policy, The Heritage Foundation, May 11, 2006.

47. James K. Glassman, "A Nation of Citizen Investors," *American Enterprise,* March 2005, available online at http://archives.evergreen.edu/webpages/curricular/2005-2006/nola/CitizenInvestors.pef.pdf.

48. Grover Norquist, "Ownership Can Be Revolutionary," *American Enterprise,* March 2005, available online at http://archives.evergreen.edu/webpages/curricular/2005-2006/nola/OwnershipRevolutionary.pdf.

49. Americans are "operational liberals" and "philosophical conservatives," public opinion analysts Lloyd Free and Hadley Cantril famously argued in their *The Political Beliefs of Americans* (New Brunswick, NJ: Rutgers University Press, 1967). Americans are skeptical of government in the abstract, yet they embrace specific public programs of social protection for workers with genuine enthusiasm. For more recent assessments, which reach the same basic conclusion, see Fay Lomax Cook and Edith J. Barrett, *Support for the American Welfare State* (New York: Columbia University Press, 1992); and Stanley Feldman and John Zaller, "The Political Culture of Ambivalence: Ideological Responses to the Welfare State," *American Journal of Political Science* 36:1 (February 1992): 268–307.

50. "I am sure," wrote one journalistic wag, "these Americans will be grateful to Paul Ryan for giving them the opportunity to make such a liberating choice." Jordan Weissmann, "Paul Ryan Says It's Fine if 22 Million Americans 'Choose' Not to

Buy Health Care," June 27, 2017, available online at http://www.slate.com/blogs/moneybox/2017/06/27/paul_ryan_says_it_s_fine_if_22_million_americans_choose_not_to_buy_health.html.

51. Julie Appleby, "Health Accounts Would Eat Up Savings," *USA Today,* February 6, 2006, 4A.
52. University of Minnesota, Office of Human Resources, "Medical Plan Description," 2006.
53. Amy Goldstein, "Uncertain Cure: Early Reaction to Health Savings Account Is Two-Sided," *Washington Post,* March 12, 2006, Fl.

Chapter 3

1. Timothy Egan, "No Degree, and No Way Back to the Middle," *New York Times,* May 24, 2005, available online at http://www.nytimes.com/2005/05/24/national/class/BLUECOLLAR-FINAL.html.
2. Nicky Woolf, "Over 50 and Once Successful, Jobless Americans Seek Support Groups to Help Where Congress Has Failed," *The Guardian,* November 7, 2014, available online at https://www.theguardian.com/money/2014/nov/07/long-term-unemployed-support-groups-congress.
3. Egan, "No Degree, and No Way Back to the Middle."
4. "The Productivity-Pay Gap," *Economic Policy Institute,* October 2017, available online at https://www.epi.org/productivity-pay-gap; see also Ian Dew-Becker and Robert J. Gordon, "Where Did the Productivity Growth Go? Inflation Dynamics and the Distribution of Income," NBER Working Paper No. 11842 (Cambridge, MA: National Bureau of Economic Research, December 2005), available online at http://www.nber.org/papers/wll842.pdf.
5. For recent overviews, see Pew Research Center, "The State of American Jobs," Pew Research Center, October 16, 2016, available online at http://www.pewsocialtrends.org/2016/10/06/the-state-of-american-jobs/; Ben Casselman, "Manufacturing Jobs Are Never Coming Back," *FiveThirtyEight,* March 18, 2018, available online at https://fivethirtyeight.com/features/manufacturing-jobs-are-never-coming-back/; and Casselman, "Americans Don't Miss Manufacturing—They Miss Unions," *FiveThirtyEight,* May 13, 2016, available online at https://fivethirtyeight.com/features/americans-dont-miss-manufacturing-they-miss-unions/; Kevin Clarke, "The Decline of Unions Is Part of a Bad 50 Years for American Workers," *America,* September 4, 2017, available online at https://www.americamagazine.org/politics-society/2017/08/23/decline-unions-part-bad-50-years-american-workers.
6. Diego Comin, Erica L. Groshen, and Bess Rabin, "Turbulent Firms, Turbulent Wages?" *Journal of Monetary Economics,* 56:1 (2009): 127.
7. Gene Sperling, *The Pro-Growth Progressive: An Economic Strategy for Shared Prosperity* (New York: Simon and Schuster, 2005), 7.
8. Peter Cappelli, *The New Deal at Work: Managing the Market-Driven Workforce* (Cambridge, MA: Harvard Business School Press, 1999), 25–26.
9. Ibid., 2–3.

10. Noah Smith, "Uber Better Not Be the Future of Work," *Bloomberg*, March 8, 2018, available online at https://www.bloomberg.com/view/articles/2018-03-08/uber-drivers-earn-pay-that-s-just-above-the-poverty-line.

11. Lydia DePillis, "Seattle Might Try Something Crazy to Let Uber Drivers Unionize," *Washington Post*, August 31, 2015, available online at https://www.washingtonpost.com/news/wonk/wp/2015/08/31/seattle-might-try-something-crazy-to-let-uber-drivers-unionize/; Laurie Penny, "Every Time We Take an Uber We're Spreading Its Social Poison," *The Guardian*, March 3, 2017, available online at https://www.theguardian.com/commentisfree/2017/mar/03/uber-spreading-social-poison-travis-kalanick

12. Peter Cappelli, "Examining the Incidence of Downsizing and Its Effects on Establishment Performance," NBER Working Paper 7742 (Cambridge, MA: National Bureau of Economic Research, June 2000), available online at http://www.nber.org/papers/w7742.

13. Henry S. Faber, "Employment, Hours, and Earnings Consequences of Job Loss: US Evidence from the Displaced Workers Survey," *Journal of Labor Economics* 35.S1 (2017): S235–S272, available online at https://www.journals.uchicago.edu/doi/10.1086/692353.

14. Henry S. Farber, "What Do We Know about Job Loss in the United States?" Federal Reserve Bank of Chicago, *Economic Perspectives* 2Q (2005): 13–27, available online at http://www.chicagofed.org/publications/publications/economic-perspectives/2005/2qtr2005_part2_farber.pdf. These are difference-in-difference estimates of earnings loss that compare changes in displaced workers earnings with changes in the earnings of workers who are not displaced.

15. For a good analysis, see Robert G. Valletta, "Rising Unemployment Duration in the United States: Causes and Consequences," Federal Reserve Bank of San Francisco, May 2005, available online at http://www.chicagofed.org/publications/publications/economic-perspectives/2005/2qtr2005_part2_farber.pdf.

16. Calculated from Bureau of Labor Statistics historical data, comparing 1969 and 2001—both business cycle peaks. Data available online at https://data.bls.gov/timeseries/LNS13008636.

17. Stacey Schreft and Aarti Singh, "A Closer Look at Jobless Recoveries," Federal Reserve Bank of Kansas City 2Q (2003), available online at https://www.kansascityfed.org/Publicat/econrev/Pdf/2q03schr.pdf; Andrew Stettner and Sylvia A. Allegretto, "The Rising Stakes of Job Loss: Stubborn Long-Term Joblessness amid Falling Unemployment Rates," EPI & NELP Briefing Paper #162 (Washington, DC: Economic Policy Institute, May 2005), available online at https://www.epi.org/publication/bp162/.

18. Stettner and Allegretto, "Rising Stakes of Job Loss."

19. For a powerful recent examination of the economic situation of today's young Americans (so-called millennials), see Michael Hobbes, "FML: Why Millennials Are Facing the Scariest Financial Future of Any Generation since the Great Depression," *Highline*, December 14, 2017, available online at https://highline.huffingtonpost.

com/articles/en/poor-millennials/. For analyses of the similar strains faced by those who grew up in the 1970s and early 1980s, see Tamara Draut, *Strapped: Why America's 20- and 30-Somethings Can't Get Ahead* (New York: Doubleday, 2006), and Anya Kamanetz, *Generation Debt: Why Now Is a Terrible Time to Be Young* (New York: Riverhead Books, 2006).

20. Farber, "What Do We Know about Job Loss in the United States?" 24.

21. Stettner and Allegretto, "Rising Stakes of Job Loss."

22. These and later figures regarding long-term unemployment are calculated from Bureau of Labor Statistics historical data, available online at https://data.bls.gov/timeseries/LNS13008636.

23. Sharon Cohen, "Faces beyond the Number of Long-Term Unemployed," KPIC.com, February 11, 2012, available online at http://online.wsj.com/article/SB1060722645367411400.html.

24. Alan B. Krueger, Judd Cramer, and David Cho, "Are the Long-Term Unemployed on the Margins of the Labor Market?" Brookings Papers on Economic Activity (Spring 2014): 261, available online at https://www.brookings.edu/wp-content/uploads/2016/07/2014a_Krueger.pdf.

25. Rand Ghayad, "The Jobless Trap," Northeastern University, 2013.

26. Cohen, "Faces beyond the Number of Long-Term Unemployed"; Austin Nichols, Josh Mitchell, and Stephan Lindner, "Consequences of Long-Term Unemployment," The Urban Institute Report, July 2013, available online at https://www.urban.org/sites/default/files/publication/23921/412887-Consequences-of-Long-Term-Unemployment.PDF; Gokce Basbug and Ofer Sharone, "The Emotional Toll of Long-Term Unemployment: Examining the Interaction Effects of Gender and Marital Status," *RSF: The Russell Sage Foundation Journal of the Social Sciences* 3:3 (2017): 222-244, available online at https://muse.jhu.edu/article/659931.

27. Mitra Toossi and Elka Torpey, "Older Workers: Labor Force Trends and Career Options," *Career Outlook*, May 2017, available online at https://www.bls.gov/careeroutlook/2017/article/older-workers.htm; Eleanor Krause and Isabel V. Sawhill, "What We Know—and Don't Know—about the Declining Labor Force Participation Rate," Center on Children and Families at Brookings Institution, February 3, 2017, available online at https://www.brookings.edu/wp-content/uploads/2017/05/ccf_20170517_declining_labor_force_participation_sawhill1.pdf.

28. Maximiliano Dvorkin and Hannah Shell, "A Cross-Country Comparison of Labor Force Participation," Federal Bank of St. Louis (2015), available online at https://research.stlouisfed.org/publications/economic-synopses/2015/07/31/a-cross-country-comparison-of-labor-force-participation/.

29. Katharine Bradbury, "Additional Slack in the Economy: The Poor Recovery in Labor Force Participation during This Business Cycle," Federal Reserve Bank of Boston Public Policy Briefs, No. 05-02 (Boston: MA, July 2005), available online at https://www.bostonfed.org/publications/public-policy-brief/2005/additional-slack-in-the-economy-the-poor-recovery-in-labor-force-participation-during-this-business-cycle.aspx.

30. Economic Policy Institute, State of Working America Data Library, "Real Entry-Level Wages of High School Graduates, by Gender, 1973–2013" and "Real Entry-Level Wages of College Graduates, By Gender, 1973–2013," 2018, available online at http://www.stateofworkingamerica.org/chart/swa-wages-figure-4p-real-entry-level-wages/ and http://www.stateofworkingamerica.org/chart/swa-wages-figure-4q-real-entry-level-wages/.

31. Economic Policy Institute, State of Working America Data Library, "Share of Recent High School Graduates with Employer Health/Pension Coverage, 1979–2010" and "Share of Recent College Graduates with Employer Health/Pension Coverage, 1979–2010," 2018, available online at http://www.stateofworkingamerica.org/chart/swa-wages-figure-4r-share-high-school-graduates/ and http://www.stateof-workingamerica.org/chart/swa-wages-figure-4s-share-college-graduates/.

32. Economic Policy Institute, "Contribution of Within-Group and Between-Group Inequality to Total Wage Inequality, 1973–2011," The State of Working America (Washington, DC: Economic Policy Institute, 2012), available online at http://www.stateofworkingamerica.org/chart/swa-wages-table-4-20-contribution-group/.

33. Paul Solman, "Analysis: Student Loan Debt and an Astonishing Number No One Is Talking About," PBS News Hour, May 21, 2018, available online at https://www.pbs.org/newshour/economy/making-sense/analysis-student-loan-debt-and-an-astonishing-number-no-ones-talking-about.

34. Mark Huelsman, "The Debt Divide: The Racial and Class Bias behind the 'New Normal' of Student Borrowing," Demos, May 19, 2015, available online at https://www.demos.org/sites/default/files/publications/Mark-Debt%20divide%20Final%20(SF).pdf.

35. Graciela Chichilnisky and Olga Gorbachev, "Volatility in the Knowledge Economy," Economic Theory 24 (2004): 531–47.

36. W. Michael Cox and Richard Alm, Myths of Rich and Poor: Why We're Better Off than We Think (New York: Basic, 2000), 201.

37. Ibid., 187.

38. U.S. Department of Labor, Bureau of Labor Statistics (BLS), "Computer Programmers," Occupational Outlook Handbook, 2006–2007 Edition (Washington, DC: BLS, 2006), available online at http://www.bls.gov/oco/ocosll0.htm.

39. Stephanie Armour, "Workers Asked to Train Foreign Replacements," USA Today, April 6, 2004, available online at http://usatoday.com/money/workplace/2004-04-06-replace_x.htm.

40. Educational qualifications from Bureau of Labor Statistics, "Occupational Outlook Handbook." Quote from Rachel Konrad, "Tech Job Decline: Computer Jobs Lose Luster as Young Techies Aspire to Other Careers," Montana Standard, June 25, 2005, available online at https://mtstandard.com/business/tech-job-decline/article_3a18e318-0929-5a38-9d0e-fe4ff295d95b.html.

41. Daniel Bell, The Coming of Post-industrial Society: A Venture in Social Forecasting (New York: Basic Books, 1973).

42. Amy Merrick, "Wal-Mart's Future Workforce: Robots and Freelancers," *The Atlantic*, April 4, 2018, available online at https://www.theatlantic.com/business/archive/2018/04/walmarts-future-workforce-robots-and-freelancers/557063/.

43. Calculated from Bureau of Labor Statistics historical data, available online at http://bls.gov/data/home.htm (accessed September 26, 2018).

44. This is the core argument of Torben Iversen and Thomas Cusack, "The Causes of Welfare State Expansion: Deindustrialization or Globalization?" *World Politics* 52 (April 2000): 313–49.

45. Griff Witte, "As Income Gap Widens, Uncertainty Spreads: More U.S. Families Struggle to Stay on Track," *Washington Post*, September 20, 2004, A1, available online at https://www.washingtonpost.com/archive/politics/2004/09/20/as-income-gap-widens-uncertainty-spreads/83cc9a83-5ee4-4e57-bd0e-d984881a1579.

46. James Manyika et al., "Jobs Lost, Jobs Gained: Workforce Transitions in a Time of Automation," *McKinsey Global Institute*, December 2017, available online at https://www.mckinsey.com/~/media/mckinsey/featured%20insights/future%20of%20organizations/what%20the%20future%20of%20work%20will%20mean%20for%20jobs%20skills%20and%20wages/mgi-jobs-lost-jobs-gained-report-december-6-2017.ashx.

47. Tiffany Hsu and Nick Wingfield, "Walmart Expands Online Grocery Delivery to 100 Cities," *New York Times*, March 14, 2018, available online at https://www.nytimes.com/2018/03/14/business/dealbook/walmart-online-delivery-groceries.html.

48. Bureau of Labor Statistics, "Share of Part-Time Workers at Lowest since November 2008," United States Department of Labor, August 11, 2015, available online at https://www.bls.gov/opub/ted/2015/share-of-part-time-workers-at-lowest-since-november-2008.htm; "Contingent and Alternative Arrangements Summary," June 7, 2018, available online at https://www.bls.gov/news.release/conemp.nr0.htm. The exact estimate of the share of the workforce that is contingent (using the Bureau's broadest definition) is 3.8 percent.

49. Claudia Goldin and Lawrence F. Katz, "Women Working Longer: Facts and Explanations," National Bureau of Economic Research Working Paper 22607, September 2016, available online at http://scholar.harvard.edu/files/goldin/files/goldin_katz_wwl_nber_wp22607.pdf.

50. Michael K. Lettau, "Compensation in Part-Time Jobs versus Full-Time Jobs: What if the Job Is the Same?" Bureau of Labor Statistics Working Paper 260, December 1994, available online at https://www.bls.gov/ore/abstract/ec/ec940080.htm.

51. Tilly, Chris. "Reasons for the continuing growth of part-time employment." *Monthly Labor Review* 114:3 (1991): 16.

52. General Accounting Office, "Contingent Workforce: Size, Characteristics, Earnings, and Benefits," May 20, 2015, available online at https://www.gao.gov/products/GAO-15-168R.

53. Kotaro Hara et al., "A Data-Driven Analysis of Workers' Earnings on Amazon Mechanical Turk," Proceedings of the 2018 CHI Conference on Human Factors in Computing Systems, 2018, available online at https://www.cs.cmu.edu/~jbigham/pubs/pdfs/2018/crowd-earnings.pdf.

54. Max Weber, *The Protestant Ethic and the Spirit of Capitalism,* trans. Talcott Parsons and Anthony Giddens (London: Allen and Unwin, 1930).

55. OECD, "Hours Worked (Indicator)," 2018, available online at https://data.oecd.org/emp/hours-worked.htm; Michael Greenstone and Adam Looney, "The Great Recession May Be Over, but American Families Are Working Harder than Ever," *Brookings Institution,* July 8, 2011, available online at https://www.brookings.edu/blog/jobs/2011/07/08/the-great-recession-may-be-over-but-american-families-are-working-harder-than-ever/.

56. Chad Stone, "Failure to Extend Emergency Unemployment Benefits Will Hurt Jobless Workers in Every State," Center on Budget and Policy Priorities Report, December 11, 2013, available online at https://www.cbpp.org/research/failure-to-extend-emergency-unemployment-benefits-will-hurt-jobless-workers-in-every-state?fa=view&id=4060#_ftn1.

57. Jamelle Bouie, "Unemployed Workers Need Benefits, but Republicans Still Say 'No,' " *Daily Beast,* December 10, 2013, available online at https://www.thedailybeast.com/unemployed-workers-need-benefits-but-republicans-still-say-no.

58. Michael J. Graetz and Jerry L. Mashaw, *True Security: Rethinking American Social Insurance* (New Haven, CT: Yale University Press, 1999), 76; Nick Buffle and Sarah Rawlins, "Declining Rate of Unemployment Insurance: Many Workers Are Unemployed Too Long to Receive Help," *Center for Economic and Policy Research,* February 14, 2017, available online at http://cepr.net/blogs/cepr-blog/declining-rate-of-unemployment-insurance-many-workers-are-unemployed-too-long-to-receive-help.

59. Claire McKenna, "The Job Ahead: Advancing Opportunity for Unemployed Workers," National Employment Law Project Report, February 2015, available online at https://nelp.org/wp-content/uploads/2015/03/Report-The-Job-Ahead-Advancing-Opportunity-Unemployed-Workers.pdf.

60. Cynthia Fagnoni, "Unemployment Insurance: Receipt of Benefits Has Declined, With Continued Disparities for Low-Wage and Part-Time Workers," *Testimony Before the Subcommittee on Income Security and Family Support, US of House of Representatives, Committee on Ways and Means. Washington, DC: General Accounting Office* (2007), available online at https://www.thedailybeast.com/unemployed-workers-need-benefits-but-republicans-still-say-no.

Chapter 4

1. This is one of the profiles of indebted families contained in Tamara Draut and Javier Silva, *Borrowing to Make Ends Meet: The Growth of Credit Card Debt in the '90s* (New York: Demos, 2003), 15.

2. The story is told in Steven K. Wisensale, *Family Leave Policy: The Political Economy of Work and Family in America* (Armonk, NY: M.E. Sharpe, Inc., 2001).

3. Lois Wladis Hoffman, "The Effects of the Mother's Employment on the Family and the Child," available online at http://parenthood.library.wisc.edu/Hoffman/Hoffman.html; Bureau of Labor Statistics, *Employment Characteristics of Families— 2017* (Washington, DC: United States Department of Labor, 2017), available online at https://www.bls.gov/news.release/pdf/famee.pdf.

4. Maria Cancian and Deborah Reed, "Changes in Married Couples' Intra-household Distribution of Work and Earnings" (paper prepared for presentation at the Population Association of America 2004 Annual Meeting, Boston, MA, March 2004)..

5. Ibid. See also Kim Parker and Gretchen Livingston, "6 Facts about American Fathers," Pew Research Center, June 15, 2017, available online at http://www.pewresearch.org/fact-tank/2017/06/15/fathers-day-facts/.

6. US Census Bureau Historical Income Tables 2005, available online at http://census.gov/hhes/www/income/histinc/f07ar.html; Heather Boushey and Kavya Vaghul, "Women Have Made the Difference for Family Economic Security," Washington Center for Equitable Growth Issue Brief, April 2016, available online at http://cdn.equitablegrowth.org/wp-content/uploads/2016/04/04153438/Women-have-made-the-difference-for-family-economic-security-pdf.pdf.

7. Boushey and Vaghul, "Women Have Made the Difference for Family Economic Security."

8. Ibid. See also Jared Bernstein and Karen Kornbluh, "Running Faster to Stay in Place: The Growth of Family Work Hours and Incomes," New America Foundation Work and Family Program Research Paper, June 2005, available online at http://newamerica.net/Download_Docs/pdfs/Doc_File_2437_l.pdf; Ben Casselman, "Number of the Week: Rise of Single Moms Drives Down Overall Income," Wall Street Journal (blog), September 21, 2013, available online at https://blogs.wsj.com/economics/2013/09/21/number-of-the-week-rise-of-single-moms-drives-down-overall-income/.

9. The memorial is at http://griefnet.org/memorials/2001b/mayl-902094727.html (accessed January 29, 2006). I have edited it slightly to fix a small grammatical error.

10. Drew Desilver, "Access to Paid Family Leave Varies Widely across Employers, Industries," Pew Research Center, March 23, 2017, available online at http://www.pewresearch.org/fact-tank/2017/03/23/access-to-paid-family-leave-varies-widely-across-employers-industries/; Drew Desilver, "Access to Paid Family Leave Varies Widely across Employers, Industries," Pew Research Center, March 23, 2017, available online at http://www.pewresearch.org/fact-tank/2017/03/23/access-to-paid-family-leave-varies-widely-across-employers-industries/.

11. That one nation is Mexico, which offers 12 weeks of paid leave. Janet C. Gornick, Marcia K. Meyers, and Katherine E. Ross, "Supporting the Employment of Mothers: Policy Variation across Fourteen Welfare States," Luxembourg Income Study Working Paper #139 (Luxembourg: LIS, 1996), http://lisproject.org/publications/LISwps/139.pdf; Gretchen Livingston, "Among 41 Nations, U.S. Is the Outlier When It Comes to Paid Parental Leave," Pew Research Center, September 26, 2016, available online at http://www.pewresearch.org/fact-tank/2016/09/26/u-s-lacks-mandated-paid-parental-leave/; Laura Addati et al., Maternity and Paternity at Work: Law and Practice across the World (Geneva: International Labour Office, 2014), available online at http://ilo.org/wcmsp5/groups/public/---dgreports/---dcomm/---publ/documents/publication/wcms_242615.pdf.

12. National Partnership for Women & Families, "State Paid Family and Medical Leave Insurance Laws, July 2018," available online at http://www.nationalpartnership. org/research-library/work-family/paid-leave/state-paid-family-leave-laws.pdf.

13. The term is from Arlie Russell Hochschild, *The Time Bind: When Work Becomes Home and Home Becomes Work* (New York: Metropolitan Books, 1997).

14. Kim Parker and Gretchen Livingston, "6 Facts about American Fathers," Pew Research Center, June 15, 2017, available online at http://www.pewresearch.org/fact-tank/2017/06/15/fathers-day-facts/.

15. Susan Dynarski and Jonathan Gruber, "Can Families Smooth Variable Earnings?" Brookings Papers on Economic Activity 1 (1997): 229–84.

16. Moreover, singles living alone and single parents have also become more common in recent decades—which might be thought to explain why the overall volatility of family incomes has increased. This explanation, however, turns out not to be true. Change in the mix of American families does not by itself seem to be a major contributor to rising volatility. Instead, income volatility has risen across all family *types*. These conclusions are based on my own investigations, as well as Neil Bania and Laura Leete, "Income Volatility and Food Insufficiency in U.S. Low-Income Households, 1991–2003," Institute for Research on Poverty Discussion Paper no. 1325-07, University of Wisconsin, April 2007, available online at http://irp.wisc.edu/publications/dps/pdfs/dpl32507.pdf; Karen E. Dynan, Douglas W. Elmendorf, and Daniel E. Sichel, "Financial Innovation and the Great Moderation: What Do Household Data Say?" (paper prepared for a conference on "Financial Innovations and the Real Economy" sponsored by the Federal Reserve Bank of San Francisco, November 2006), available online at http://frbsf.org/economics/conferences/0611/2_Sichel.pdf; and Olga Gorbachev, "Has the Increased Attachment of Women to the Labor Market Changed a Family's Ability to Smooth Income Shocks?" *The American Economic Review* 106:5 (May 2016): 247–51, available online at https://search.proquest.com/docview/1788239142?accountid=15172..

17. Elizabeth Warren and Amelia Warren Tyagi, *The Two-Income Trap: Why Middle-Class Mothers and Fathers Are Going Broke* (New York: Basic Books, 2003), 6.

18. Ibid, 7.

19. U.S. Census Bureau, "Single Parent Day," Release Number CB18-SFS.38, March 21, 2018 (based on Current Population Survey, Annual Social and Economic Supplements 1950 to 2017), available online at https://www.census.gov/newsroom/stories/2018/single-parent.html.

20. Carlen Hempel, "Middle Class and Out of Work," *Boston Globe Magazine,* June 15, 2003.

21. "U.S. Savings Rate Hits Lowest Level since 1933," Associated Press, January 30, 2006; Jeanna Smialek, "Why the Savings Rate Is a Reason to Worry about 2018 U.S. Growth," Bloomberg.com, January 26, 2018, available online at https://www.bloomberg.com/news/articles/2018-01-26/why-the-savings-rate-is-a-reason-to-worry-about-2018-u-s-growth.

22. Calculated from Federal Reserve Board, Survey of Consumer Finance, 2016, available online at https://www.federalreserve.gov/econres/files/BulletinCharts.

pdf. All results are weighted; Daniel Dowdy, "Are Plummeting Savings and Rising Debt Red Flags for Household Finances?" The Aspen Institute Blog, May 14, 2018, available online at http://www.aspenepic.org/plummeting-savings-rising-debt-red-flags-household-finances; Gloria G. Guzman, "Household Income: 2016," United States Census Bureau America Community Survey Brief, September 2017, available online at https://www.census.gov/content/dam/Census/library/publications/2017/acs/acsbr16-02.pdf.

23. Dynarski and Gruber, "Can Families Smooth Variable Earnings?"

24. Kasey Wiedrich et al, "On Track of Left Behind?: Findings from the 2017 *Prosperity Now Scorecard*," Prosperity Now Scorecard Summary, July 2017, available online at https://prosperitynow.org/files/PDFs/2017_Scorecard_Report.pdf.

25. http://www.pewtrusts.org/-/media/assets/2015/01/fsm_balance_sheet_report.pdf; Robert Haveman and Edward N. Wolff, "Who Are the Asset Poor? Levels, Trends, and Composition, 1983–1998," Discussion paper 1227-01 (Institute for Research on Poverty, 2001): table 7, available online at http://irp.wisc.edu/publications/dps/pdfs/dpl22701.pdf.

26. Bricker et al, "Recent Changes in U.S. Family Finances from 2013 to 2016: Evidence from the Survey of Consumer Finances," Federal Reserve Bulletin 103, no. 3 (September 2017): 20; Toluse Olorunnipa, "Trump Asks 'How's Your 401(k)?' But Most Voters Don't Have One," Bloomberg.com, December 19, 2017, available online at https://www.bloomberg.com/news/articles/2017-12-19/trump-asks-how-s-your-401-k-but-most-voters-don-t-have-one.

27. Robert J. Samuelson, "Pressure of the American Dream," *Washington Post,* July 26, 2004, All, available online at http://www.washingtonpost.com/wp-dyn/articles/A14226-2004Jul25.html.

28. Cited in Elizabeth Warren and Amelia Warren Tyagi, "What's Hurting the Middle Class," *Boston Review,* September/October 2005, available online at http://bostonreview.net/BR30.5/warrentyagi.html.

29. Warren and Tyagi, *Two-Income Trap.*

30. Diane W. Schanzenbach, Ryan Nunn, and Megan Mumford, "Where Does All the Money Go: Shifts in Household Spending over the Past 30 Years," *The Hamilton Project*, Brookings Institution, June 2, 2016, available online at http://www.hamiltonproject.org/assets/files/where_does_all_the_money_go.pdf;   Erin El Issa, "2017 American Household Credit Card Debt Study," *NerdWallet*, 2017, available online at https://www.nerdwallet.com/blog/average-credit-card-debt-household/.

31. Christian Weller, "The Middle Class Falls Back," *Challenge* 49: 1 (January/February 2006): 16–43.

32. Warren and Tyagi, "What's Hurting the Middle Class," 9.

33. Robert Shiller, *Irrational Exuberance,* 2nd ed. (Princeton, NJ: Princeton University Press, 2005).; Stacey V. Smith, "Rising Home Prices Lead to Worries of Another Housing Market Bubble," *NPR.org*, May 11, 2018, available online at https://www.npr.org/2018/05/11/610315734/rising-home-prices-lead-to-worries-of-another-housing-market-bubble; Brad Finkelstein, "Housing Bubble or Not, the Real Estate Market Is in Trouble," *National Mortgage News*, March

28, 2018, available online at https://www.nationalmortgagenews.com/news/housing-bubble-or-not-the-real-estate-market-is-in-trouble.

34. Heather Boushey, "The Debt Explosion among College Graduates" (Center for Economic and Policy Research, 2005), available online at http://cepr.net/publications/debt_college_grads.htm#_ftnref4; Sandy Baum and Marie O'Malley, "College on Credit: How Borrowers Perceive Their Education Debt" (Nellie Mae Corporation, February 2003).

35. Those familiar with research on wealth will know that the PSID generally finds lower levels of household wealth than the Federal Reserve Board's Survey of Consumer Finances (SCF). This is because the SCF "oversamples" wealthy Americans (that is, includes a disproportionate number of them in the survey) and provides a somewhat more detailed picture of assets and debts. Conversely, the PSID includes a disproportionate number of low-income Americans, so it is generally better at measuring wealth at the bottom of the economic ladder. For the analyses reported here, my interest is changes over time in wealth levels, rather than the levels themselves, so the discrepancies between the two surveys are not a major issue. Moreover, PSID wealth levels come remarkably close to SCF levels for all but the richest families—which, again, are not my concern here. Median household wealth, for example, is about 90 percent as large in the PSID as in the SCF. Thomas Juster, James P. Smith, and Frank Stafford, "The Measurement and Structure of Household Wealth," *Labour Economics* 6 (1999): 253–75.

36. Calculated from Panel Study of Income Data Wealth Supplement, 1984, 2004, and 2015.

37. Jeff Grabmeier, "Credit Card Debt: Younger People Borrow More Heavily and Repay More Slowly, Study Finds," *Phys.org*, January 14, 2013, available online at https://phys.org/news/2013-01-credit-card-debt-younger-people.html.

38. Federal Reserve Board, *Survey of Consumer Finances Chartbook*, 2016, "Median Value of Debt for Families with Holdings, By Age of Head," available online at https://www.federalreserve.gov/econres/files/BulletinCharts.pdf. See also Jesse Bricker, et al., "Changes in U.S. Family Finances from 2013 to 2016: Evidence from the Survey of Consumer Finances," *Federal Reserve Bulletin* (September 2017), available online at https://www.federalreserve.gov/publications/2017-september-changes-in-us-family-finances-from-2013-to-2016.htm; and Tamara Draut and Javier Silva, *Generation Broke: The Growth of Debt among Young Americans* (New York: Demos, October 2004), available online at http://demos.org/pubs/Generation_Broke.pdf.

39. Calculated from Panel Study of Income Data Wealth Supplement, 1984, 2004, and 2015; see also Ray Boshara, William R. Emmons, and Bryan J. Noeth, "The Demographics of Wealth: How Age, Education, and Race Separate Thrivers from Strugglers in Today's Economy Essay No. 3," Federal Reserve Bank of St. Louis, July 2015, available online at https://www.stlouisfed.org/~/media/Files/PDFs/HFS/essays/HFS-Essay-3-2015-Age-Birth-year-Wealth.pdf?la=en.

40. Geoffrey Paulin and Brian Riordan, "Making It on Their Own: The Baby-Boom Meets Generation X," *Monthly Labor Review* 121:2 (February 1998): 18, available online at http://bls.gov/opub/mlr/1998/02/art2full.pdf.

41. Adam Wesolowski-Mantilla, "Generational Spending Habits of under 25 Year Olds: The Way of the Millennial," *Northwestern Business Review*, February 12, 2018, available online at https://northwesternbusinessreview.org/generational-spending-habits-of-under-25-year-olds-the-way-of-the-millennial-4980c3e09132.

42. Stef W. Kight, "Being 30: Spending Way Less on Booze, Cigarettes, Books," Axios, August 26, 2018, available online at https://www.axios.com/millennial-spending-income-demographics-trends-153a5f33-7f56-4f1d-b72b-501e30ae6003.html

43. Anne L. Alstott, *No Exit: What Parents Owe Their Children and What Society Owes Parents* (New York: Oxford University Press, 2004).

44. Two children cost slightly less than twice the cost of a single child, because some costs can be pooled. Mark Lino, Kevin Kuczynski, and Nestor Rodriguez, *Expenditures on Children by Families, 2015*. Miscellaneous Publication No. 1528-2015. U.S. Department of Agriculture, Center for Nutrition Policy and Promotion, January 2017, available online at https://www.cnpp.usda.gov/sites/default/files/crc2015.pdf

45. Joan Blades and Kristin Rowe-Finkbeiner, *The Motherhood Manifesto: What American Moms Want—And What to Do about It* (New York: Nation Books, 2006); Warren and Tyagi, *Two-Income Trap*, 6.

46. These findings are based on an analysis of the Gallup Poll Social Series (April 2003, 1,000 adults) with an ordered probit model, controlling for age, education, race, income, marital status, and gender (all respondents were employed). See also Jeffrey Jones, "Job Loss Would Quickly Lead to Hardship for Many in U.S.," Gallup, April 18, 2014, available online at https://news.gallup.com/poll/168563/job-loss-quickly-lead-hardship.aspx.

47. Susanna Loeb, *Missing the Target: We Need to Focus on Informal Care rather than Preschool* (Washington, D.C.: Brookings, June 16, 2016), available online at https://www.brookings.edu/research/missing-the-target-we-need-to-focus-on-informal-care-rather-than-preschool/.

48. On the amount of time parents spend with children, see Eugene Smolensky and Jennifer Appleton Gootman, *Working Families and Growing Kids* (Washington, DC: National Academies Press, 2003), 32–35. For a good review and extension of the time-use research, see Jerry A. Jacobs and Kathleen Gerson, *The Time Divide: Work, Family and Gender Inequality* (Cambridge, MA: Harvard University Press, 2004). The statistic on sleep comes not just from personal experience but also from Andrew Cherlin and Prem Krishnamurthy, "What Works for Mom," *New York Times*, May 9, 2004, sec. 4, 13.

49. Paul W. Newacheck et al., "An Epidemiologic Profile of Children with Special Health Care Needs," *Pediatrics* 102:1 (July 1998): 117–23; MaryBeth Musumeci and Julia Foutz, "Medicaid's Role for Children with Special Health Care Needs: A Look at Eligibility, Services, and Spending," *Kaiser Family Foundation*, February 2018, available online at http://files.kff.org/attachment/Issue-Brief-Medicaids-Role-for-Children-with-Special-Health-Care-Needs-A-Look-at-Eligibility-Services-and-Spending.

50. Alstott, *No Exit*, 118; Anna Lukemeyer, Marcia K. Meyers, and Timothy Smeeding, "Expensive Children in Poor Families: Out-of-Pocket Expenditures for the Care of

Disabled and Chronically Ill Children in Welfare Families," *Journal of Marriage and Family* 62:2 (May 2000): 413.

51. AARP, *Caregiving in the United States* (Washington, D.C.: AARP, June 2015), available online at https://www.aarp.org/content/dam/aarp/ppi/2015/caregiving-in-the-united-states-2015-report-revised.pdf; Debby Feyerick, "Baby Boomers Feeling Strain of Caring for Older Parents," *CNN.com*, July 31, 1998, available online at http://cnn.com/HEALTH/9807/31/elder.care.

52. Wan He and Luke J. Larsen, *Older Americans with a Disability: 2008–2012*, U.S. Census Bureau (Washington, DC: U.S. Government Printing Office, December 2014), 1–20.

53. Richard W. Johnson and Joshua M. Wiener, *A Profile of Frail Older Americans and Their Caregivers* (Washington, DC: Urban Institute, February 2006), 64.

54. Feyerick, "Baby Boomers Feeling Strain."

55. Michelle J. Budig and Paula England, "The Wage Penalty for Motherhood," *American Sociological Review* 66 (2001): 204–25; Deborah J. Anderson, Melissa Binder, and Kate Krause, "The Motherhood Wage Penalty: Which Mothers Pay It and Why?" *American Economic Review* 92:2 (May 2002): 354–58; Graciela Chichilinsky, "Catastrophic Risks: The Need for New Tools, Financial Instruments and Institutions" (paper prepared for Social Science Research Council Project on the Privatization of Risk, 2005), available online at http://privatizationofrisk.ssrc.org/Chichilnisky/.

56. Torben Iversen and Frances Rosenbluth, "The Political Economy of Gender: Explaining Cross-National Variation in the Gender Division of Labor and the Gender Voting Gap," *American Journal of Political Science* 50:1 (January 2006): 1–19.

57. Centers for Disease Control, "Cohabitation, Divorce, Marriage, and Remarriage in the United States," *Vital and Health Statistics*, ser. 23, no. 22. Department of Health and Human Services, 2002, available online at http://cdc.gov/nchs/data/series/sr_23/sr23_022.pdf.

58. Pamela J. Smock, "The Economic Costs of Marital Disruption for Young Women over the Past Two Decades," *Demography* 30 (1993): 353–71; Matthew McKeever and Nicholas H. Wolfinger, "Reexamining the Economic Costs of Marital Disruption for Women," *Social Science Quarterly* 82:1 (March 2001): 202–17; Laura M. Tach and Alicia Eads, "Trends in the Economic Consequences of Marital and Cohabitation Dissolution in the United States," *Demography* 52:2 (April 2015): 401–32.

59. U.S. Government Accountability Office, "Retirement Security: Women Still Face Challenges," Report to the Chairman, Special Committee on Aging, U.S. Senate, July 2012, available online at https://www.gao.gov/assets/600/592726.pdf.

60. David K. Shipler, *The Working Poor: Invisible in America* (New York: Knopf, 2004), 21–26.

61. Patricia A. McManus and Thomas A. DiPrete, "Losers and Winners: The Financial Consequences of Separation and Divorce for Men," *American Sociological Review* 66 (2001): 246–69.

62. Stacy Rapacon, "Why Women Should Rethink Their Finances after Divorce", *U.S. News & World Report*, August 14, 2017, available online at https://money.

usnews.com/money/personal-finance/family-finance/articles/2017-08-14/why-women-should-rethink-their-finances-after-divorce.

63. Recent research suggests that the costs of divorce have fallen since the 1980s—though they still represent, on average, a one-third drop in household income from the year prior to divorce to the year afterward. At the same time, however, the costs of family breakup for unmarried mothers living with male partners—a growing share of the population—has simultaneously risen and is now similar to the cost for divorced mothers. Tach and Eads, "Trends in the Economics Consequences of Marital and Cohabitation Dissolution in the United States."

64. Lee Lillard and Linda Waite, "Marriage, Divorce, and the Work and Earning Careers of Spouses," University of Michigan Retirement Research Center, 2003, available online at http://mrrc.isr.umich.edu/publications/briefs/pdf/ib_003.pdf; Katherine Weisshaar, "Earnings Equality and Relationship Stability for Same-Sex and Heterosexual Couples," *Social Forces* 93:1 (September 2014): 93–123.

Chapter 5

1. Associated Press, "United Flight 175 Victims at a Glance," *USA Today* (September 25, 2001), available online at https://usatoday30.usatoday.com/news/nation/2001/09/12/victim-capsule-flight175.htm.

2. Emily Brandon, "The 10 Biggest Failed Pension Plans" *U.S. News & World Report,* August 23, 2010, available online at https://money.usnews.com/money/blogs/planning-to-retire/2010/08/23/the-10-biggest-failed-pension-plans.

3. Dale Russakoff, "Human Toll of a Pension Default," *Washington Post,* June 13, 2005, A1.

4. Brandon, "The 10 Biggest Failed Pension Plans."

5. Alexei Barrionuevo, "Enron Prosecutors Have Another Key Witness, From Jail," *New York Times,* March 20, 2006, C1.

6. BBC News, "Regulators Probe Enron Stock Selloff," January 14, 2002, available online at http://news.bbc.co.uk/2/hi/americas/1758345.stm.

7. "Enron Ex-workers Forlornly View Rubble," *New Hampshire Sunday News,* December 16, 2001, Business.

8. Pension Benefit Guaranty Corporation (PBGC), *Pension Insurance Data Book 2006* (Washington, DC: PBGC, 2007), 19, available online at https://www.pbgc.gov/documents/2006databook.pdf.

9. Albert B. Crenshaw, "A 401(k) Post Mortem: After Enron, Emphasis on Company Stock Draws Scrutiny," *Washington Post,* December 16, 2001, H1.

10. Employee Benefits Research Institute, *EBRI Databook on Employe Benefits* (Washington, D.C.: EBRI, October 2015), Chap. 5.

11. Investment Company Institute, "The US Retirement Market, First Quarter 2017," June 2017, available online at https://www.ici.org/faqs/faq/401k/faqs_401k.

12. Alicia H. Munnell and Annika Sunden, *Coming Up Short: The Challenge of 401(k) Plans* (Washington, DC: Brookings Institution, 2004), 75–77.

13. Edward A. Zelinsky, "The Defined Contribution Paradigm," *Yale Law Journal* (December 2004): 451–534.

14. Peter Wehner, "Memo on Social Security" (January 5, 2005), 1, available online at http://house.gov/etheridge/WhiteHouseMemo.pdf.

15. Eduardo Porter and Mary Williams Walsh, "Retirement Turns into a Rest Stop as Benefits Dwindle," *New York Times,* February 9, 2005, available online at http://nytimes.com/2005/02/09/business/09retire.html.

16. Frank Newport, "Update: Americans' Concerns about Retirement Persist," *Gallup,* May 9, 2018, available online at https://news.gallup.com/poll/233861/update-americans-concerns-retirement-persist.aspx.

17. See AARP website, http://aarp.org.

18. Calculated from real stock-price data collated by Robert Shiller and available online at http://irrationalexuberance.com/ie_data.xls.

19. Jonathan Peterson, "Many Forced to Retire Early," *Los Angeles Times,* May 15, 2004, available online at http://latimes.com/business/la-fi-forcedout15May15,0,7334343.story?coll=la-home-headlines.

20. Jon Elster, *Ulysses and the Sirens: Studies in Rationality and Irrationality* (New York: Cambridge University Press, 1979).

21. Although AT&T's plan is usually treated as the first formal pension, it was closer to a form of disability insurance, providing a minimal stipend to workers when they could no longer work, rather than providing a true retirement income. I am grateful to John Langbein for alerting me to this fact.

22. U.S. Senate Subcommittee on Labor, *Legislative History of the Employee Retirement Income Security Act of 1974* (Washington, DC: U.S. Government Printing Office, 1976), 4747, 4775.

23. Joint Committee on Taxation, *General Explanation of the Revenue Act of 1978,* 95th Cong., 1979, Joint Committee Print, 84.

24. Alan S. Blinder, "Why Is Government in the Pensions Business?" in *Social Security and Private Pensions: Providing for Retirement in the Twenty-First Century,* ed. Susan M. Watcher (Lexington, MA: Lexington Books, 1988), 17–34; Steven Sass, *The Promise of Private Pensions: The First Hundred Years* (Cambridge, MA: Harvard University Press, 1997).

25. These estimates are based on my own calculations from the National Income and Product Accounts ("Private Pension and Profit Sharing" as a share of "Compensation of Employees" within corporate and non-corporate businesses and nonprofits (that is, excluding public-sector workers' compensation, as well as compensation paid directly by households)). I am grateful to Steve Rose for his guidance in analyzing these figures.

26. Hewitt Associates, *How Well Are Employees Saving and Investing in 401(k) Plans, 2005 Hewitt Universe Benchmarks* (Lincolnshire, IL: Hewitt Associates, 2005).

27. "Ten Questions with Ted Benna," *Journal of Financial Planning* (January 2003): 16.

28. Jason Zweig, "Look Back and Learn," *Money* 28:4 (1999): 94–95.

29. Ibid., 551, 548, 551.

30. Assistant Labor Secretary David George Ball, quoted in Albert Crenshaw, "Pension Proposals Offer Workers Options, Control," *Washington Post,* March 10, 1991, H3.

31. "President Participates in Social Security Conversation in New York," news release, Office of the Press Secretary, White House, May 24, 2005, available online at http://whitehouse.gov/news/releases/2005/05/20050524-3.html.

32. Donald Lambro, "Is the 401(k) a GOP Secret Weapon?" *Human Events Online*, April 20, 2006, available online at http://humaneventsonline.com/article.php?id=14147.

33. All the figures in the previous two paragraphs come from Edward Wolff, *Retirement Insecurity* (Washington, DC: Economic Policy Institute, 2002), Tables 1 and 2.

34. Dan Dadlec, "Why Retirement Savers Are in Better Shape than Ever" *Time*, February 2, 2017, available online at http://time.com/money/4656003/retirement-savers-better-shape-than-ever/; Tom Anderson, "Trump Rally Helps Boost 401(k) balances to Record $92,500" CNBC, February 2, 2017, available online at https://www.cnbc.com/2017/02/02/trump-rally-helps-boost-401k-balances-to-record-92500-fidelity-says.html; Employee Benefit Research Institute, "401(k) Plan Asset Allocation, Account Balances, and Loan Activity in 2016," EBRI Issue Brief No.458 (September 10, 2018), 14–15 available online at https://www.ebri.org/docs/default-source/ebri-issue-brief/ebri_ib_458_k-update-10sept18.pdf?sfvrsn=bca4302f_2.

35. EBRI, "401(k) Plan Asset Allocation, Account Balances, and Loan Activity in 2016," 14–15.

36. Bureau of Labor Statistics, U.S. Department of Labor, *The Economics Daily*, Higher Paid Workers More Likely to Have Access to Retirement Benefits than Lower Paid Workers," June 23, 2017, available online at https://www.bls.gov/opub/ted/2017/higher-paid-workers-more-likely-to-have-access-to-retirement-benefits-than-lower-paid-workers.htm.

37. Peter Orszag, "Progressivity and Savings: Fixing the Nation's Upside-Down Incentives for Savings" (testimony before the House Committee on Education and the Workforce, February 25, 2004), available online at http://brookings.edu/views/testimony/orszag/20040225.pdf; Monique Morrissey, "The State of American Retirement" (Economic Policy Institute, Retirement Inequality Chartbook, March 2016), available online at http://www.epi.org/files/2016/state-of-american-retirement-final.pdf.

38. Assistant Labor Secretary David George Ball, quoted in Crenshaw, "Pension Proposals Offer Workers Options," H3.

39. Brigitte C. Madrian and Dennis F. Shea, "The Power of Suggestion: Inertia in 401(k) Participation and Savings Behavior," *Quarterly Journal of Economics* 116:4 (2006): 1159.

40. Leonard E. Burman, Norma B. Coe, and William G. Gale, "What Happens When You Show Them the Money: Lump Sum Distributions, Retirement Income Security and Public Policy" (prepared for Second Annual Joint Conference for the Retirement Research Consortium, 2000), available online at http://bc.edu/centers/crr/papers/SV-2%20Burman%20Coe%20Gale.pdf.

41. Gary V. Engelhardt, "Reasons for Job Change and the Disposition of Pre-retirement Lump Sum Pension Distributions," *Economics Letters* 81:3 (2003): 333-39.

42. Edward N. Wolff, "Is the Equalizing Effect of Retirement Wealth Wearing Off?" New York University, March 29, 2002, 39, available online at https://www.econ.

nyu.edu/user/wolffe/RetirementWealthInequalityApril02.pdf; Edward N. Wolff, *The Transformation of the American Pension System: Was It Beneficial to Workers?* (Kalamazoo, MI: W.E. Upjohn Institute for Employment Research, 2011).

43. Munnell and Sunden, *Coming Up Short*, ch. 4.

44. Gary Burtless, "Risk and Returns of Stock Market Investments Held in Individual Retirement Accounts," Task Force on Social Security Reform, House Budget Committee, (May 11, 1999), available online at http://brookings.edu/views/testimony/burtless/19990511.htm.

45. Olivia Mitchell, James Poterba, Mark Warshawsky, and Jeffrey Brown, "New Evidence on the Money's Worth of Individual Annuities," *American Economic Review* 89: 5 (1999): 1299–318.

46. Munnell and Sunden, *Coming up Short,* 143–51.

47. Alicia H. Munnell, Anthony Webb, and Francesca Golub-Sass, *The National Retirement Risk Index: An Update* (Boston: Boston College Center for Retirement Research, October 2012), available online at http://crr.bc.edu/wp-content/uploads/2012/11/IB_12-20-508.pdf. Other reports on the index are available online at http://crr.bc.edu/special-projects/national-retirement-risk-index/ .

48. Government Accountability Office (GAO), Most Households Approaching Retirement Have Low Savings (Washington, DC: GAO, June 2, 2015), available online at https://www.gao.gov/products/GAO-15-419.

49. Employee Benefit Research Institute (EBRI), *Debt of the Elderly and Near Elderly, 1992–2016* (Washington, DC: EBRI, March 2018), available online at https://www.ebri.org/pdf/briefspdf/EBRI_IB_443.pdf; and *Debt of the Elderly and Near Elderly, 1992–2004* (Washington, DC: EBRI, September 2006), available online at http://ebri.org/pdf/notespdf/EBRI_Notes_09-20061.pdf.

50. Bureau of Labor Statistics, "Civilian Labor Force Participation Rate by Age, Sex, and Ethnicity," October 24, 2017, available online at https://www.bls.gov/emp/tables/civilian-labor-force-participation-rate.htm; and Barry Bosworth, Gary Burtless, and Kan Zhang, *Later Retirement, Inequality in Old Age, and the Growing Gap in Longevity between Rich and Poor* (Washington, D.C.: Brookings, 2016), available online at https://www.brookings.edu/wp-content/uploads/2016/02/BosworthBurtlessZhang_retirementinequalitylongevity_012815.pdf.

51. Jeffrey R. Brown, "How Should We Insure Longevity Risk in Pensions and Social Security?" (Center for Retirement Research, an Issue in Brief 4, August 2000), available online at http://bc.edu/centers/crr/issues/ib_4.pdf.

52. Mary Jordan and Kevin Sullivan, "The New Reality of Old Age in America," *Washington Post*, September 30, 2017, available online at https://www.washingtonpost.com/graphics/2017/national/seniors-financial-insecurity.

53. Wolff, *Retirement Insecurity.*

54. Michael Clingman, Kyle Burkhalter, and Chris Chaplain, "Replacement Rate for Hypothetical Retired Workers," Actuarial Note Number 2018.9, Social Security Administration, June 2018, available online at https://www.ssa.gov/OACT/NOTES/ran9/an2018-9.pdf.

55. Stuart Butler and Peter Germanis, "Achieving a 'Leninist' Strategy," *Cato Journal* 3:2 (Fall 1983): 548.

56. Butler and Germanis, "Achieving a 'Leninist' Strategy," 552.

57. The articles are too numerous to list here, but see in particular Martin Feldstein, "Social Security, Induced Retirement and Aggregate Capital Accumulation," *Journal of Political Economy* 82:5 (1974); and Feldstein, "Toward a Reform of Social Security," *Public Interest* 40 (Summer 1975). The finding in the first publication that Social Security greatly reduces private savings turned out to be the result of a programming error. Dean R. Leimer and Selig D. Lesnoy, "Social Security and Private Savings: New Time Series Evidence," *Journal of Political Economy* 90:3 (June 1982): 606–29.

58. For a good compendium of the charges, look no further than the 2001 report of the President's Commission to Strengthen Social Security, available online at https://www.ssa.gov/history/reports/pcsss/Report-Final.pdf. See also Michael Tanner, *Social Security and Its Discontents* (Washington, DC: Cato Institute, 2004).

59. In 1994, the advocacy group Third Millennium gained widespread attention with its claim that more eighteen- to twenty-year-olds believed that "UFOs exist" than that "Social Security will still exist" when Generation X retires. The poll on which the claim was based, however, was tailor-made to reach this misleading conclusion. In 1997, the Employee Benefit Research Institute, an independent research organization that forswears taking stands on policy issues, directly tested the Third Millennium claim and found that a large majority of young Americans believed more strongly that they would receive Social Security than that alien life exists. See Fay Lomax Cook and Lawrence R. Jacobs, "Americans' Attitudes toward Social Security: Popular Claims Meet Hard Data," National Academy of Social Insurance, Social Security Brief, No. 10, March 2001, available online at http://nasi.org/usr_doc/ss_brief_10.pdf.

60. Butler and Germanis, "A 'Leninist' Strategy for Privatizing Social Security," 555.

61. Jason Furman and Robert Greenstein, "An Overview of Issues Raised by the Administration's Social Security Plan" (Washington, DC: Center on Budget and Policy Priorities, February 2005), 1, available online at http://cbpp.org/2-2-05socsec4.pdf.

62. Robert J. Shiller, "The Life-Cycle Personal Accounts Proposal for Social Security: An Evaluation" (unpublished manuscript, Yale University, March 2005), available online at http://irrationalexuberance.com/shillersocsec.doc. The 50-50 portfolio is touted in the previously cited 2001 report of the President's Commission to Strengthen Social Security.

63. Peter J. Ferrara, *Social Security: The Inherent Contradiction* (Washington, DC: Cato Institute, 1980).

Chapter 6

1. David U. Himmelstein, Elizabeth Warren, Deborah Thorne, and Steffie Woolhandler, "Illness and Injury as Contributors to Bankruptcy," *Health Affairs*, Web Exclusive, February 2, 2005, available online at http://content.healthaffairs.org/cgi/reprint/hlthaff.w5.63vl.pdf. The upper-bound estimate is based on the study's finding that 46 percent of bankruptcy filers cited illness or injury as a specific reason for bankruptcy and/or had medical bills exceeding $1,000. The lower-bound estimate limits the definition of medical bankruptcy just to filers who cited illness or injury.

2. John Leland, "When Even Health Insurance Is No Safeguard," *New York Times,* October 23, 2005, A1.

3. Leland, "When Even Health Insurance Is No Safeguard."

4. Between 2000 and 2007, the share fell from 68 percent to 59 percent. Kaiser Family Foundation, "2017 Employer Health Benefits Survey," September 19, 2017, sec. 2, available online at https://www.kff.org/health-costs/report/2017-employer-health-benefits-survey/.

5. Albert Crenshaw, "Workers' Family Coverage Reaches $10,880 Average; Small Employers Dropping Plans as Costs Rocket Another 9 Percent," *Washington Post,* September 15, 2005, D2, available online at http://washingtonpost.com/wp-dyn/content/article/2005/09/14/AR2005091400693.html; Milt Freudenheim, "Fewer Employers Totally Cover Health Premiums," *New York Times,* March 23, 2005, available online at http://cohealthinitiative.org/NYTfewer.htm.

6. Sara R. Collins, Karen Davis, Michelle M. Doty, Jennifer L. Kriss, and Alyssa L. Holmgren, "Gaps in Health Insurance: An All-American Problem," The Commonwealth Fund, Washington, DC, April 2006, available online at http://cmwf.org/usr_doc/Collins_gapshltins_920.pdf.

7. General Motors, "Letter to Stockholders: 2003 Annual Report" (General Motors Corporation, 2003), 3, available online at http://gm.com/company/investor_information/docs/fin_data/gm03ar/letter_3.html.

8. Leland, "When Even Health Insurance Is No Safeguard."

9. Susan Brink, "What Country Spends the Most (And Least) on Health Care Per Person?" *NPR,* April 20, 2017, available online at http://www.npr.org/sections/goatsandsoda/2017/04/20/524774195/what-country-spends-the-most-and-least-on-health-care-per-person.

10. Steffie Woolhandler and David U. Himmelstein, "Paying for National Health Insurance—And Not Getting It," *Health Affairs* (July/August 2002): 88–98, available online at http://content.healthaffairs.org/cgi/reprint/21/4/88.

11. Tax Policy Center, "How Does the Tax Exclusion for Employer-Sponsored Health Insurance Work?" *Tax Policy Center Briefing Book* (Washington, DC: Tax Policy Center, 2018), available online at https://www.taxpolicycenter.org/sites/default/files/briefing-book/tpc-briefing-book_0.pdf.

12. Jacob S. Hacker, *The Divided Welfare State: The Battle over Public and Private Social Benefits in the United States* (New York: Cambridge University Press, 2002), 257.

13. Emily M. Mitchell and Steven R. Machlin, "Concentration of Health Expenditures and Selected Characteristics of High Spenders, U.S. Civilian Noninstitutionalized Population, 2015," Agency for Healthcare Research and Quality Statistical Brief #506, December 2017, available online at https://meps.ahrq.gov/data_files/publications/st506/stat506.pdf.

14. George A. Akerlof, "The Market for Lemons: Quality Uncertainty and the Market Mechanism," *Quarterly Journal of Economics* 84:3 (1970): 235–51.

15. Amy Goldstein, "Nearly 12 Million People Enrolled in 2018 Health Coverage Under the ACA," *Chicago Tribune,* April 3, 2018, available online at https://www.chicagotribune.com/business/ct-obamacare-enrollment-20180403-story.html.

16. Technical Board on Economic Security, Minutes of the Meeting of the Executive Committee, September 27, 1934, Materials Related to the CES, "Committee

Activities," SSAHA. I found this document thanks to the careful review of the CES materials by Jaap Kooijman, "Condition Critical: The Exclusion of a National Health Insurance Program from the Social Security Act of 1935" (PhD dissertation, University of Amsterdam, 1994), 33–34.

17. Theodore R. Marmor, *The Politics of Medicare* (Chicago: Aldine, 1973).

18. According to the AFL-CIO's point man for health insurance, Medicare was presented as "a public Blue Cross program. This was our pitch, our strategy: 'Now, we can get this through collective bargaining for our members up to retirement, but we can't do it for the older people.'" Nelson H. Cruikshank, interview, Social Security Administration Project, pt. 3, no. 151, tape-recorded November 18,1965 (New York: Columbia University Oral History Collection, 1976), 200.

19. Paul Starr, *The Social Transformation of American Medicine* (New York: Basic Books, 1982).

20. Hacker, *Divided Welfare State,* 257.

21. DeNavas-Walt, Proctor, and Lee, "Income, Poverty, and Health Insurance Coverage," table C-1, 60.

22. Starr, *Social Transformation.*

23. Dan Balz and Ronald Brownstein, *Storming the Gates: Protest Politics and the Republican Revival* (Boston: Little, Brown, 1996).

24. Joseph Newhouse, *Free for All? Lessons from the Rand Health Insurance Experiment* (Cambridge, MA: Harvard University Press, 1993).

25. Robert Dreyfuss and Peter H. Stone, "Medikill," *Mother Jones* (January/February 1996), available online at http://motherjones.com/news/feature/1996/01/medikill.html#start.

26. Jonathan Cohn, "Crash Course," *New Republic* 233:19 (2005), available online at https://newrepublic.com/article/63360/crash-course.

27. See, for example, John C. Goodman and Gerald Musgrave, *Patient Power: The Free Enterprise Alternative to Clinton's Health Plan* (Washington, DC: Cato Institute, 1994). For a more recent example, see R. Glenn Hubbard, John F. Cogan, and Daniel P. Kessler, *Healthy, Wealthy, and Wise: Five Steps to a Better Health Care System* (Washington, DC: AEI Press/Hoover Institution, 2005).

28. David Cutler and Richard Zeckhauser, "Adverse Selection in Health Insurance," in *Frontiers in Health Policy Research,* vol. 1, ed. A. Garber (Cambridge, MA: MIT Press, 1998), 1–31.

29. John C. Goodman, "Health Savings Accounts Will Revolutionize American Health Care," National Center for Policy Analysis, Brief Analysis no. 464 (January 15, 2004), available online at http://ncpa.org/pub/ba/ba464/.

30. Stephen Miller, "More Employees Satisfied with Consumer-Driven Health Plans," Society for Human Resource Management, July 24, 2015, available online at https://www.shrm.org/ResourcesAndTools/hr-topics/benefits/Pages/CDHP-satisfaction-rises.aspx Employee Benefit Research Institute, "Early Experience with High-Deductible and Consumer-Driven Health Plans: Findings from the EBRI/Commonwealth Fund Consumerism in Health Care Survey," Issue Brief no. 288 (December 2005), available online at http://ebri.org/publications/ib/index.cfm?fa=ibDisp&content_id=3606.

31. Julie Appleby, "Health Savings Accounts Are Back in the Policy Spotlight," NPR. org, February 2, 2017, available online at http://www.npr.org/sections/health-shots/2017/02/02/513060189/health-savings-accounts-are-back-in-the-policy-spotlight; Kaiser Family Foundation, "2016 Employer Health Benefits Survey," September 14, 2016, 158, available online at http://files.kff.org/attachment/Report-Employer-Health-Benefits-2016-Annual-Survey.

32. Almost immediately after its creation, the key architect of the legislation in the Johnson administration started developing secret plans for extending Medicare to all children in the United States. Hacker, *Divided Welfare State,* 251.

33. Kaiser Family Foundation, *2017 Employer Health Benefits Survey,* sec. 11. This is percentage of larger employers offering retiree health coverage *among large employers that offer health benefits to workers,* as the overwhelming majority do.

34. Jacob S. Hacker, "Privatizing Risk without Privatizing the Welfare State: The Hidden Politics of Social Policy Retrenchment in the United States," *American Political Science Review* 98:2 (May 2004): 253.

35. Hacker, *Divided Welfare State,* 326.

36. Social Security Administration (SSA), *Income of the Aged Chartbook,* 2000 (Washington, DC: SSA, September 2004), available online at http://ssa.gov/policy/docs/chartbooks/income_aged/2002/index.html.

37. Henry J. Aaron and Robert D. Reischauer, "The Medicare Reform Debate: What Is the Next Step?" *Health Affairs* 14:4 (1995). Proposals differ on how the level of this support would be determined; in most, it would be geared to some sort of average of private and Medicare premiums.

38. See Jacob S. Hacker and Paul Pierson, *Off Center: The Republican Revolution and the Erosion of American Democracy* (New Haven, CT: Yale University Press, 2005), 85–93.

39. Kaiser Family Foundation (KFF), *An Overview of The Medicare Part D Prescription Drug Benefit* (Washington, DC: KFF, October 12, 2018), available online at https://www.kff.org/medicare/fact-sheet/an-overview-of-the-medicare-part-d-prescription-drug-benefit/; Patricia Neuman et al., "Medicare Prescription Drug Benefit Progress Report: Findings from a 2006 National Survey of Seniors," *Health Affairs,* web exclusive, August 21, 2007, available online at http://content. healthaffairs.org/cgi/reprint/hlthaff.26.5.w630vl.

40. Marilyn Moon, "Restructuring Medicare's Cost-Sharing," The Commonwealth Fund (December 1996), available online at http://cmwf.org/Publications/Publications_show.htm?doc_id=221428.

41. Mark Merlis, "Opening the Federal Employees Health Benefits Program to Individual Purchasers," study conducted for the U.S. Department of Health and Human Services (July 31, 2001), 10–11, available online at http://markmerlis. com/FEHBP.pdf.

42. Adam Clymer, "Of Touching Third Rails and Tackling Medicare," *New York Times,* October 27, 1995, 21.

43. Medicaid.gov, "June 2018 Medicaid and CHIP Applications, Eligibility Determinations, and Enrollment Report," August 31, 2018, available online at https://www.medicaid.gov/medicaid/program-information/downloads/june-

2018-enrollment-data.zip; Georgetown University Health Policy Institute, "Medicaid's Role for Young Children, December 2016, available online at https://ccf.georgetown.edu/wp-content/uploads/2017/02/MedicaidYoungChildren.pdf; Kaiser Family Foundation, "Medicaid's Role in Nursing Home Care," KFF, June 2017, available online at http://files.kff.org/attachment/Infographic-Medicaids-Role-in-Nursing-Home-Care.

44. Martha Shirk, with the assistance of Cathy Trost and Susan Schultz, *In Their Own Words: The Uninsured Talk about Living without Health Insurance* (Washington, DC: KFF, 2000), available online at http://kff.org/uninsured/2207-index.cfm.

45. Janet Currie, *The Invisible Safety Net: Protecting the Nation's Poor Children and Families* (Princeton, NJ: Princeton University Press, 2006), 60.

46. Andrea Campbell, *Trapped in America's Safety Net: One Family's Struggle* (Chicago: University of Chicago Press, 2014), x–xii.

47. Kaiser Family Foundation, "Status of State Action on the Medicaid Expansion, September 11, 2018, available online at https://www.kff.org/health-reform/state-indicator/state-activity-around-expanding-medicaid-under-the-affordable-care-act.

48. Rachel Garfield, Anthony Damico, and Kendal Orgera, "The Coverage Gap: Uninsured Poor Adults in States That Do Not Expand Medicaid," Kaiser Family Foundation, June 12, 2018, available online at https://www.kff.org/medicaid/issue-brief/the-coverage-gap-uninsured-poor-adults-in-states-that-do-not-expand-medicaid/.

49. Jacob S. Hacker and Paul Pierson, "The Dog that Almost Barked: What the ACA Repeal Fight Says about the Resilience of the American Welfare State," *Journal of Health Politics, Policy, and Law* 43:4 (2018): 551–77, available online at https://read.dukeupress.edu/jhppl/article/43/4/551/134450/The-Dog-That-Almost-Barked-What-the-ACA-Repeal.

50. Karen Pollitz and Gary Claxton, "Proposals for Insurance Options That Don't Comply with ACA Rules: Trade-offs In Cost and Regulation," Kaiser Family Foundation, April 18, 2018, available online at https://www.kff.org/health-reform/issue-brief/proposals-for-insurance-options-that-dont-comply-with-aca-rules-trade-offs-in-cost-and-regulation/.

Conclusion

1. Margot Sanger-Katz, "Why Trump's Obamacare Promise Will Be So Hard to Keep," *New York Times*, January 11, 2017, available online at https://www.nytimes.com/2017/01/11/upshot/trumps-obamacare-plan-still-optimistic-still-vague.html. Amber Phillips, "'They're rapists.' President Trump's Campaign Launch Speech Two Years Later, Annotated," Washington Post, June 16, 2017, available online at https://www.washingtonpost.com/news/the-fix/wp/2017/06/16/theyre-rapists-presidents-trump-campaign-launch-speech-two-years-later-annotated/?utm_term=.0f97a8bcd38f#annotations:12172445.

2. Meera Jagannathan, "Here Are the Times Trump Swore He'd Save Medicaid—as GOP Health Bill with $800 Billion Cut Heads to Senate," *New York Daily News*, May 4, 2017, available online at http://www.nydailynews.com/news/politics/times-president-trump-swore-save-medicaid-article-1.3137291.

3. Haeyoun Park, "The Outcomes of the Many Republican Health Plans Are Not So Different," *New York Times*, July 24, 2017, available online at https://www.nytimes.com/interactive/2017/07/24/us/republican-health-bill-versions.html.

4. Hannah Katch, "Like Other ACA Repeal Bills, Cassidy-Graham Would Cap and Deeply Cut Medicaid," Center on Budget and Policy Priorities, September 25, 2017, available online at https://www.cbpp.org/research/health/like-other-aca-repeal-bills-cassidy-graham-would-cap-and-deeply-cut-medicaid.

5. Dylan Matthews, "The Republican Tax Bill Got Worse: Now the Top 1% Gets 83% of the Gains," *Vox*, December 18, 2017, available online at https://www.vox.com/policy-and-politics/2017/12/18/16791174/republican-tax-bill-congress-conference-tax-policy-center.

6. Peggy Bailey et al., "Health Proposals in President's Budget Would Reduce Health Insurance Coverage and Access to Care," Center on Budget and Policy Priorities, February 16, 2018, available online at https://www.cbpp.org/research/health/health-proposals-in-presidents-budget-would-reduce-health-insurance-coverage-and; Dylan Matthews, "Donald Trump's Budget Proposal Breaks His Promise to Not Cut Social Security," *Vox*, May 22, 2017, available online at https://www.vox.com/policy-and-politics/2017/5/22/15674822/donald-trump-social-security-disability-budget; and Samuel Chamberlain, "Trump Budget to Cut Medicaid, Food Stamps—'Put Taxpayer First,' Officials Say," *Fox News,* May 22, 2017, available online at http://www.foxnews.com/politics/2017/05/22/trump-budget-to-cut-medicaid-food-stamps-put-taxpayer-first-officials-say.html.

7. Gillian B. White, "The Dismal Future of Trump's Least Favorite Agency," *The Atlantic*, November 17, 2017, available online at https://www.theatlantic.com/business/archive/2017/11/cfpb-mulvaney-trump/546131/.

8. Two lively introductions to these biases are Daniel Kahneman, *Thinking, Fast and Slow* (New York: Farrar, Straus and Giroux, 2011) and Richard H. Thaler, *Misbehaving: The Making of Behavioral Economics* (New York: Norton, 2015).

9. Annie Baxter, "Majority of Americans Feel 'Forgotten' by Government," *Marketplace*, April 26, 2017, available online at https://www.marketplace.org/2017/04/26/economy/most-americans-feel-government-has-forgotten-them; Pew Research Center, "The State of American Jobs," October 6, 2016, available online at http://www.pewsocialtrends.org/2016/10/06/the-state-of-american-jobs/ ("Americans think the responsibility for preparing and succeeding in today's workforce starts with individuals themselves: 72% say 'a lot' of responsibility should fall on individuals. . . . 40% assign a lot of responsibility to state governments, and 35% say the federal government should assume a lot of responsibility"); "David Kusnet, Lawrence Mishel, and Ruy Teixeira, *Taking Past Each Other: What Everyday Americans Really Think (and Elites Don't Get) about the Economy* (Washington, DC: Economic Policy Institute), 5–6. Available online at https://www.epi.org/files/page/-/old/books/talking/TalkingPastEachOther(full).pdf

10. Adam Seth Levine, *American Insecurity: Why Our Economic Fears Lead to Political Inaction* (Princeton, NJ: Princeton University Press, 2015).

11. Nathan Goldschlag and Alex Tabarrok, "Is Regulation to Blame for the Decline in American Entrepreneurship," *Economic Policy* 33:93 (January 2018): 5–44;

Ian Hathaway and Robert E. Litan, "Declining Business Dynamism in the United States: A Look at States and Metros" Brookings Institution, May 5, 2014 available online at https://www.brookings.edu/wpcontent/uploads/2016/06/declining_business_dynamism_hathaway_litan.pdf; Alison Wellington, "Health Insurance Coverage and Entrepreneurship," *Contemporary Economic Policy* 19:4 (2001): 465–78; Robert Fairlie, Kanika Kapur, and Susan M. Gates, "Is Employer-Based Health Insurance a Barrier to Entrepreneurship?" (Santa Monica: Kauffman-RAND Institute for Entrepreneurship Public Policy, 2010).

12. Tahira M. Probst, Claudio Barbaranelli, and Laura Petitta, "The Relationship between Job Insecurity and Accident Under-Reporting: A Test in Two Countries," *Work & Stress* 27:4 (2013): 383–402; Wendy R. Boswell, Julie B. Olson-Buchanan, and T. Brad Harris, "I Cannot Afford to Have a Life: Employee Adaptation to Feelings of Job Insecurity," *Personnel Psychology* 67:4 (2014): 887–915; Jennie E. Brand, "The Far-Reaching Impact of Job Loss and Unemployment," *Annual Review of Sociology* 41 (2015): 359–75.

13. Greg J. Duncan, Richard J. Murnane, and Editors, *Whither Opportunity? Rising Inequality, Schools, and Children's Life Chances* (New York: Russell Sage Foundation, 2012); Vivek Wadhwa, Krisztina Holly, Raj Aggarwal, and Alex Salkever, "The Anatomy of an Entrepreneur: Family Background and Motivation" (Kansas City, MO: The Ewing Marion Kauffman Foundation, 2009), available online at https://ssrn.com/abstract=1431263; Heather Boushey and Adam S. Hersh, "The American Middle Class, Income Inequality, and the Strength of Our Economy" (Washington, DC: Center for American Progress, 2012), available online at https://cdn.americanprogress.org/wp-content/uploads/issues/2012/05/pdf/middleclass_growth.pdf.

14. There is evidence, for example, that economic instability, as distinct from low income, impairs childhood development, at least in lower-income families. See Lindsey Leininger and Ariel Kalil, "Economic Strain and Children's Behavior in the Aftermath of the Great Recession," *Journal of Marriage and Family* 76 (2014): 998–1010; Ariel Kalil and Kathleen Ziol-Guest, "Parental Job Loss and Children's Academic Progress in Two-Parent Families," *Social Science Research* 37 (2008): 500–15; Philip Oreopoulos, Marianne Page, and Ann Huff Stevens, "The Intergenerational Effects of Worker Displacement," *Journal of Labor Economics* 26:3 (July 2008): 455–83, available online at https://www.journals.uchicago.edu/doi/abs/10.1086/588493.

15. Lloyd Free and Hadley Cantril, *The Political Beliefs of Americans* (New Brunswick, NJ: Rutgers University Press, 1967).

16. The term is of course Joseph Schumpeter's from *Capitalism, Socialism and Democracy* (New York: Harper Perennial, 1962).

17. @EricCantor, "Today, we celebrate those who have taken a risk, worked hard, built a business and earned their own success," *Twitter*, September 3, 2012, 9:06 a.m., https://twitter.com/ericcantor/status/242654833218293760?lang=en.

18. Jacob S. Hacker and Ruy Teixeira, "It Wasn't Just Iraq," *The American Prospect*, November 19, 2006, available online at http://prospect.org/article/it-wasnt-just-iraq.

19. Benjamin Page and Lawrence Jacobs, *Class War? What Americans Really Think about Economic Inequality* (Chicago: University of Chicago Press, 2009), ch. 3.
20. Ronald Brownstein, "America's Persistent Economic Gloom," *The Atlantic*, January 27, 2016, available online at https://www.theatlantic.com/business/archive/2016/01/american-pessimism-economy/431574/.
21. Jacob S. Hacker, Philipp Rehm, and Mark Schlesinger, "The Insecure American: Economic Experiences, Financial Worries, and Policy Attitudes," *Perspectives on Politics* 11 (2013): 23–50.
22. Jacob S. Hacker, Philipp Rehm, and Mark Schlesinger, *Standing on Shaky Ground: Americans' Experiences with Economic Insecurity* (New Haven, CT: Economic Security Index Project, December 2010), http://www.economicsecurityindex.org/upload/media/ESI%20report%20final_12%2013.pdf.
23. Ruy Teixeira, "Public Opinion Snapshot: Universal Health Care Momentum Swells," Center for American Progress, Washington, DC, March 23, 2007, available online at http://americanprogress.org/issues/2007/03/opinion_health_care.html.
24. The phrase is from David Osborne and Ted Gaebler, *Reinventing Government: How the Entrepreneurial Spirit Is Transforming the Public Sector* (New York: Penguin, 1993).
25. Rachel West, Indivar Dutta-Gupta, Kali Grant, Melissa Boteach, Claire McKenna, and Judy Conti, "Strengthening Unemployment Protections in America: Modernizing Unemployment Insurance and Establishing a Jobseeker's Allowance" (Washington, DC: Center for American Progress, June 2016), available online at https://cdn.americanprogress.org/wp-content/uploads/2016/05/31134245/UI_JSAreport.pdf; George Wentworth, "Closing Doors on the Unemployed: Why Most Jobless Workers Are Not Receiving Unemployment Insurance and What States Can Do about It" (New York: National Employment Law Project, December 2017), available online at https://s27147.pcdn.co/wp-content/uploads/Closing-Doors-on-the-Unemployed12_19_17-1.pdf.
26. Daron Acemoglu and Robert Shimer, "Productivity Gains from Unemployment Insurance," *European Economic Review* 44 (2000): 1195–224, available online at https://economics.mit.edu/files/5685.
27. See Andrew Stettner, Michael Cassidy, and George Wentworth, "A New Safety Net for an Era of Unstable Earnings," The Century Foundation, December 15, 2016, available online at https://tcf.org/content/report/new-safety-net-for-an-era-of-unstable-earnings.
28. Lori G. Kletzer, "Why the U.S. Needs Wage Insurance," *Harvard Business Review*, January 25, 2016, available online at https://hbr.org/2016/01/why-the-u-s-needs-wage-insurance.
29. Stettner, Cassidy, and Wentworth, "A New Safety Net for an Era of Unstable Earnings."
30. Jeffrey B. Liebman, "Understanding the Increase in Disability Insurance Benefit Receipt in the United States," *Journal of Economic Perspectives* 29:2 (2015): 123–50, available online at https://assets.aeaweb.org/assets/production/articles-attachments/jep/app/2902/29020123_corr.pdf.

31. "Chart Book: Social Security Disability Insurance" (Washington, DC: Center on Budget and Policy Priorities, August 2018), available online at https://www.cbpp.org/sites/default/files/atoms/files/7-21-14socsec-chartbook.pdf.

32. Nicole Maestas, Kathleen J. Mullen, and Alexander Strand, "Does Disability Insurance Receipt Discourage Work? Using Examiner Assignment to Estimate Causal Effects of SSDI Receipt" *American Economic Review* 103:5 (2013): 1797–829, available online at https://eml.berkeley.edu/~saez/course/maestas-mullen-strandAER13.pdf.

33. Heather Boushey, *Finding Time: The Economics of Work-Life Conflict* (Cambridge, MA: Harvard University Press, 2016).

34. Quoted in Tamara Draut, *Strapped: Why America's Twenty- and Thirty-Somethings Can't Get Ahead* (New York: Doubleday, 2005), 156.

35. Wage and Hour Division, United States Department of Labor, *Balancing the Needs of Families and Employers: Family and Medical Leave Surveys* (Washington, DC: U.S. Department of Labor, 2000), available online at https://www.dol.gov/whd/fmla/toc.htm.

36. Elise Gould, "Providing Unpaid Leave Was Only the First Step; 25 years after the Family and Medical Leave Act, More Workers Need Paid Leave," Economic Policy Institute, February 1, 2018, available online at https://www.epi.org/blog/providing-unpaid-leave-was-only-the-first-step-25-years-after-the-family-and-medical-leave-act-more-workers-need-paid-leave/.

37. Robert C. Bird and Liz Brown, "The United Kingdom Right to Request as a Model for Flexible Work in the European Union," *American Business Law Association* 55:1 (2018): 53–115, available online at https://onlinelibrary.wiley.com/doi/epdf/10.1111/ablj.12117.

38. Raj Chetty et al., "Active vs. Passive Decisions and Crowd-Out in Retirement Savings Accounts: Evidence from Denmark," *The Quarterly Journal of Economics* 129:3 (2014): 1141–1219.

39. Ben Miller, "The Student Debt Problem Is Worse Than We Imagined," *New York Times*, August 25, 2018, available online at https://www.nytimes.com/interactive/2018/08/25/opinion/sunday/student-debt-loan-default-college.html

40. Robert Kelchen, "How Much Do For-Profit Colleges Rely on Federal Funds?" (Washington, DC: Brookings Institution, January 11, 2017), available online at https://www.brookings.edu/blog/brown-center-chalkboard/2017/01/11/how-much-do-for-profit-colleges-rely-on-federal-funds/. Kelchen notes that this estimate may be "several percent off" because existing sources are not wholly consistent in their definition of an academic year.

41. For a recent comprehensive review, see Emmanuel Saez, Joel Slemrod, and Seth H. Giertz, "The Elasticity of Taxable Income with Respect to Marginal Tax Rates: A Critical Review," *Journal of Economic Literature* 50:1 (2012): 3–50.

42. Jack VanDerhei, Sarah Holen, Luis Alonso, and Steven Bass, "401(k) Plan Asset Allocation, Account Balances, and Loan Activity in 2014" (Washington, DC: Employee Benefit Research Institute, April 2016), available online at https://www.ebri.org/pdf/briefspdf/ebri_ib_423.apr16.401k-update.pdf.

43. The "replacement rate" is even lower when Medicare Part B (physicians' insurance) and Part D (drug insurance) premiums are taken into account. See Michael Clingman, Kyle Burkhalter, and Chris Chaplain, "Replacement Rates for Hypothetical Retired Workers," *Actuarial Note.* (Baltimore, MD: Social Security Administration, July 2017), available online at https://www.ssa.gov/oact/NOTES/ran9/an2017-9.pdf; Paul N. Van De Water and Kathy Ruffing, "Social Security Benefits Are Modest: Benefit Cuts Would Cause Hardship for Many," Center on Budget and Policy Priorities, August 7, 2017, available online at https://www.cbpp.org/research/social-security/social-security-benefits-are-modest.

44. The Retirement Risk Index is based on calculating future retirement income (based on projected wealth holdings and assuming retirement at age sixty-five) and then comparing this income with the "replacement rate" needed to maintain consumption in old age—a target that varies from 65 percent of previous income for higher-income single people to 85 percent for lower-income one-earner couples. Households that are projected to fall 10 percent or more short of this target are considered "at risk." Alicia H. Munnell, Wenliang Hou, and Geoffrey T. Sanzenbacher, "National Retirement Risk Index Shows Modest Improvement in 2016" (Newton, MA: Center for Retirement Research at Boston College, January 2018), available online at http://crr.bc.edu/wp-content/uploads/2017/12/IB_18-1.pdf.

45. In 2017, tax breaks for defined-contribution plans cost the federal government an estimated $117 billion, Individual Retirement Accounts cost $25.5 billion, and defined-benefit plans cost $77 billion. Joint Committee on Taxation, *Estimates of Federal Tax Expenditures for Fiscal Years 2017–2021* (JCX-34-18), May 25, 2018, available online at https://www.jct.gov/publications.html?func=startdown&id=5095.

46. "Distribution Table 2017 005A: Percent of Families with Tax Benefits for Retirement Savings, 2017 Income Levels and Law," United States Department of Treasury: Office of Tax Analysis, March 2016, available online at https://www.treasury.gov/resource-center/tax-policy/tax-analysis/Documents/Retirement-Savings-2017.pdf; "Distribution Table 2017 005b: Percent Value of Tax Benefits for Retirement as a Share of After-Tax Income, 2017 Income Levels and Law," United States Department of Treasury: Office of Tax Analysis, March 2016, available online at https://www.treasury.gov/resource-center/tax-policy/tax-analysis/Documents/Retirement-Savings-2017.pdf.

47. Jacob Hacker "Restoring Retirement Security: The Market Crisis, the 'Great Risk Shift,' and the Challenge for Our Nation," *Elder Law Journal* 19:1 (2011): 32–36, available online at http://jacobhacker.com/assets/hacker_baum_lecture.pdf.

48. Ian Ayres and Jacob S. Hacker, "Social Security Plus," *Elder Law Journal* (forthcoming 2018).

49. Jacob S. Hacker, *The Divided Welfare State: The Battle over Public and Private Social Benefits in the United States* (New York: Cambridge University Press, 2002), 101.

50. Irene Papanicolas, Liana R. Woskie, and Ashish K. Jha, "Health Care Spending in the United States and Other High-Income Countries," *Journal of American Medical*

Association 319:10 (2018): 1024–39, available online at https://jamanetwork. com/journals/jama/fullarticle/2674671.

51. See Atul Gawande, "Health Care's Price Conundrum," *New Yorker*, December 18, 2015, available online at https://www.newyorker.com/news/news-desk/health-cares-cost-conundrum-squared. For a compendium of Cooper's findings, see http://www.healthcarepricingproject.org.

52. Jason Furman and Matt Fielder, "The Economic Record of the Obama Administration: Reforming the Health Care System," The White House: President Barack Obama, December 13, 2016, available online at https:// obamawhitehouse.archives.gov/blog/2016/12/13/economic-record-obama-administration-reforming-health-care-system.

53. Sara R. Collins, Munira Z. Gunja and Michelle M. Dotty, "How Well Does Insurance Coverage Protect Consumers from Health Care Costs? Findings from the Commonwealth Fund Biennial Health Insurance Survey, 2016" (New York: The Commonwealth Fund, October 2017), available online at https://www.commonwealthfund.org/publications/issue-briefs/2017/oct/ how-well-does-insurance-coverage-protect-consumers-health-care?redirect_ source=/publications/issue-briefs/2017/oct/insurance-coverage-consumers-health-care-costs.

54. During the 2016 campaign, Senator Bernie Sanders put forth a plan for universal Medicare that he said would cost "only" around $1.5 trillion a year, though other experts suggested it would much cost more. But taking the number at face value, $1.5 trillion represents around 8 percent of our economy. By way of comparison, the 1942 tax hike to fund World War II amounted to 5 percent of GDP. The 1993 tax hike under President Bill Clinton that Republicans (falsely) claimed was the "largest in history" equaled just over half a percent of GDP. Committee for a Responsible Federal Budget, "Is Clinton's Tax Increase One of the Largest in History?" October 6, 2016, available online at http://www.crfb.org/blogs/ clintons-tax-increase-one-largest-history.

INDEX